the other road to serfdom and the
path to sustainable democracy

the other road to

SERFDOM

& the **path to sustainable**
democracy

ERIC ZENCEY

university press of new england

hanover and london

University Press of New England
www.upne.com
© 2012 University Press of New England
All rights reserved
Manufactured in the United States of America
Designed by Eric M. Brooks
Typeset in Calluna by Passumpsic Publishing

For permission to reproduce any of the material in this
book, contact Permissions, University Press of New England,
One Court Street, Suite 250, Lebanon NH 03766; or visit
www.upne.com

"Ending the Culture War" first appeared as "Transcending the
Culture Wars: Environmental History as Meta-metanarrative"
and is reprinted with permission from *Liberal Education*.
Copyright 2008 by the Association of American Colleges
and Universities.

Library of Congress Cataloging-in-Publication Data
Zencey, Eric.
The other road to serfdom and the path to sustainable
democracy / by Eric Zencey.
      p. cm.
Includes bibliographical references and index.
ISBN 978-1-58465-961-7 (cloth : alk. paper) —
ISBN 978-1-61168-367-7 (ebook)
  1. Sustainable development. 2. Environmental economics.
  I. Title.
✓ HC79.E5Z443   2012
338.9'27 — dc23   2012018385

5 4 3 2 1

For
Kathryn,
Daphne,
Anne, &
Joe

contents

introduction
the weather on factory planet

n the summer of 2010 an unprecedented heat wave in Russia lasted two months, baking Moscow, drying up peat bogs and forests in the region, and leading to fires that blanketed the city with acrid, suffocating smoke. Thousands died. Also that summer a monsoon in Pakistan dumped half the usual annual rainfall—ten inches—in one night; the flooding killed thousands and displaced 20 million. There were more deaths and displacement from floods in China, drought and fire in Australia, drought in Central Africa and East Africa. In the American Southwest, ongoing drought led to water rationing in Phoenix, Flagstaff, Las Vegas. Lake Mead, the major reservoir on the Colorado River, dropped to its lowest level since the water had been impounded by the Hoover Dam three-quarters of a century ago.

The weather news from the summer of 2010 was so consistently extreme, and the number of people affected so large, that by the time September arrived the rains and flooding in Burkina Faso passed with little notice in the Western press: only a few thousand dead and a hundred thousand made homeless. In many papers that didn't make the front page.

The largest domestic environmental story from the summer of 2010 was the blowout and explosion on the Deepwater Horizon drilling platform in the Gulf of Mexico. Twelve men were killed, and more than 5 million barrels of oil were released into the Gulf of Mexico before the undersea gusher was finally stanched.

What do these environmental catastrophes have in common?

Except for the Deepwater Horizon blowout, they're all instances of anomalous and deadly weather, making them presumptive evidence of climate change driven by global warming. "Climate is what you expect," Mark Twain said, "and weather is what you get." Lately we haven't been getting what we expect. Science, speaking with precision, has to offer up a boilerplate caution that is much misunderstood and misused: "No particular incident of weather can with any confidence be ascribed to changing climatic patterns." Even so, the weather the planet experienced in the summer of 2010 is consistent with what atmospheric scientists have been predicting since they first sounded the alarm about greenhouse gases and their potential to disrupt the climate more than half a century ago. Storms are stronger and more frequent. Rain and snow fall (or don't fall) in places and amounts that are without precedent in living memory. In the winter of 2010 a freak snowstorm dumped two feet of snow on Washington, DC; Republican Senator James Inhofe of Oklahoma loudly trumpeted this as proof positive of his long-standing assertion that climate change, which he persists in calling global warming, is a hoax. (In this he was simply displaying his ignorance; whether it stems from political calculation or congenital defect is difficult to know.)

Historical experience of weather is no guide to the future. In retrospect, you'd have thought that insurance companies would have had a strong incentive to study and respond to the problem; their profit margins depend on predicting payouts, including payouts for storm damage. But they came rather late to a recognition of the issue. As a technical paper noted in 2005, "Although insurers first expressed concern about climate change more than three decades ago, fewer than one in a hundred appear to have seriously examined the business implications," and those that have haven't published what they found; their strategies for coping became proprietary trade secrets. But one of the ways insurers are coping is readily apparent: some refuse to underwrite coverage in vulnerable areas. Having taken a beating in Florida because of hurricane damage, State Farm dropped 125,000 customers after its request for a 67 percent rate increase was denied.

In a larger, whole-systems view, even the oil catastrophe in the Gulf of Mexico is a climate change story. We drill deeper and riskier wells because we haven't controlled our demand for oil, which, when burned, releases CO_2, one of the gases changing our climate and weather. But there's another thread of connection, one that comes into focus when we see the whole system, economy and ecology, evolving over time. When we add this temporal dimension, each of the major stories in the environmental news from the summer of 2010 becomes an episode in an even more disturbing tale: the story of how our industrial civilization is systematically reducing the ability of the planet to support human life.

The heat wave in Russia led to the failure of most of the summer grain crop, one-quarter of that country's annual wheat harvest. The thousand-year monsoon in Pakistan produced flooding that not only killed ten thousand and displaced millions but also drowned farmland: another national granary taken offline for at least a year, probably two or three, maybe longer. In Nigeria, ongoing drought means 10 million people live with "food insecurity"—they have little to no idea where tomorrow's food is coming from. The idled shrimpers and fishermen of the Gulf didn't harvest the tonnage of seafood that they harvested last year, and that missing harvest represents protein that humans, somewhere, had been expecting to ingest.

In the very long timescale in which planetary processes evolve and change, the Gulf fishery is likely to rebound and return to its pre–Deepwater Horizon productivity. There's even a chance (small, but still within the range of possibility) that this will happen within the lifetimes of the human members of Gulf Coast ecosystems—the shrimpers and fishers and communities that have expanded into the economic niche offered by this extractive base. (Being human, they'll calculate the rate of recovery against the yardstick of their own lives, not the millennia and eons that are the usual measure of environmental history.) We'll find out in years to come whether the Russian heat wave will be repeated. Future monsoons in Pakistan may regress to normal, and rains may eventually return to Somalia and Nigeria, to Australia, to the American Southwest. I wouldn't bet on it. Weather will vary, but our new climate will continue to give us unprecedented catastrophes. The future will resemble the present.

Of this too we can be certain: as long as oil is pumped from the ground and transported long distances, there will be accidents, some large enough to cause productivity-diminishing damage to ecosystems. The amount of oil that finds its way into world oceans because of human act and accident is a very small percentage of the oil we use—just .025 percent each year goes astray. But the world burns 87.4 million barrels of oil every day, enough to fill 16,000 supertankers a year; all told, about four of those tanker loads—9 million barrels of oil—find their way directly into world oceans. To this must be added spillage on land. Oil is toxic stuff that doesn't break down easily, and much of what we spill on land and sea ends up in coastal aquatic ecosystems, where it diminishes their health and productivity. These are the nurseries of marine life. Poison them and you diminish the marine food pyramid, which concentrates solar energy into increasingly larger life-forms: sunlight is fixed into biomass by phytoplankton, phytoplankton are eaten by zooplankton, zooplankton are eaten by fish, fish are eaten by bigger fish. We eat from the top of that pyramid.

Along with the certainty that some small but significant percentage of oil will be spilled by human act, we can be certain that as long as processes of climate change are under way, unprecedented weather will play havoc with our agricultural expectations. Both kinds of changes are reducing the ability of the planet to feed us. When you add in the effects of other human acts — irrigation practices that salinate soils and make them sterile, farming practices that draw down soil nutrients faster than natural processes can restore them, and an expanding urban population that transforms farmland into building sites and roadways — feeding humans doesn't look to be a long-term growth industry. We've built our population out to and beyond the edge of what's sustainable, leaving little resilience, little slack, in our food delivery system. When we connect the dots — assembling them as a historian might, as linked episodes in a single narrative — a clear trajectory emerges: climate change and the industrial activities that produce it are diminishing the planet's capacity to feed us.

The wealthy nations of the world aren't at immediate risk. Money gives human populations in First World nations the power to command food from other sources, other ecosystems. (An MSN webstory, "How the Gulf Coast Oil Spill Will Affect Your Dinner Plate," blithely told Americans accustomed to eating Gulf Coast seafood that "now's a good time to develop a taste for red snapper from the Hawaiian Islands, where fisheries are better managed" — as if the catastrophe in the Gulf were simply a case of poor fisheries management.) But while there are substitutes in the market for "Gulf Coast shrimp" and even "marine-sourced protein," in planetary terms there is no substitute for "food." Wherever the American gustatory footprint lands, it will displace other consumption, depriving other humans of a life necessity: the food they had expected to eat.

Economists have long celebrated something called Say's Law: "Supply creates its own demand." It states a favored principle — the idea that everything that's produced produces, at the same time, the income needed to buy it. There's an appealing symmetry to it, a Newtonian balance of equal and opposite movement. The law certainly seems to apply to food. Increase the supply and you eventually increase the population and hence demand. Unfortunately, the obverse isn't true: hunger doesn't put food on the table. Only people working with and within natural processes can do that, and what we're doing to the planet is diminishing the ability of nature to make its expected contribution to the partnership.

In 2008, America's sudden enthusiasm for ethanol made from corn drove up food prices worldwide, leading to riots in Mexico, Haiti, Egypt, Bangladesh. We didn't have to see the connection between their hunger and our energy policy unless we wanted to. That's part of the beauty of the market system that we operate under: when it works, it works impersonally, like a force of nature, reconciling supply and demand at a market-clearing price. Like a healthy ecosystem, a well-functioning market is adaptive and resilient, responding to changing circumstance readily and quickly, without central organization or control. No one person decided that the price of corn should go up. In an effective market the price seems to come "naturally," falling on everyone, rich and poor, buyer and seller alike.

To the Austrian economist Friedrich Hayek and the several generations of thinkers who have been influenced by him, these qualities make free markets the foundation of democratic freedom. No coercion, no planning, no bureaucrats imposing decisions: free markets, Hayek said, are crucial to a free society. The idea has been carried over to democratic decision making, the "marketplace of ideas" that in theory lies behind elections: in politics as in markets, what Adam Smith called the "invisible hand" of collective decision making is thought to guide us, automatically, to create the common and social good from individual pursuit of individual self-interest. To many of the free-market faithful, there is and can be no such thing as a social good or a public interest separate and apart from the individual interests that markets, and elections, tally.

That's the theory. But what happens in practice when the free market is a market for food, and the supply suddenly shrinks? No matter what the market does or doesn't do, if there isn't enough food to go around, some people—maybe a lot of people—starve or go hungry. That's hardly a social good.

One implication is that food production and distribution ought not to be left completely to market forces. That's the position taken by Wendell Berry, who has written passionately and repeatedly about the psychic, social, and ecological consequences of commodifying agriculture. "A man who would value a piece of land strictly according to its economic worth," he tells us, "is as crazy, or as evil, as the man who would make a whore of his wife." To Berry this is not an analogy but an equation. A healthy relationship to land comes from understanding that soil is a living thing, a community in which we participate in a visceral, physical way: when we eat we take in the not-self and transform it, literally, into the self. Pimping out your acreage is no different than pimping out any other intimate partner.

In our culture Berry's perspective has fewer subscribers than the sentiment expressed rhetorically by Supreme Court Justice Antonin Scalia in his decision in *Lucas v. South Carolina Coastal Council* in 1992: "For what is property but the profits thereof?" Land, like any productive property, is reducible to money, and for legal purposes that's all it is.

This biblically cadenced support for the commodification of land notwithstanding, we do try to moderate the effects of market relations on our food supply; rarely are we so cold-blooded as to look people in the eye and tell them they deserve to starve because they don't have enough money to buy food. But charity, or even the establishment of a God-given and socially guaranteed right to food, won't solve the problem. Feed as many individuals as you can when- and wherever you choose, if there isn't enough food in the system, then someone in the system will go hungry.

There are other troubling implications to sudden diminishment of the world's food-producing capacity. In a world where significant numbers of people experience "food insecurity" or outright starvation, a nation rich enough to be well-fed—rich enough to command food resources from other regions—is likely to become a target of envy, anger, censure, and resentment. When those emotions find political expression, wealthy nations and their citizens become literal targets—of riots and protests abroad and of low-budget, terrorist violence against their people and property wherever they're most vulnerable. In the face of that anger and violence, one response of wealthy nations will be to with-draw, fortify, and self-protect. That response has political costs. "There are no atheists in foxholes," says the old saw from World War II. True or not, it's clear that there aren't many civil liberties in foxholes either. In the "war on terror" every citizen is a potential soldier, and a soldier has little right to privacy and no right to be left alone. Pursuit of security in an ecologically degraded, increasingly hungry, increasingly belligerent world will challenge our commitment to maintain a free and open soci-ety, one in which we enjoy personal freedom and civil liberties.

We got to this difficult passage in part because markets operate not on clean white pages in textbooks, but in the actual world, where reality—including the reality of unprecedented weather—tests the assumptions on which economic theory is based. And this is one of the themes un-derlying this book: if our system of market exchange is to function as a bulwark of democratic freedom, markets need to be rooted in systems as resilient and flexible as they are—in healthy ecosystems, ecosystems that have the capacity to absorb sudden change in their operating envi-ronment without being permanently disabled. When an economy is not rooted in resilient ecosystems, market forces are far from being imper-sonal, noncoercive, and automatic. As the food riots in 2008 showed, when people are starving they're likely to view property law as a nicety belonging to fatter times and to see looting and pillage as necessary sur-vival strategies. When people aren't being fed, the "impersonal alloca-tion of the market" isn't consensual and uncoerced; it has to be enforced very personally, at the point of a gun.

Economics is conventionally divided into two subfields. Microeco-nomics studies individual choices in markets, the behaviors that are the foundation of the economy: other things being equal, we prefer to pay less for something rather than more and to allocate our spend-ing in ways that produce the maximum amount of positive return—in happiness, in life satisfaction, in well-being. Macroeconomics looks at whole systems, analyzing the economy's overall dynamics, finding pat-terns and making predictions that have clear policy consequences. But economic science has not yet developed a specialization in what might be called meta-macroeconomics, the study of how economies evolve over time in relation to their host ecosystems as those systems evolve and are changed by human action. That's because according to standard economic theory, that field has no reason to exist. From its origins in the eighteenth and nineteenth centuries, economic theory has explicitly taken nature as a given, defining it as an element of production immune to change. What can't change can't be harmed.

In its very definitions, then, mainstream economic theory thoroughly but implicitly presumes that nature can infinitely absorb our acts and works. In the summer of 2010 the news from Russia and Pakistan and China and Somalia and Nigeria and the Gulf of Mexico was this: standard economics is wrong.

This will be the major theme in what follows. If we are to establish our civilization on an ecologically sustainable basis — if we are to retain and in many cases reestablish the resilient ecosystems that are the necessary foundation that allows our market system to be a bulwark of civil liberties — we must transform our economic thinking.

In focusing on economics I don't mean to say that there aren't other claimants for the title "biggest worst problem." Clearly there are other hurdles we need to pass if we're to move our culture toward a sustainable relationship with nature. Increasing human population is, as William Ryerson has said, "the multiplier of everything else," so a strong case can be made that population control is the most effective way to begin to solve the problem. Our technology lets us do ill-considered things without taking time to consider; more regulation to enforce better design and to prevent the imposition of harms on nature, and on other humans, might be the most effective effort we could make. Then too, deep structures in our thinking might be the fundamental problem. We believe that nature can be infinitely tinkered with and that we can learn enough to succeed in our tinkering. We don't believe we're personally responsible for the commission of a moral wrong when collectively our acts cause species to go extinct. Ideas like these have led us to where we are today, so changing them might be the best way to put us on the path toward sustainability.

But all of these are manifestations of a deeper idea, a faith that underlies all our problematic acts and works: the idea that for economic purposes the planet is effectively infinite. That mistaken idea is what allows us to grow our population and our technological reach with little thought of the collective consequences of each individual act. And it's economic theory that has told us that our individual acts lead to a common good, a good that none of us need to intend. It's becoming increasingly clear that this hasn't been working out. Our economy is our primary vehicle for interacting with the planet, which means that if we can manage to get the economy right, we'll be well on the way to getting our relationship to the planet right. We need a new economic vision, an economics grounded on fundamental assumptions that are a better fit to reality, the reality of a finite planet.

A story, to illustrate this by way of analogy: when I was a boy, my family moved to a rambling Victorian house in a small town on the banks of the Chesapeake and Delaware Canal. My imagination had recently been captured by a child's mystery novel set in an old mansion with secret passageways and hidden rooms, and once we had settled in, I busily set about thumping walls, measuring rooms and hallways, hoping to find spaces that no one knew were there. The house was old and large; anything seemed possible. But my investigations soon showed me that the back of *this* — my grandmother's closet — was the front of *that* — the stairs to an alcove above her room; that the depth of wall between two bedrooms held not a secret passageway but an old chimney. There were no mysterious hidden rooms, no spaces left unaccounted for. When I was done with all my measuring and thumping, there was no place in the house's large and complicated floor plan into which I could project my eight-year-old imagination and my essentially romantic desire to believe that there was more, always more waiting to be discovered. That realization seems to me to model the condition we find ourselves in today, as we make a similar, if more gradual and drawn-out, shift in our thinking. I don't mean that we have demystified our world completely; there are still plenty of obscurities, unknowns, and undiscovered truths out there waiting for us, and it's likely — even desirable — that some of them will always escape the grasp of our rational understanding. I mean that we are being forced to recognize and admit that *the back of this is the front of that* — protein not netted from the Gulf is protein not eaten somewhere in the system; corn turned to ethanol in Kansas and wheat scorched to death in Russia become tortillas not eaten in Mexico and bread not eaten in Egypt and Bangladesh. There is no magical opening to an infinite world; there is no mysterious undiscovered space into which we can expand our thinking, our population, our agriculture, our economy.

Seduced by a vision of infinite increase in any- and everything we value, we have been as children, putting our faith in unrealistic hopes and romantic chimeras, refusing to acknowledge reality. It's time, frankly, for us to grow up.

The realization that *the back of this is the front of that* is a novelty in the history of Western industrial civilization, which has for several centuries consciously styled itself as gathering its energies behind an expansive frontier. For most of that time, the frontier was a literal line of demarcation separating land (and ecosystems and resources) that were subsumed under Western economic control from land that was not. As the Western colonial project — the encompassing of all the land masses of the world under a globally integrated system of trade, making all the Earth's resources available for use by Western-style industrial economies — came nearer and nearer to completion, the frontier ceased to be a geographical, spatial referent on land and was projected elsewhere: undersea, into space. For a time in the 1960s and 1970s the oceans seemed the next logical place to look for infinity, and technologies were developed to mine the seabed, to drill for oil offshore, and to find and catch fish with industrial efficiency. Expansion into outer space — the "High Frontier" — was consistently promoted with rhetoric about economic benefits, including the eventual appropriation of "off-planet" resources. But the oceans turned out to be all too finite, as the collapse of the commercial cod fishery in the Atlantic soon showed; and no matter what sorts of technologies we might invent, the pull of gravity is unchanging and makes getting off the surface of the planet energetically expensive — so expensive that exploitation of extraterrestrial resources is not now and (I predict with confidence) never will be routine, economically profitable behavior. By default, the frontier has become a rather more abstract thing: the moving edge of technological development in service to a more thorough, increasingly rapid creation of wealth.

We persist in thinking that the frontier can be pushed ever outward. Our political and economic systems evolved on a planet that offered the appearance, if not the reality, of an infinite expanse in which our economy could grow. Gradually, we're discovering what it means to realize that our world is finite. But Infinite-Planet Theory lives on.

You see Infinite-Planet Theory in the thinking of those who believe that the problem of feeding a hungry world can and must be solved by increasing agricultural output. Is that even possible? The short answer: no. The amount of food we can grow is ultimately limited by three factors: soil fertility, water, available sunlight. In our cheap-energy petroleum economy we've pushed against the limits set by the first two constraints, using the energy of oil to fix nitrogen into artificial fertilizers and to pump freshwater into dry lands that are, in nature's design, inhospitable to farming. The prospects for continuing that effort are not good; when the oil runs out (as it must, being finite), so too will end its enormous subsidy to agriculture. Even with cheap energy, there's not much hope of pushing back the third constraint by substantially increasing the amount of sunlight dedicated to agriculture for humans. The *back of this*, it turns out, is *the front of that*: sunlight used by human agriculture can't be used for anything else. We currently appropriate an astounding 40 percent of what biologists call the Net Primary Product (NPP) of nature — the biomass available within ecosystems as food energy, produced by green plants that turn sunlight into edible energy. (As recently as two centuries ago, the human "take" was insignificant: less than 1 percent.) To take any more of that NPP would be to further hamper the ecosystems of the planet on whose health and resilience our lives collectively depend. And short of erecting huge reflectors in space, it's beyond our power to increase the amount of sunlight falling on the planet. (Putting reflectors out there, as some ambitious engineering schemes have suggested, would tend to aggravate, not counter, global climate change. More recently, the fantasies of geo-engineers have turned to halting climate change by doing just the opposite: using huge stratospheric shades or clouds of smoke to reduce the amount of sunlight falling on the planet.)

The planet's solar income is mind-bogglingly large. All told, in one year the planet receives about twice as much energy as we'll ever get from all the Earth's nonrenewable resources — coal, oil, natural gas, and mined uranium — combined. The sun delivers more energy in one hour than the world uses in a year. These facts can seem reassuring: if what we need is such a small percentage of what's available, then how could we possibly have an energy crisis? But it's important to remember that in nature nothing goes to waste. The amount of energy falling on the Earth is considerable, yes, but that sunlight is already doing something: it's being used by ecosystems as the motive force of their cycles of life, cycles that support our human civilization. No doubt in many cases we could insinuate a bit more use by humans into its flow without imposing any undue losses on the ecosystems that this use would affect, but it's equally certain that in many cases larger interventions will have ecological consequences. Solar energy is free and ubiquitous, but its exploitation for any human purpose—food, direct conversion to electricity, even passive solar gain to warm a house—is not a completely costless benefit. In many, many cases the cost in lost solar income to ecosystems will be negligible; in others, it won't.

It's time to admit that sunlight is crucial to growing food, and the amount of arable land that can catch that sunlight is finite. This means the Earth has a finite capacity to grow food—for us and for other species.

Because human population has grown in response to a growing food supply, and because more of everything that humans want has always seemed better, the ecosystems that support our civilization limp along on 60 percent of their design income. Think for a moment of what would happen to us—to our households, our families, our communities and nations—if human incomes were cut, everywhere and across the board, to 60 percent of what we had grown accustomed to expect. Not a pretty sight: the social world as we know it would radically change for the worse, and if the change came suddenly enough, civilization itself would collapse. The effect of this loss on the planet's ecosystems has been similarly dire, though few of us have been schooled in the understandings we need in order to be able to see it.

The simple fact is, were we to expand agriculture further, increasing our take of Net Primary Product to an even larger percentage, more ecosystems would collapse. Many are in collapse already. The planet is losing arable land to desertification and soil degradation. The great forests of the tropics are being cut at a rate we can measure in acres per second. We do this to make room for cattle—food for humans. The loss severely reduces the genetic diversity that allows those ecosystems to survive and thrive by adapting to change, and even compromises the ability of the planet to breathe for us, to recycle oxygen into the atmosphere. Riparian ecosystems have disappeared as major rivers (the Colorado, the Ganges, the Yellow, the Tigris, the Euphrates, the two rivers that replenish the Aral Sea) no longer reliably reach an outlet, having been diverted for irrigation; once-lush deltas have become dry and stony deserts. Dead zones in our oceans, produced by agricultural runoff, are growing. And on and on.

We could try to bring even more land into cultivation—but only at the cost of increasing the rate at which we lose something else, something that Infinite-Planet Theory has never thought to value: the ecosystem services on which our civilization, including our capacity to feed ourselves, depends. These services generally come to us as the free gift of nature, outside of any market. To take a simple example: sunlight evaporates water from the oceans of the world, forming vapor that travels on the wind as clouds, which release their water to us, replenishing lakes and rivers and aquifers, bringing clean water to our wells and reservoirs and eventually to our faucets and sinks. Absent this ecosystem service, we'd have to desalinate, transport, and distribute clean water ourselves at considerable expense.

An appreciation of ecosystem services has led some economists— ecological economists—to talk about healthy resilient ecosystems as natural capital. Like built capital—the tools and machinery that contribute to production without being consumed by it—natural capital provides a steady stream of services that are economically valuable. In a later chapter we'll look at those services in more detail; here, we can note that among those services are climate moderation; water desalination, transport, and delivery; flood control; and the creation and maintenance of soil fertility. Our agriculture depends on all of these ecosystem services, and they are in increasingly short supply.

Notice the positive feedback loop: food scarcity leads to expanded agriculture, which diminishes natural ecosystems and their ecosystem services, which eventually leads to agricultural losses, which leads to food scarcity. That cycle led to the disappearance of many a previous civilization, and unless we find a way to break out of it, our civilization will be no exception.

For two centuries we've tackled the problem of feeding ourselves by addressing the supply side of the equation, trying to eliminate food scarcity by increasing agricultural output to meet the demands of whatever population arrives to consume it. But the human population responded to increased agricultural largess the way every other living thing on the planet responds when its food niche expands. It grew, matching, again, the limits of the food supply: Say's Law. Or, more pungently, "we're pond scum," as Gary Flomenhoft, of the Gund Institute for Ecological Economics, puts it. "Given the right conditions algae flourishes, reproducing exponentially, until it hits a resource limit and crashes." Though our nervous systems are orders of magnitude more complex than that of algae, our collective behavior is just as unreflective and self-destructive. It's true that for a generation or two the Green Revolution offered us the hope that we'd feed everyone by using petroleum-based fertilizers and pesticides and expanding the use of fossil-fueled machinery. World agriculture was transformed as "backward" (pre-petroleum, organic) practices were modernized and farmers everywhere were encouraged (and given market incentives) to emulate the industrial model developed in wealthy nations. But the Green Revolution—even in its current incarnation as a move to genetically engineer domesticated plants to make them more salt-resistant, drought-resistant, and more productive—can't escape the underlying thermodynamic reality, a reality ignored by those who enthusiastically supported the export of Western industrial agricultural practices to the world. Basically, the Green Revolution consisted of using antique solar income, stored as fossil fuel, to augment the current solar income captured and made edible by agriculture. On a net energy basis—calories in compared to calories out—industrial agriculture is an energy sink, using more energy than it delivers into the economy. (It takes between seven and ten calories of energy to put a calorie of food energy on an American plate.) This is all the more remarkable, given that agriculture is a vast net to capture falling sunlight—the easiest, most economical, most accessible way an economy can capture solar flow and introduce it as useful products into our lives. Not only has industrial agriculture been a bad energy bargain, costing more than it produced, but even in the shorter run it didn't achieve its goal: as food supply expanded, population expanded along with it, reducing the rate of food insecurity only slightly (and increasing, in absolute numbers, the population that lives with food insecurity). A good proportion of the 7 billion souls on the planet today are oil incarnate, walking *fait accomplis* who will be bereft of sustenance when the oil runs out, as it must.

It's time to start talking about preserving ecosystem services, which means acknowledging limits to our capture of Net Primary Product, which means moderating our demand for food, which means halting human population increase. We need policies that cease to encourage and actively discourage population increase until our population stabilizes at a number that can be fed through a sustainable agriculture: an agriculture that doesn't rely on fossil fuels, an agriculture that doesn't destroy its own preconditions for existence by mining soil fertility faster than natural processes can replenish it.

Centuries of industrial development driven by our use of antique solar energy have obscured this essential fact: at bottom, an economy depends on extraction from nature, and the extraction of food calories for human use is the base on which all else is built. In their quarter of a million years as an identifiable species on the planet, humans have undergone two major shifts in the way they get their food. The shifts are so far-reaching in their consequences that it's fair to say that humans have, in their course, inhabited three distinctly different planets.

As a species we emerged on the savannahs of Africa to live in small tribes, getting our sustenance through hunting and gathering. The planet was relatively unaffected by our presence. Some hunting and gathering tribes managed the landscapes they inhabited (notably, through use of fire) to maximize the game and plant life they found useful, but only rarely did their exploitation of those resources carry them beyond the bounds of what their host ecosystems could supply, absorb, and adapt to. The human population was small — 1 million, maybe 10 or 50 million — and widely dispersed. In consequence, the planet was large and expansive, filled with a bounty that human appropriation could scarcely diminish. We can call this planet Wilderness Planet — though the term is an anachronism, the product of a distinction that belongs to the next phase of human history. Hunters and gatherers didn't think of their home as wilderness; it was their territory, their place, and no sharp distinction was needed or made between the land they physically occupied and the land that held the natural systems from which they drew their sustenance.

With the invention of agriculture ten thousand years ago came a distinction between cultivated and uncultivated land, and the gradual transformation of Wilderness Planet into Garden Planet. Slowly at first, and then with increasing energy, humans transformed natural ecosystems into cultivated ecosystems that produced more of what they wanted, garnering for themselves a greater proportion of the Earth's photosynthetic product. Farming societies achieved surpluses of food that allowed the expansion of population and the development of towns and cities (and of civilization — literally, "life in cities"). Agriculture seemed (and for some societies, or at least some members of those societies, actually was) a more efficient way to secure food; certainly it allowed for the development of wealth beyond what could be achieved by the most opulent hunter-gatherer society. With agriculture came a division of labor and an increase in the workforce that was not occupied with securing food. That historic shift enabled the development of trade and technics, and also of property law and social and economic classes — and formal and institutional systems of governance. As French philosopher Jean-Jacques Rousseau (who sided with the hunters) put it, "The first man to plant a stick in the ground and say 'this is mine,' and find others foolish enough to believe him, is the true originator of civil society." To the gardener's point of view, nature was what lay beyond the city walls and garden fences. On Garden Planet, nature left to itself is wilderness — a realm of threat and danger and inscrutably spontaneous processes, or, later (as the expansion of the garden proceeded and dangerous predators were eliminated), a realm to which the weary city-dweller could retreat for safe repose, for renewal and aesthetic stimulation, for escape from the fumes and sewage of the city, and from the occasionally burdensome duty of giving civil other-regard to strangers (a necessity for social life in close quarters with thousands, tens of thousands, eventually millions of others).

This transition — from Wilderness Planet to Garden Planet — was not accomplished in an instant by the first human to plant a seed in the expectation that he or she would be there to see and own the result. It proceeded at different speeds in different regions, with the garden pressing ever outward across the surface of the Earth. Among its other products, the garden brought conflict with hunters and gatherers at its expanding border. The two systems are structurally and conceptually antagonistic. Territory — land you chase others away from — doesn't entail legal concepts of sole ownership and use, doesn't bring fences and lawsuits and sheriffs. To a hunter-gatherer, a field of tasseled corn or a pen full of nursing piglets would seem like a fortuitous accident, one that's ripe for exploitation. To farming peoples, respect for an individual's property interest in nature and its products is the self-evident foundation of rational human behavior. Non-agricultural tribes, then, were by definition savage, not fully human. They lived out there in the Wilderness, after all, beyond the reach of both plow and law; as outlaws they could have no civil rights.

By Rousseau's standard, hunters and gatherers were no fools. Even so, they lost what was, historically, the first and longest of all world wars. (Mop-up actions continued well into the nineteenth century and some of the twentieth.) The victors can indulge themselves in generosity: some small hunting and gathering tribes remain today, on lands that are generally reserved for their use, though their cultures are still vulnerable to the subtler corrosions and seductions brought by Garden Planet.

For most of the agricultural societies that developed under its sway, the logic of Garden Planet was dynamic and inexorably expansionist. "Go forth and multiply" was the Old Testament version of this charge. There's a formal, if not literal, accuracy to the history that's recounted in that text: with the development of agriculture we left the Eden of hunting and gathering and were consigned to the toil of getting food by the sweat of our brows. But the logic of Garden Planet didn't need validation by the Word of a Judeo-Christian God. Other cultures, too, responded to the impulse, heeding the call to grow more, feed more, multiply. And the imperative to expand agricultural production led to other imperatives. Agriculture allowed humans to build bigger cities, which required them to invent solutions to the problems big cities create—police, armies, sewers, roads, toilets, trains, elevators, markets, aqueducts, plumbing, hygiene, medicine, fertilizer, zoning laws, civil liberties.

And as the culture of Garden Planet consolidated itself on the face of the Earth, bringing into full development the idea of maximally efficient appropriation of the products of nature for human use, the Earth was transformed again, becoming something else: Factory Planet. Every gardener knows that a garden is an artificial creation, a collaborative work of art that represents the continual accommodation of the gardener's purpose to the constraints and dynamics that characterize natural systems. As a partnership between nature and human artifice, the garden includes live things that pursue their own purposes and embody the trial-and-error design intelligence of evolution. A factory is another thing entirely. There is little partnership with nature evident within it (although, as we shall see, industrial processes are rooted in nature and are not exempt from natural law). For better and sometimes worse, the factory's every piece and part reflects not a time-tested natural purpose but a purpose, and a degree of knowledge and ignorance, that is wholly and solely human. Like any machine, a factory is made of numerous components that are easily isolated one from another: parts that can be removed, replaced, repaired, tinkered with. Its form is wholly dictated by its humanly purposed function, and that function—efficiency in the production of value for humans—is its sole reason for being.

The transformation of Garden Planet into Factory Planet would not have been possible but for the trick humans learned of using past solar income, stored as fossil fuel, to make wealth in the present. Today our global ecological-economic system is operated like a mechanical factory humming along at maximum output for the benefit of human beings, whose increase we passively welcome without limit. As in any factory operating at peak capacity, the smallest perturbation ripples through the whole and results in a loss of output. In an industrial factory, when glitches arise the line can be shut down, broken parts replaced, inventories expanded or reduced, production shifted elsewhere. On Factory Planet, there is no "elsewhere," no downtime. The pursuit of maximum efficiency in the production of use value for humans is the effort to reduce slack—resiliency—in the system. On Factory Planet, "glitches" like oil spills, droughts, and floods mean loss of output, and that means human misery, suffering, and death.

We've built a Factory Planet but have yet to implement the accounting systems we need to operate it. Every business uses capital equipment (the factories, machines, offices, and equipment, the tools-of-the-trade that allow its workers to do their jobs with speed and efficiency). If a business sold off its capital, it would have a sharp increase in cash intake—for a while. If it were to treat that intake as income by distributing it to partners and owners and shareholders, it would soon go out of business. The owners of a pizza store don't sell the ovens in order to make payroll—not if they want to stay in business. On Factory Planet, we do just that, cashing out our natural capital as income, spending it, and leaving the world a poorer, less resilient, less beautiful, less productive place. We need to adopt a system of global income accounting that treats drawdown of natural capital as an operating loss, not an income item. One of the chapters here shows how this can be done through adoption of an alternative indicator set, such the Genuine Progress Indicator (now used in Maryland and several Canadian provinces) or the index of Gross National Happiness (which originated in Bhutan and is being adapted by other nations) or—more promising—a blend of the two, which I call "GPI Plus."

Ultimately this book is about what we must do to achieve a sustainable democratic society, one capable of preserving the civil freedoms we value. Sustainability is a difficult taskmaster, for nature deals in realities and physical truths, not human intention or theory or hope. We will have more to say about what sustainability is and isn't later in this volume. Here we can simply note that whether we embrace a sustainable culture or not, it will most assuredly come. The one thing we can know for certain about an unsustainable system is that it will not last. The most disturbing environmental news from the summer of 2010 is this: the consequences of failing to make the changes we need to make in order to establish our culture on an ecologically sustainable basis won't fall on our descendants in some distant future. On Factory Planet, environmental history, whose rhythms usually move in thousands and tens of thousands of years, is now revealed in current event. You can read the sobering story of our civilization's ecological collapse in your daily paper.

In the third century BCE, the Greek mathematician Archimedes quantified the physical principles behind the lever. Of course people had long known that with a sturdy pole and a fulcrum, a solitary man could move objects that were too heavy for him to budge by muscle alone. But it was Archimedes who first articulated the principles involved and saw that the power of the lever was scalable, upward, to ever larger objects. "Give me a place to stand," he's reputed to have declared, "and I will move the Earth!" (In his enthusiasm he overreached; he would also have needed a lever of considerable length, and a suitable fulcrum.)

Factory Planet needs moving. Gradually more and more of us have come to see that if our civilization is to continue in anything like its present form, we need to rebuild our physical infrastructure on new principles: We need to use renewable sources of energy, so we need solar photovoltaic cells and hydroelectric and wind power. We need the efficiencies gained by white roofs and green roofs and better insulation and mass transit, by pedestrian-friendly cities and low-wattage lighting, by better designs — less energy- and resource-intensive designs — for everything. We need to establish our agriculture and forestry and fisheries on a sound, sustainable basis, harvesting no more than each year's annual growth rather than drawing down finite stocks of soil fertility, trees, fish. In these physical matters, the direction we need to move is fairly clear (although the political path toward achieving these changes is not). Intelligent planning and development of a new, green infrastructure will minimize human pain and suffering as we make the transition from our unsustainable society to one that is capable of being maintained over time.

But it's important to acknowledge that the unsustainable patterns and practices of Factory Planet didn't develop accidentally. As unplanned and inchoate as they seem, they stand together as the result of an underlying cause: Infinite-Planet Theory. These idea systems have roots that reach back a century and more ago, to Garden Planet, when the world seemed infinitely capable of absorbing our acts and works, infinitely capable of absorbing the perpetual expansion of the human estate. Those ideas and theories told us that the world as we've made it today would be a good and beautiful thing. Only as that world comes into full realization have a sizable number of us begun to realize that all is not as promised and that therefore there must have been some systematic flaw in the design.

Which is to say: along with a green physical infrastructure, we need also a green intellectual infrastructure. This book is my attempt to articulate what some elements of that infrastructure will be. It has been my aim to identify Archimedian fulcrum points: the key places in which the lever of rational argument may be inserted and heaved for maximum effect.

Quite a few of those leverage points fall within economic theory — mainstream economic theory, where Infinite-Planet Theory has its castle keep: its most protected, fortified, sturdiest redoubt. Most of what follows represents an assault on that conceptually hermetic enclave. Academics of all kinds, economists included, are a notoriously disputatious lot, and success in changing minds comes from anticipating objections, documenting arguments, arguing carefully. If at times in what follows the discussion seems to turn on a hair too finely split, on recondite points of analysis and fine-grained wrangling over obscure ideas, I ask that the general reader forgive me. Behind you lies the economist reading over your shoulder, the skeptical Infinite-Planet Theorist whose world is nearly impervious to being shaken but, for the sake of all of us, profoundly needs that shaking.

Some of the work collected here has been published — sometimes on paper, sometimes online. I've taken the occasion of this book to extend and elaborate some subjects whose presentation elsewhere was limited by space constraints. I've tried to eliminate repetitive coverage of the fundamental ideas that lie behind subjects as disparate as abortion rights and the American taste for SUVs, Carlos Ponzi's pyramid scheme and the early years of the oil industry, terrorism and neoclassical economic theory. Still, some ideas (the laws of thermodynamics, for instance) are so fundamental to the project of sustainability that repeated mention of them is unavoidable. As these ideas recur, I've tried to give an appropriate amount of context and explanation without being unduly repetitious. I hope I have not misjudged.

Threaded through what follows is an emergent view that readers of my previous work will find familiar: energy and the laws describing its use have enormous explanatory power for human society, and understanding them is crucial to any effort to integrate economy into ecology, as we must if we are to have a sustainable civilization. That's the ultimate end-in-view of this book: to articulate some of the essential changes we need to make in our thinking if we are to accommodate our culture to the reality of a finite planet. This we must do if we are to have any hope of preserving the freedoms and civil liberties that we enjoy under constitutional democracy, including especially the fundamental right underlying all the rest: the right to privacy, to be let alone in all matters that have no effect on others. As a review of the work of Infinite-Planet Theorist Friedrich Hayek makes clear, if we fail to change our infinite-planet thinking, we travel on his road to serfdom.

the other road to serfdom and the
path to sustainable democracy

the other road to serfdom

A hundred and fifty years ago, in a remarkable chapter in his *Principles of Political Economy*, John Stuart Mill looked ahead to the sort of world we'd have if human population and economic activity continued growing at the rates he was seeing in 1848. He did this in order to argue against the idea that more is always better, but today his reductio ad absurdum, offered as justification for "the stationary state," reads more like a dismally accurate prediction. There isn't much to like, he said, in a world

> with nothing left to the spontaneous activity of nature; with every rood of land brought into cultivation, which is capable of growing food for human beings; [with] every flowery waste or natural pasture ploughed up, all quadrupeds or birds which are not domesticated for man's use exterminated as his rivals for food, [with] every hedgerow or superfluous tree rooted out, and scarcely a place left where a wild shrub or flower could grow without being eradicated in the name of improved agriculture.

Mills's dystopian vision has, by and large, been achieved. Of course it's not literally true to say that we have exterminated every animal we haven't domesticated, or that "every rood of land" has been brought into cultivation; some land is desert or otherwise inhospitable to farming, and we've set aside some potentially arable land as wilderness and habitat for wild species. In most nations there's a sturdy consensus that this is right and necessary and appropriate (though in some nations that consensus is under assault). Nevertheless, worldwide the human estate continues to expand, as forests are clear-cut to make way for cattle, as rocky slopes and other marginal lands are brought under the plow, as human population grows by about a quarter million souls a day. Growth in arable land has slowed in the past decade, and it now no longer outpaces the rate at which it is lost to erosion and urbanization and soil degradation. As population continues to grow, arable land per person is declining even more rapidly; thirty-five years ago each human resident of the planet could draw sustenance from a third of a hectare, but by 1995 that figure had fallen to a quarter of a hectare — a decrease of 25 percent. One result: land that's farmed has to be farmed hard — with intensive use of unsustainably sourced fossil fuel fertilizers and pesticides, and with techniques that amount to "soil mining," an unsustainable drawdown of soil fertility that will further reduce the amount of arable land in the future. This degradation of agricultural land is nothing new: nearly one-third of all land that was used for agriculture forty years ago has become unusable for that purpose now. The biblical "land of milk and honey" is far from being lush and verdant today. But we shouldn't be reassured by the thought that loss of arable land has a long history. The process has gone on so long only because the soils of the planet were so enormously fertile and productive to begin with.

The nondomesticated species that continue to share our planet with us are here largely because we allow them to be — or because there's a time lag between our acts (like dumping greenhouse gases into the atmosphere) and the consequences of our acts (the disappearance of polar bear habitat, and hence polar bears, because of climate change); or because the extinction-producing processes currently under way (the cutting of rainforest, for instance) have not yet reached their full expression in the world. We who are alive today are living through the largest, fastest episode of species extinction the planet has seen since the meteor impact ended the Cretaceous era and wiped out the dinosaurs. Geologists have begun to refer to our era as the Anthropocene — the humanly shaped era.

In many places, including the United States, the few remaining ecosystems that register as "wild" are not large enough to support the spontaneous operation of nature within their borders. We have to manage the wilderness in order to sustain it — and the oxymoron inherent in "wilderness management" has long since faded from view, as necessity has made routine what logical consistency would have forbidden.

To those born into the fossil fuel era, it seems normal and ordinary that we should have vast energies available to us to effect our will in nature. It's all we've ever known, and until the recent rise of interest in environmental history, few scholars of the subject managed to make headway against the cultural perception that anything that happened much before the late nineteenth century could be treated as the quaint folkways of a remote and benighted time. This attitude is visible in Henry Ford's well-known judgment: "History is bunk." History has nothing to teach us, because petroleum changed everything, forever.

Except it didn't. Seen in the context of environmental history, the handful of generations since exploitation of petroleum began in earnest (even the centuries that comprise the fossil fuel era as a whole) are just an instant in geological time. That longer context is the time scheme in which life evolved and in which the natural processes of the planet largely operate. Humans have been an identifiable species for about a quarter of a million years, and if we represent that history by a line six feet long (the width of a six-footer's arm spread), the petroleum era—Factory Planet—is but a paper slice coming right at the end. Life itself begins well over thirteen miles in the other direction. Most of that six-foot arm spread is Wilderness Planet; Garden Planet, at ten thousand years, is less than a palm width.

Because of the power unleashed by oil, the dystopia that Mill envisioned in 1848 is very much the world we have today—not an Edenic paradise, not even a Garden Planet, but a world in which the "spontaneous activity of nature" has been circumscribed, bounded, broken, eliminated.

Factory Planet, as it's operated now, is not sustainable. But even if we made it so—even if we throttled back our productive engines to the level the planet can sustainably support—there's another problem: our conversion of nature into wealth at the maximum rate practicable within environmental limits would still leave very little room for something we cherish. I don't mean wilderness hikes or the possibility of encountering whales or polar bears or virgin forest—things that only some of us seem to cherish—but something more far-reaching and widely valued: democracy and civil liberty.

By "civil liberty" I mean freedoms like those encoded into the US Bill of Rights, which is no longer a particularly ambitious statement of rights, no longer the aspirational model to the world that it once was. The view of rights built into the US system is primarily negative: freedom from arbitrary arrest and conviction, freedom from uncompensated taking of property for public use, freedom from authoritative control of speech, thought, assembly, affiliation. Other statements of basic rights—from the United Nations, for instance—stake out additional positive rights: freedom from hunger, freedom from environmentally caused harm, freedom to enjoy a standard of living that is consistent with the levels of health, well-being, economic security, and personal dignity that prevail in the society in which you reside. But crucial to both is the idea that citizens have a right to be left alone in all things except those that directly affect others. This distinction between what's public and what's private, and not the false ground of release from work or duty or responsibility, is the true foundation of our experience of freedom, as Wendell Berry has told us. That distinction lies behind the founding premise of democratic theory as articulated by John Locke: "Every man has a Property in his own Person. This no Body has any Right to but himself."

This democratic ideal was fresh and new when it evolved three hundred years ago on Garden Planet—a world that offered a vast distance between what culture took from nature and what nature could sustainably provide. On Garden Planet humans lived in ecosystems that were by and large lush, healthy, resilient, and so expansive that they could be and were taken for granted. But on Factory Planet we capture 40 percent of the income stream represented by Net Primary Product (NPP), and our appropriation of this much solar energy strains ecosystems to the breaking point.

Humans, we can assume, have a strong and collective interest in avoiding ecological collapse and the destruction of society. In consequence, on Factory Planet acts that were private on Garden Planet have public and social consequences that make them legitimate subjects of public regulation and control.

For instance: fifty years ago if you burned a bit of carbon fuel or clearcut a forest, it was pretty much nobody's business but your own. (This simplifies things: nuisance law meant that you couldn't directly damage the interest that other property owners have in the "quiet enjoyment" of their property, and in some circumstances courts have recognized that clear-cutting and use of fuels imposes damages on others.) In our era, when every ton of CO_2 emissions puts a burden on the planet's limited ability to absorb it, and when forests and their necessary services to civilization are becoming scarcer and scarcer worldwide, it's clear that carbon emissions and deforestation impose real and measurable damage on us all and are therefore legitimately controlled by public authority in pursuit of the public good. It would seem that what can be legitimately controlled in whole can be legitimately controlled in part; the logic says that the felling of a single tree, the burning of a single gallon of gas, have clear and undeniable consequences for humanity in general. Unpleasant as the reality is, we make no progress by denying it: any act that releases carbon or diminishes ecosystems is no longer a wholly private act.

Or suppose you live in Colorado and want to catch the rainwater falling on your roof so that you can use it to water your lawn. This is a fundamental prerogative; rain is the free gift of nature, right? Not in Colorado Compact states. In the watershed of the Colorado River every drop (and then some) of the river is assigned to a use — mostly irrigation to grow food, *pace* Mill — and law forbids property owners to impede the flow of rainwater to the river. Property owners object, and in truth the imposition of this rainwater regulation seems absurd and unfair, a violation of the fundamental precepts on which our society was founded. But in focusing their wrath on the government that sets the rules rather than on the reasons the rules are needed, angry citizens are mistaking the messenger for the message, the agent for the source.

Or suppose you fancy making a living as a lobsterer in coastal New England. Sorry — there's no room for you on the water anymore, not unless you can be taken on by one of the existing license holders. Every pound of lobster that nature is capable of sustainably producing in those ecosystems has been anticipated, counted, assigned to a harvester, a market, a use. In some of the fishery management regions, the waiting list for a lobstering permit is twenty to thirty years. Basically you wait in line for existing permit holders to die or retire. This sort of regulation is like the stranglehold that medieval craft guilds once exercised on their trades — except here the choke point is the size of the resource that's being worked, not the limited ability of skilled craftspeople to take on apprentices.

Because our economy exceeds the limits of what nature can sustain, we are experiencing an increasing need for regulatory regimes for all manner of resources: an International Whaling Commission to limit the harvest of whales; a fishing treaty to apportion tonnages of catch from world oceans; a greenhouse gas treaty to apportion the planet's strained carbon-absorption capacity; intra- and international water compacts to apportion river flow among rival users, and on and on. On Factory Planet, the realm of private action—the realm in which our freedoms can be exercised without legal constraint—grows smaller and smaller, as the rule of law is turned toward regulating our collective ecological footprint.

One alternative to such rule of law is the absence of the rule of law—and a world headed for ecosystem collapse, a world in which "extralegal" conflict (war, vendetta, feuds, privateering, armed expropriation) over increasingly scarce resources will flourish. A society in which individuals find it necessary to threaten each other with violence in order to secure access to life-sustaining resources is not a society that offers its citizens the full benefits of civil, democratic society. Nor do countries in a state of war find it easy to hang on to civil liberties. Resource shortages displace populations, create failed states, breed resentments on which terrorism feeds, and send nations to war—circumstances under which we'll see further erosion of civil liberties.

The one option that is not available is to continue things as they once were: no resource regimes—no authoritative, coercive management of our collective ecological footprint—and growth without apparent limit. The sad truth is that there are limits to sustainable economic growth, and our transgression of those limits will force change of one sort or another upon us.

The conclusion is inescapable: if we grow further beyond the planet's ability to support us, more and more of our private acts will have public consequences, and the momentum of the choices we're been making will carry us to a politically unpleasant place: a world in which our lives will be hemmed in by the imperative to control our collective environmental impact while maximizing our production of food and wealth. A factory being run at maximum capacity is a marvelously efficient system, but it's not a system whose human participants are given much room to exercise prerogative, discretion, choice, or free will; a factory is no place for someone to insist on their right to privacy. A Factory Planet, budgeted right up to the edge of what's ecologically sustainable and run for the sole purpose of maximizing the wealth that the human species enjoys, is a planet from which we've eliminated the literal ground on which democratic freedoms flourish.

Support for this thesis comes from an unexpected place: *The Road to Serfdom*, Friedrich Hayek's influential 1944 treatise on free-market capitalism as the necessary foundation for democratic freedom.

The book was an expansion of a magazine article, "Freedom and the Economic System," that Hayek published in 1938, which itself had been an elaboration of a memo that he wrote in the early 1930s to his employer, Sir William Beveridge, director of the London School of Economics. In that memo Hayek took issue with the notion being advanced by his socialist colleagues, and by Beveridge himself, that the future of democracy lay in centralized, socialist control of the economy like that being practiced by the Soviet Union.

Like many another paradigm-defining work in political economy, Hayek's had its origin in crisis. As the argument that Hayek fashioned grew from memo to article to book, the world went to war. The Allied nations found it necessary to imitate the systems of industrial organization that had been developed in Germany to build its war machine: centralized planning with government control of heavy industry, and a shift away from consumer production to the production of armaments and other supplies for the armed forces. With fewer consumer goods of all kinds, including basics and staples, available in the market, the resulting upward pressure on consumer prices was checked by price controls, and scarcity was addressed through rationing. Because so much of the workforce had gone into uniform, labor was scarce, and demand put upward pressure on wages; these, too, were controlled by administrative decision. Thus, large sectors of the economies of the wartime Allies, including the functions of production, distribution, and income distribution, came under administrative command-and-control rather than market allocation.

To many on the political Left in Britain (where Hayek had emigrated in 1931), this arrangement of the wartime economy had desirable features. It was productive, efficient, and equitable. Rationing and price controls distributed the burden of home-front sacrifice across income groups instead of letting price rationing place it squarely on the less well-to-do. Decisions made centrally, by command, could be made rationally, without the hit-or-miss, trial-and-error quality of free-market capitalism, in which those who make decisions about production undertake a degree of risk and either fail (resulting in wasted resources) or are rewarded (which adds the cost of private profit to whatever is produced). Under conditions of perfect competition, private profit is supposed to disappear anyway. (As entrepreneurs suss out where money is to be made and enter into that market, production goes up and returns to capital are, in theory, reduced to the lowest level that will sustain the investment.)

As the pro-planning argument saw things, business as usual in a free-market economy, with free-market movement of capital in and out of different productive activities, always involves some degree of waste, because capital is not perfectly fungible. Machinery and other physical investments built for one purpose are not perfectly adapted to others. And falling profit margins — the signal that tells entrepreneurs that demand for what they make has been sufficiently sated by current production — are also a signal that resources and time and effort have been wasted by being embodied in goods and services that are not being demanded. When an economy is composed mostly of small firms engaged in relatively uncomplicated production (which is to say, when the prerequisite conditions of perfect competition are to some degree achieved), these inefficiencies are small and are easily justified as a price worth paying for the higher overall efficiencies of market allocation. But when firms and industries are large and their productive activities complex, the costs of misjudging the market, or of shifts in consumer preferences, are proportionately larger. When large enough, advocates of planning said, those costs can overwhelm the efficiencies achieved by market allocation. In those conditions it seems reasonable — seems economic, in the sense of getting a greater benefit for a smaller cost — to try to achieve through administrative decision making the allocative decisions that a more perfectly structured market would have produced itself.

And to its advocates, planning had another advantage. Administrative decision making — centralized planning of the economy — allows for more optimal production of those goods and services that every economist knows markets don't handle well at all: public goods. These are goods, like education and national defense and public health, whose benefit can't be limited strictly to purchasers, either because (like national defense) enjoyment of them can't be denied to nonpurchasers, or because (like sewers and hospitals and schools) many of the benefits of their use accrue to people other than the users. Left to itself, the market overproduces consumer goods (the goods whose benefits are completely capturable by those who pay for them) and underproduces everything else. And what if, thanks to the prevailing income distribution, the economy produces luxuries for the rich and stints on producing life necessities for the poor? There are moral arguments to be made about a democratic society's duty to provide equal access to life necessities; but even if we set morals aside, sheer cynical practical considerations tell us that there is considerable public benefit to be had in ensuring that the poorer classes are healthy, working, and economically satisfied enough to be politically quiescent. These benefits aren't valued in any market and therefore can't be reflected in market allocations. Planners could, in their decision making, correct these obvious misallocative biases of the market.

For reasons like these, planning began to gain favor in England. It seemed logical and reasonable and desirable to retain the wartime model in peacetime. In 1942, well before the end of the war, the Labour Party issued a pamphlet titled *The Old World and the New Society*, outlining the principles it thought should direct postwar reconstruction:

> There should be no return to the unplanned competitive world of the inter-War years, in which a privileged few were maintained at the expense of the common good. . . . The basis for our democracy must be planned production for community use. . . . The main Wartime controls in industry and agriculture should be maintained to avoid the scramble for profits which followed the last war.

In hope, and as a gesture of confidence in their ultimate success in the war, Britons turned to consideration of what their postwar world would look like. An influential report produced by Hayek's former director, Beveridge, outlined the possibilities achievable after the war through planning. These included universal health care coverage — a continuation and a modest extension of the wartime arrangement by which coverage was provided to those injured by German bombardment and to anyone whose work was tied to the war effort. (And because in the modern era entire economies, not just armies, go to war, that included just about everyone.) Beveridge's proposal included a system of family allowances to ensure a minimum income; a program of comprehensive social insurance; a government obligation to maintain full employment. The report found favorable reception among Britons who felt that the sacrifices and hardship of the war should not be endured simply to restore the British economy to the unsatisfactory state it had been in before the war, with workers idled and incomes cut by the Depression. "Now, when the war is abolishing landmarks of every kind," Beveridge wrote, "is the opportunity for using experience in a clear field. A revolutionary moment in the world's history is a time for revolutions, not for patching."

Thanks in part to the public stumping done by Beveridge in support of his report, planning became the byword of the day. Enthusiasm for central coordinated control and the elimination of competition seemed to come from every quarter, and Hayek was deeply troubled by that emerging consensus. For him, planning was the definitive element of the socialism he had seen develop into Nazism and Stalinism. All of them involved "the abolition of private enterprise, of private ownership of the means of production, and the creation of a system of 'planned economy' in which the entrepreneur working for profit is replaced by a central planning body." *The Road to Serfdom* was written to halt the rush to planning.

It's true, as the editor of the recent reissue of *The Road to Serfdom*, Bruce Caldwell, says in his celebratory introduction, that Hayek's main point is one that most today would accept as self-evident: "Fascism and communism both represent totalitarian systems that have much more in common with each other than either does with the sorts of governments and economic systems that exist under liberal free market democracies." Both were systems in which centralized planning replaced the market-based allocation decisions that, by Hayek's lights, were essential to democracy. But popular perception of self-evidence, even as influenced and supported by economists, is not always correct. Hayek's easy collapse of categories stands in need of rethinking.

All three systems (fascism, communism, and the governments and economic systems that have existed in liberal free-market democracies) are more similar than different in three large and interrelated aspects. First and foremost, they are systems designed for an infinite planet, dedicated to the idea of perpetual economic growth. The fact that we have reached the limits of the planet's ability to provide us with sustainable flows of inputs, and the limits of its ability to absorb our flow of effluents without undergoing dramatic, civilization-threatening change, makes this similarity at least as important, today, as any differences between or among them.

The second way that the systems are similar: they are systems for controlling capital. It's fairly easy to see that fascism and socialism are systems for doing this, but at first glance it seems misguided to place liberal free-market economies in the same category. Far from exerting control over capital, liberal free-market economies are defined by the freedom with which capital can enter and leave markets in pursuit of profit wherever opportunity seems to lie. Social control of capital is socialism, and free-market economies, popular opinion has it, are by definition not socialist.

But every society exerts some measure of control over the social effects of capital; every political economy is, in some measure, socialist. No current economic system confers legal authority on the owner of a factory to lock people inside it and work them to death, as I. G. Farben and the Nazis did to Jews and others in the slave labor camps of Germany. This avenue in pursuit of profit is forbidden, even if it maximizes output and minimizes costs (which, the experience of Nazi industry demonstrated, it will do as long as the labor that's worked to death can be freely replenished). The Nazi-industrial system went so far in pursuit of profit-maximizing efficiency as to experiment with nutrition, searching for the least-cost, optimum number of calories to feed a prisoner-worker each day. (Too few calories, and output suffered; too many, and the slave lived longer than was necessary or useful.)

What the Nazis did at Auschwitz and Bergen-Belsen and Dachau and the other slave camps violated fundamental principles of humanity. Those violations were so unspeakably horrible that we may not fully appreciate the economic function of those fundamental principles: they operate as social limits to what capital can and can't do. What was done in the Nazi slave-labor system was a fulfillment of a fundamental urge of capital — to maximize return on investment, to gain the greatest surplus of income over expense. The industrial nations of the world have always set social limits on that pursuit (some more ambitiously than others), though they haven't always recognized that that was what they were doing. The question, therefore, isn't whether we should or shouldn't have some degree of social control of capital; that issue has long been decided. We are, all of us, socialist to some degree or another.

The only questions that remain are: to what extent and for what purposes should this social control be exerted?

And this leads to the third way that these systems are similar, which is intimately related to the first: when those questions are answered, the voice of capital and its managers tends to speak a whole lot louder than the voices of ordinary citizens. None of these three systems is particularly effective at insulating its system of controlling capital from influence by capital and its agents. These owners and managers of productive resources seek to maximize their returns, sometimes by imposing harms and damage and loss on citizens. The loss and harm can be direct and mechanical, as from dangerous products, unsafe working conditions, and toxic effluents. The loss can be indirect but no less real, as when elements of the public commons — clean air, clean water, healthy ecosystems, and planetary endowment of natural resources — are enclosed and diminished for private gain.

Another similarity: in all three systems, owners and managers of capital seek to reduce the uncertainties that threaten the maintenance and expansion of their returns. In whatever system it finds itself, whether administered by publicly chartered corporations or by publicly appointed commissars, and whether the returns it seeks are profits for shareholders or fulfillment of five-year plans (or year-end bonuses for investment bankers or dachas on the Caspian for its managers), a productive enterprise seeks to reduce the uncertainty of achieving those ends by seeking to control rather than be controlled by the forces that bear upon it. This it will do so far as the effort is *economic* — so far as it has a higher benefit than cost. This basic self-interested motivation on the part of the owners and managers of capital isn't unique to organizations operating in free markets; benefit maximization is rational behavior in any system.

To reduce uncertainty in achieving its ends, a productive enterprise in a market system may spend huge amounts on advertising, promoting brand loyalty to insulate itself from market forces. It may use the criminal justice system to sue close competitors for real or trumped-up offenses against patents and licenses. It may file lawsuits it has no hope of winning in order to harass and impose legal costs on individuals whose purposes threaten organizational goals, as companies do when they sue whistle-blowers and critics for defamation and damages. (These are called SLAPP suits — "Strategic Lawsuit Against Public Participation" — and no one knows how many are filed every year, although one estimate puts the number in the thousands.) The goal-directed behavior of any organization is shaped by a legal environment that determines what kinds of harms and damage do and don't have to be compensated, and about what parts of the commons can and can't be appropriated for private, profitable use. An organization with sufficient resources need not take that legal environment as a given. It can invest time and effort to shape it to its own purposes — sometimes directly through lobbying and other interventions into the political system, sometimes by spending money on advertising to influence the public opinion that is expressed through voting.

Few economists have protested that these sorts of actions are a violation of the precepts that make the free-market economy an efficient allocator of resources; there was no outcry from the economics discipline about the recent *Citizens United* decision, which lifted limits on what corporations can spend to influence elections. With market restraints loosened in these ways, the rational, benefit-maximizing behavior of large organizations doesn't always and automatically line up with the interests of citizens in a free society. This is Hayek's point — but for some reason he thought that the problem was limited to capital brought under greater social control through collectivization. It isn't.

The ready ability of capital to influence the systems and dynamics that would otherwise control it wouldn't matter so much if the disposition and use of capital didn't have far-reaching effects on society. But the management of any large organization has plenty of consequences for humans and ecosystems beyond its organizational borders. Economists call these "externalities" — consequences that fall on others besides the two parties, willing buyer and willing seller, who enter into the contract of a market relation. Some externalities are positive: a factory offers employment opportunities, contributing to the economic life and material security of the broader community. Some are negative — harms and damage (or, in the softer language of economists, "disamenities") that fall far from the factory gates, on people other than the individual buyer and seller. One large disamenity is, of course, the degradation of ecosystems that comes from the unsustainable use of resource streams;

this wouldn't matter at all if the planet were infinite, for then every economic act would leave "enough and as good" ecosystem services in place after it was done. On an infinite planet, owners and managers of productive resources could be given freer rein to pursue the ends for which their enterprise is organized. But even on an infinite planet, externalities would justify some degree of social control of capital.

Given that capital should not be free to work its workers to death, should social control of capital also guarantee some other, higher minimum standards of health and safety on the job? Mine workers are inclined to think so, as the imperative to maximize profit leads mine operators to miscalculate or flat-out ignore the dangers of the work. Safety costs money, and the free-market solution — "Let workers freely choose to work in dangerous conditions if they want, or seek employment elsewhere if they don't; the market will enforce an appropriate level of safety" — is unrealistic, if not downright inhumane. (The labor contract between an individual worker and an employer is not a contract freely entered between equals; individual workers have little power to negotiate the terms and conditions of their employment. This is the basic justification for unions, and it is underappreciated in a society that has long been propagandized by neoconservative free-market ideology.)

Should social control of capital delve into recondite technical matters about when and how and where drilling mud should be tested to make sure it will do the job assigned to it? Gulf Coast residents whose lives and livelihoods suffered from the Deepwater blowout would be inclined to think so; the capital equipment used to extract oil from beneath the seafloor has a very large potential to impose costs and harms on members of society not immediately involved in the extraction process, so society has a legitimate claim to set standards and to regulate its use.

Should social control extend to macroplanning of allocation decisions, to maximize the social benefits of the economy more efficiently? This is the nub of the controversy Hayek sought to influence with *The Road to Serfdom*, offering a variety of arguments. Caldwell summarizes the book's main point: "Planning . . . would not work in practice . . . unless the western democracies were prepared to accept severe constraints on personal liberty of the sort on display in the system against which they were currently fighting."

But couldn't there be a *little* planning? Couldn't the negative political consequences of planning be recognized, controlled, eliminated? On this question — whether the road that leads from planning to serfdom is a slippery slope that, once entered, leads to an inevitable result — Hayek and his readers, even his sympathetic ones, were in some disagreement.

Paul Samuelson, recounting Hayek's thesis in his introductory textbook, reported him as having argued that "government modification of laissez faire must lead *inevitably* to serfdom," a statement he emphasized twice. Hayek took offense, writing to Samuelson, "I am afraid in glancing through the 11th edition of your *Economics* I seem to have discovered the source of the false allegation about my book *The Road to Serfdom* which I constantly encounter, most resent, and can only regard as malicious distortion which has largely succeeded in discrediting my argument." Hayek went on to scold Samuelson further, saying most emphatically that he had not said the decline from planning to serfdom was inevitable: "How anyone who has read my book can in good faith say this [is remarkable,] when, ever since the first edition, I say right at the beginning . . . 'Nor am I arguing that these developments are inevitable.'"

In his reply, Samuelson apologized and promised to emend his text. But Hayek had engaged in a bit of selective emphasis. The next two sentences in the passage he cited to Samuelson — sentences that Hayek included in the letter — say, "If they were [inevitable], there would be no point in writing this. They can be prevented if people realize in time where their efforts may lead." In scolding Samuelson, Hayek was at least uncharitable and perhaps a bit grandiose. It seems that in place of Samuelson's formulation of his basic idea — that "abandonment of *laissez faire* leads inevitably to serfdom" — Hayek would have him substitute "leads inevitably to serfdom *if you don't listen to Hayek*." The disagreement turns on the definition of "inevitable": granted it means "bound to happen," should it also mean "bound to happen if we don't do something to stop it"?

The dictionary says no; common usage, alas, says yes. If Samuelson's reading was a misreading, it was a common one. Most of Hayek's readers took him to be saying that any degree of central planning in an economy inevitably leads to more central planning and that (as the book does say) "planning and democracy are irreducibly in conflict." That was the clear conclusion offered by the condensed, popular version of the book published by *Reader's Digest* in 1945, which sold in the millions.

It's also the emphasis in the eighteen-page, five-hundred-word cartoon pamphlet version that Hayek prepared for *Look* magazine that year, and which was also issued as a bit of anti–New Deal propaganda by General Motors. Neither of these shorter versions included the (ineffective) denial quoted above.

The *Reader's Digest* edition did emphasize, with italics, a phrase not emphasized in the original: "The rise of fascism and naziism," the passage says, "was not a reaction against the socialist trends of the preceding period *but a necessary outcome of those tendencies.*" Other passages support the slippery-slope reading. Planning isn't just the road to serfdom — it *is* serfdom: "It is impossible to be just or to let people live their own life if the central authority doles out raw materials and allocates markets, if every spontaneous activity has to be 'approved' and nothing can be done without the sanction of the central authority." And "the only alternative to the submission to the impersonal and seemingly irrational forces of the market is submission to an equally uncontrollable and therefore arbitrary power of other men."

These are ringing, anthemic statements that have none of the nuance that Hayek claimed for his presentation in his letter to Samuelson. They're absolute statements, and they undercut Hayek's insistence that he never said that serfdom under totalitarian rule was a necessary, inevitable result of central planning.

And both statements are wrong.

The assertion that freedom is impossible if the economy is subject to macroplanning commits a category error by insisting that a quality ascribable to an individual component of a system must be evident in the system taken as a whole. And large corporations are islands of planning in a competitive, fluid economy; product differentiation and consumer loyalty supported by strategic marketing campaigns — advertising — help to reduce the uncertainties of sales and diminish the enterprise's subjection to the "impersonal forces of the market." Direct lobbying (and now, in the United States, massive infusions of campaign money for "issues" advertising) help to reduce what might be called the operational uncertainties of business in a democratic political environment. Corporate plans are laid and, to the extent that money, advertising, and political influence can achieve them, they're implemented. If Hayek is correct here — if his argument does not commit a category error — then the "doling out of resources" and the allocation of markets done by those economic powers makes it impossible for us to be free.

I suspect that part of the appeal of Hayek's argument here is that it very nearly reduces to an idea that feckless adolescents of a particularly romantic bent eagerly accept: freedom lies in the spontaneous expression of the self, and being constrained by plans of any sort is the antithesis of spontaneity. Again, this is a category error, as is shown by natural processes, in which individual organisms are completely free to pursue their own individual and spontaneous growth, development, and life course but are subject to immutable macrolimits set by the availability of the resources they need (for plants, water and sunlight and nutrients; for animals, water and caloric intake). The presence of others seeking the same things establishes a limit as well. Humans are of course subject to the same physical limits as other organisms, but unlike plants and nonhuman animals they have the power to theorize that their environment is infinite and to behave — and to think up economic theory — consistent with that belief.

The second of these statements, the choice that Hayek gives us between control by an impersonal market or control by the arbitrary power of other humans, contains a false dichotomy. One other possible choice has already been mentioned: submission to the uncontrollable but nonarbitrary forces of nature. Another: submission to the controlled, limited, nonarbitrary power of other humans as vested in government, particularly democratic and constitutional forms of government. In the intersection of these two choices lies the hope for achieving a sustainable civilization that preserves democratic freedoms.

The assertion that the "power of other men" is necessarily arbitrary and uncontrolled is all the more remarkable here, given that Hayek's announced intention is to defend from encroachment the civil freedom we enjoy in democracy. "The power of other men" is uncontrollable and arbitrary only if the rule of law and the mechanisms of democratic governance — majority rule constrained by constitutional limits and the civil rights of citizens — are illusory or useless. Here, then, at the heart of a supposed defense of democracy, is an assertion that democracy is unworkable.

Given that he doesn't believe in democracy, it's no wonder that Hayek finds we are on a slippery slope away from it.

A more charitable reading of Hayek on this point might suppose that, like Archimedes in his boast about the lever, in his enthusiasm to make a point he overreached. "Of course," we can give him the opportunity to say, "limited government with rule of law and civil liberty is not 'the arbitrary power of other men.' This is precisely what I want to preserve by letting the ferment of the market determine the ultimate ends for which society organizes its economic production. To preserve it, we have to abide by a limit that keeps government — even if it represents the will of the people — out of the business of macromanaging the economy, because macromanagement leads inevitably to micromanagement."

This is rather a different argument than the one Hayek actually makes, but it preserves his insistence that microfreedom is impossible within a system whose macrogoals are determined or in any way constrained. It would be a fine bit of reasoning on an infinite planet, or in a world where some natural constraint (predation by a larger and hungrier species, say) kept human numbers in check. But on the planet we actually have, this Hayekian argument is easily controverted by pointing out one finite-planet fact: like pond scum, humans, when left to pursue their individual purposes without limit, eventually bring about conditions in which all of their purposes, including their efforts to remain politically free, must be frustrated. It can hardly be morally compulsory, civically desirable, or pragmatically wise to let rigid enforcement of an instrumental end — the anarchic play of "free-market" economic activity as an expression of political and civil freedom — become the vehicle by which the ultimate end — the security of democratic freedom within society — is lost to us.

Hayek, unlike Mill, implicitly and comfortably assumed that we could have infinite economic growth on a finite planet, and his argument against macromanagement of the economy for social purposes depends on that assumption. Ecological limits to economic development, so clear to Mill a hundred years earlier, played no part in Hayek's theory. From our perspective fifty years after Hayek it's easier to see that planning is planning whether it's done to minimize poverty and injustice (as socialists were advocating then) or to preserve the minimum flow of ecosystem services that civilization requires (as we are stumbling toward today). In a finite world, free markets built on infinite-planet assumptions are just the other road to serfdom.

friedrich hayek, socialist, and his fallacy of the excluded middle

ontrary to the perception of many conservatives who hold Hayek in high esteem, he did not think that the establishment of a welfare state was incompatible with the operation of a free-market system, or that social insurance and a safety net would destroy democracy. Perhaps in an effort to co-opt the popularity of the Beveridge proposals, Hayek specifically justified the creation of a welfare state—a stingy and rather minimal version, but a welfare state nonetheless. In a chapter in *The Road to Serfdom* titled "Security and Freedom" he speaks of two kinds of security: security "against severe physical privation" and the security of a guaranteed standard of living at some other, higher level. He was adamantly against public authority providing the latter. But as to the former: "There is no reason why, in a society which has reached the general level of wealth which ours has attained, the first kind of security should not be guaranteed to all without endangering general freedom."

From here it is a relatively small step—a step Hayek certainly wouldn't take—to recognize that poverty and wealth are not absolute, but relative within an economy. In terms of their general standard of living and distance from "physical privation," many poor people in industrial societies today live better than many of the wealthiest did half a millennium ago, but this knowledge is no consolation to those who experience their poverty in the present. They measure their condition, reasonably enough, against what others in society have and what seems possible today. In this their judgment is uncoerced; everyone is free to judge for themselves the relative degree of privation they experience. This free market in human judgment comes to an unassailable and sturdy conclusion: poverty is relative. In contrast, Hayek's presumption that poverty is not relative but absolute asks us to impose the judgment of some small group of authoritative (and fallible) humans—humans who have presumably been influenced by Hayek—on everyone else. His approach is condescending and undemocratic, and in being undemocratic it violates the values he supposes to profess.

Because poverty is relative and not absolute, the distinction that Hayek drew between two kinds of security simply doesn't hold up. Both kinds of security result from the establishment of a base-level standard of living for members of a society, and rather than being opposites, they fall on a scale. Hayek wants to deny the continuity of that scale by creating two absolute types and drawing a line between them, which he does in order to express his preference that the minimum standard be set low—presumably higher than the standards of welfare that Nazis experimented with at Auschwitz, but still low. But if we admit that as a practical matter poverty is relative, Hayek's argument falls apart. And if we import into his discussion of social welfare programs the admission that most people would, if surveyed, allow that they experience "severe physical privation" when their physical standard of living falls more than, oh, two standard deviations below the social mean, then he has justified a considerable social welfare net.

That Hayek thought some such net was necessary and appropriate (and no threat to freedom) is clear: "There can be no doubt that some minimum of food, shelter, and clothing, sufficient to preserve health and the capacity to work, can be assured to everybody." He also allows that there's a role for government-sponsored health insurance: as long as the insurance won't destroy the motivation to avoid accidents and sickness, "the case for the state's helping to organize a comprehensive system of social insurance is very strong." In the real world, where people are not completely the self-interested calculators of material benefit that economics texts take them to be, who among us ever actually thinks, "I'd like to get sick or have a disabling accident now, because I'm well insured and will be taken care of"? A careful follower of Hayek would be led to support a single-payer, government-organized health insurance program. Health and a guaranteed minimum of food, shelter, and clothing are public goods—their benefits redound generally, to society, not just to the fed, sheltered, clothed, and healthy person—and because they are public goods, the market fails to provide them in optimal quantity. While not using the terms "market failure" or "public good," Hayek clearly recognized their application to this issue and allowed that publicly organized health insurance and public provision of a minimum standard of living would not compromise the freedoms we enjoy in democracy.

Perhaps Hayek had in mind the public clamor for rectifying the market failures of free-market capitalism when he wrote, "It is now often said that democracy will not tolerate 'capitalism.'" And he made his position clear: "If 'capitalism' means here a competitive system based on free disposal over private property, it is far more important to realize that only within this system is democracy possible." But we can see today, as he might have begun to see if he had read and taken seriously Mill's dark vision of infinite growth, that on Factory Planet, budgeted up to and beyond the ecological limits to economic activity, "free disposal over private property" means freedom to impose costs and harms on others without facing any limits or any consequences. That's not democratic freedom. That's the freedom of the tyrant, the freedom to impose the sort of injustice that Hayek intended to forestall.

On an infinite planet, we might all reasonably claim the right to have such freedom. "Every self a tyrant!" would be that world's apt slogan; each of us could be oblivious to the consequences of our acts for others, because our acts and works would have little (perhaps, for the hermit, no) inescapable effect on others. Unlike Mill, Hayek failed to recognize that the economic energies he celebrated would transform the world, giving us the more populous, ecologically straitened world we have today: a Factory Planet on which there is no longer any room for truly private economic acts, no longer any room for truly private economic property.

Hayek can be seen as having placed into the public conversation a passionate accounting of the previously underappreciated social costs that come from centralized planning of economic affairs. Yes, he allowed, centralized planning, especially as it mobilizes economies in wartime, *looks* efficient. But that efficiency comes only because there is one overarching end to which all members of the society are willing to ascribe, and the efficiencies disappear when the tightness of that focus is loosened, as it properly ought to be once the war-crisis is over. For their part, the advocates of planning who were his contemporaries can be seen as having advocated that once the war was won, a different central focus could animate the economy: the efficient expansion of wealth production through an extension of the human domination of nature, and an equitable distribution of the result. Progress — more stuff, more wealth, an expansion of the economy's ecological footprint — could stand as the universally acknowledged, socially desirable end that would support pursuing the efficiencies achievable by planning; economic growth would be the moral equivalent of war.

What Hayek wanted was a continuation of the principles of property and social organization that prevailed during the phase of economic growth on Garden Planet, when the planet was large enough that "free disposal over private property" did not automatically mean "freedom to impose costs, harms, damage, and loss on others." What his opponents sought was the efficiency of planned production appropriate to economic growth on Factory Planet. But today neither path is especially attractive, for neither can succeed. It is impossible to have infinite economic growth on a finite planet.

We need not be stymied by this dilemma, because there's another option. In finding that a planned economy necessarily led to a totalitarian suppression of individual liberty, Hayek committed yet another instance of the fallacy of the excluded middle. He dismissed, on flimsy grounds, any talk of a third possibility: an economy that uses price signals in markets to achieve efficient allocation decisions but also brings capital under some degree of shared and social control by ensuring that the market signals sent by prices contribute to improved (ambitiously we could say "optimal") societal outcomes. Such a system could pursue an outcome that wasn't under discussion then but whose contemporary value no rational person can deny: the creation of an ecologically sustainable civilization.

In the 1940s Oskar Lange had proposed something that fell in this middle way, arguing that a central price board could set prices, adjusting them by trial and error to achieve the desired outcomes. Hayek criticized the reliance on price boards, which would never, he said, operate as promptly and effectively as a market. But real markets don't operate as promptly and effectively as Hayek's imaginary perfect markets do, so the comparison is unjust. In an efficient free market, firms are "price takers" — the market price is the market price, and there is nothing an individual seller can do about it. But vast areas of the modern industrial economy come nowhere close to meeting this ideal. The pricing of most products reflects competitive pressure, yes, but also "imperfections" in the market: market concentration (with a few dominant sellers or a few dominant buyers having the ability to affect the whole market); real and imagined differentiation between similar products; brand loyalty supported by customer experience, or by sophisticated and expensive advertising, or by patents and copyrights. As most free-market economists will admit, about the only products that meet the criteria for being sold in an efficient and fully competitive market — and which are therefore sold at prices dictated by those markets — are minerals and basic commodities. Gypsum or wheat sold by one supplier is pretty much the same as gypsum or wheat from another. But it's the Apple Corporation, not the market, that decides the price of an iPad or iPhone.

The fact that price making, rather than price taking, is an established feature of the modern economy is attested to by other facts: many corporations devote considerable resources in their marketing and planning departments to determining what product pricing should be; the Small Business Administration offers helpful advice on pricing to firms too small to support the overhead of developing that expertise in-house; and most programs leading to an MBA degree offer coursework in strategic pricing decisions. All of these would be useless — an inefficient waste of resources — if firms simply took prices as given by the market, as Hayek's argument assumes. If private enterprise is efficient and doesn't waste money on useless activity, then these expenditures tell us that private enterprise has considerable power to engage in the administrative setting of prices. There's no reason to suppose that prices set by a public authority — Lange's price boards — would be any less efficient. It seems that the argument that administered prices are inherently inefficient falls apart on the reality of how the economy actually operates. Lange's proposal is not, on its face, impractical, absurd, inefficient, or impossible to achieve.

But (the Hayekian argument against Lange might reply) there are, in fact, important differences between a system with a centralized, public-authority price administration and the variety of private price administrations that operate in our industrial economy. Public authority is remote from economic experience and the influence of consumer-citizens, remote from the feedback loops that would let their decisions about prices be efficient. Private price administrators, working to please managers and shareholders and improve a corporation's bottom line, have a greater incentive to get prices right.

Yes and no. On the yes side: Most firms making pricing decisions are ultimately subject to some degree of discipline from the market, even as they exert some degree of influence or even control on it. That discipline sets limits on their ability to administratively set their prices — unless, of course, public authority judges them "too big to fail." (It's worth noting that in an efficient factory run at peak capacity, every part, no matter how small, is "too big to fail.") Publicly employed price administrators have no such check on the range of their authority, their degree of latitude and prerogative.

This objection is easily answered. Publicly employed price administrators would be subject to a discipline imposed by law and by the supervision of elected officials. In an effective democracy, that discipline and supervision would be as much an instrument of popular will as are the decisions, made in markets, that set limits to what corporate price-setters can do. Any argument to the contrary is an argument about the flaws of the particular democratic system being used, not an argument against a public price administration as such. That is to say, the flaw in the system lies with democracy as practiced, not with administrative price setting. One strong step toward achieving the kind of democracy that would allow price administration to function efficiently would be campaign finance reform: eliminating the ability of corporations (and money in general) to exert strong influence — influence to the point of control — over our elections. The failure to make one necessary reform is not a creditable argument against making another.

A different and convincing argument in favor of administrative pricing is suggested by an oft-repeated aphorism attributed to Oystein Dahle. "Socialism," he said, "collapsed because it did not let prices tell the ecological truth." To this the Hayekian can nod in agreement: just so; planned economies are foolish — unsustainable — because they try to lie to themselves with pricing. But Dahle went on to warn: "Capitalism will collapse if it does not let prices tell the ecological truth."

And what is that truth? Certainly one part of it is this: use of carbon fuels emits greenhouse gases; these impose the costs of climate change, which are considerable, on all of us. If carbon prices told the truth, carbon energy would be very expensive, and the invisible hand of the market would encourage us to economize its use. An ecologically true price for use of carbon fuel is a price high enough to ensure that the sum total of all CO_2 emissions would fall under the cap implied by the planet's finite capacity to absorb and recycle those gases without producing climate change. In any market, prices ration access to goods, balancing demand with supply. An ecologically accurate price for carbon fuel would ration access to the "carbon sink" services of global ecosystems, ensuring that demand for this service is constrained to available supply.

There will be differences of opinion about what that price is. But the ecological price itself is not a matter of opinion; it is a matter of technical (chemical, atmospheric, economic) fact. Opinions vary because we are ignorant, not because the thing itself is variable and uncertain. The price of our most ubiquitous carbon fuel, petroleum, is in no sense set by the market (as is made clear in my discussion, in a later chapter, about the functional equivalence of the Texas Railway Commission and OPEC). Given that the price of oil is already set by a pricing authority — ministers of oil-producing nations — it's no great leap in economic theory or practice to add to that pricing an additional increment to account for social harms — costs — that the current pricing system conveniently ignores.

Price boards like those Lange advocated, common in democracies during the Second World War, are only one way of getting prices to contribute to socially optimal outcomes. Many economists argue that a more efficient way to achieve the same end would be to use taxation and subsidy policies to ensure that prices are a better reflection of the otherwise untallied social costs and social benefits of producing particular things. Economists have long been familiar with this approach. It employs what are called *Pigouvian* taxes and subsidies, after A. C. Pigou, who laid out the case for them in 1920. The basic idea: markets can't be efficient if prices don't accurately reflect all costs and benefits. Prices rarely include all costs and benefits — some costs of production (like environmental degradation and depletion of finite resources) are not included in the price, and some benefits of consumption (for instance, the net gain for all members of society that occurs when the younger generation is effectively educated) aren't captured by the purchaser of a good. Economists say that such costs and benefits are *externalized*: they fall outside the price. If markets are going to function to give us the optimal amounts of goods and services, those externalized costs and benefits have to be internalized. Pigouvian taxes internalize costs; Pigouvian subsidies internalize benefits.

Every modern economy is characterized by some degree of Pigouvian market structuring in this way. No market economy has ever failed to incorporate the value of at least some externalities into the prices of some goods: here a society gives a subsidy to schools or students or hospitals; there it gives a tax deduction for charitable donations, elsewhere a tax on alcohol or cigarettes; and, pretty broadly throughout advanced industrial societies, governments set regulations that increase the costs of consumer goods by forcing prices to include the expense of protecting workers' lives and safety. Pigouvian "green tax" policy extends this approach into a more comprehensive treatment of environmental harms and benefits and is one effective way to balance the need to give free choice to consumers and entrepreneurs with the necessity of recognizing ecological (and social and cultural) limits to that freedom.

Work is good; use of nonrenewable matter and energy is bad. Under an appropriately fashioned green tax system, the income tax — a tax on working and on job creation, both of which are social goods — could be abandoned, replaced by an appropriate tax on matter and energy throughput. Thus, a "green tax shift" is a shift in revenue, not an increase in government revenues or in the percentage of total economic production that is assigned to the overhead of maintaining government and its provision of public goods. Taxing throughput at the origin is conceptually easier and in practice much cheaper than developing the expertise needed to set prices across the entire range of products, even product categories, offered in a modern economy. A throughput tax would ripple out into the economy and — if set accurately — would make additional price control and a whole lot of other environmental regulation unnecessary.

For instance: a tax on extraction of carbon energy (administered at the wellhead, at the mine shaft) would reduce the use of carbon energy by incorporating into its price the external costs its use imposes on society, costs that include the certainty of occasional toxic spills and the certainty of contributing to climate change. It could be phased in gradually to minimize disruption and would begin to get price signals into alignment with physical reality. Similar taxes on use of resource flows that are capable of being regenerated (forestry products, say, or fish, or the consumption of soil fertility in agriculture) could bring their rates of exploitation down from unsustainable to sustainable levels. With prices sending accurate signals about social and ecological cost, there would be far less need for command-and-control regulation — the setting of minimum mileage standards for vehicles, the monitoring of forestry and agricultural practices in the field, the monitoring of CO_2 output from coal-fired electricity generation, of fish tonnages landed at the wharf. That sort of regulation is notoriously expensive to administer. It requires a large workforce — inspectors and field agents, everything from weighers of fish to samplers of smokestacks, along with hordes of technicians to test products and processes against whatever standards are written and hordes of administrators, judicial personnel, and lawyers to handle complaints and appeals. And the regulatory approach is more directly experienced as an encroachment on individual prerogative. Once implemented, a tax-and-subsidy system becomes a mostly invisible hand steering private choice toward publicly desirable ends.

If a carbon tax were set at a rate that brought total carbon exhaust under the cap implied by the planet's limited ability to absorb and recycle CO_2 without climate change, fuel users would be free to use carbon when, where, and however they choose. (You could drive a Hummer if you wanted — if you were willing to pay a lot more carbon tax per mile than your neighbor in a smaller car.) Socially desirable outcomes in the use of capital — fewer Hummers, more hybrids, more mass transit, sustainable post-petroleum agriculture — would thus be encouraged without sacrificing the efficiencies achieved by market allocations, and without encroaching on the realm of discretionary choice that Hayek defended as a necessary component of the experience of freedom.

Our sprawling, energy- and resource-profligate civilization wasn't built in a day; it evolved gradually as self-interested consumers and producers pursued their ends in markets that told us energy and other resources are cheap and would be cheap forever. Green taxes would begin to run that evolution toward a better end — the establishment of a sustainable civilization capable of preserving human dignity, including the dignity ensured by civil liberty and open, participatory government.

This approach to taxation isn't new. Green taxes have been under discussion for more than two decades. "Many European countries," the Tax Policy Center at the Brookings Institution notes, "have used pollution taxes" — one element of a comprehensive green tax program — but the United States imposes "virtually none." Pollution taxes are but one kind of Pigouvian environmental taxation, and some nations have used them mostly to augment revenues and to defray (some of) the costs of cleanup. The first isn't a shift at all, but an augmentation, and the second doesn't address the goal of developing an ecologically sustainable economy. And as our years of experience with internal combustion engines show, it's more efficient to regulate throughput by metering inputs than by choking the tailpipe.

The movement for a more comprehensive "green tax shift" is gaining momentum, with support from environmental organizations, policy institutes, and Green Party candidates. In Australia, a group called Conservatives for Climate and Environment has run candidates for office in New South Wales, Victoria, and Western Australia, and a featured plank in their platform has been a carbon tax. (The appeal to conservatives: like its chief competitor, a system of cap-and-trade, a carbon tax would achieve carbon reduction by letting markets find the most efficient solutions; and the tax is easier and cheaper to administer, requiring less government and offering fewer opportunities for corruption or "gaming" its system than cap-and-trade does.) The World Bank, under Robert Zoellick, recently announced the adoption of a key element that's needed to implement a green tax shift: in future development decisions, the bank will take into account the value of unpriced ecosystem services when it assesses the potential costs and benefits of development. (You have to know what the costs are before they can be internalized into a green tax pricing system.) At the Gund Institute, Gary Flomenhoft has prepared a green tax proposal for the state of Vermont, and other organizations have laid similar proposals in front of policy makers elsewhere.

The kind of socialism that Lange advocated, in which markets are structured by public policy so that prices send better, more accurate signals about the social costs and social benefits of the goods that are sold within them, was neither the centralized planning that Hayek criticized nor the free-market approach that he celebrated. It is not a single thing, but a scale of possible alternatives depending on the extent to which the monetary value of externalized social costs and benefits are incorporated into market prices. Because of this it's fair to say that market socialism is the system we have now, have had in the past, and will have in the future.

The adoption of a green tax system doesn't represent a departure from current practice, then, but an effort to bring coherence and order to a system that already exists and to establish ecological sustainability as one of the goals of that system. Tweaking prices to make them better indicators of social costs and benefits will let the "invisible hand" of the market be a better, more efficient vehicle of producing the common good — a good that includes the preservation of civil freedom through the development of a stable, sustainable, finite-planet democracy that continues to enjoy the efficiencies and freedoms afforded by the uncoerced, free interplay of individuals contracting with each other in markets.

Will a green tax shift accomplish everything that needs to be accomplished to place our economy on a sound and sustainable footing? No, of course not. Some activities will still have to be enjoined, through outright prohibition, rather than taxed: destruction of habitat of endangered species, for instance. Our political institutions and systems need structural reforms to make them consistent with finite-planet thinking — a point I've elaborated elsewhere. But a Pigouvian environmental tax shift is one strong way to begin getting prices to tell the ecological truth, which is itself one effective instrument for prompting us to begin making the choices that will put us on the path to a sustainable economy.

It's going to take some work to preserve democracy in an era of ecological constraint. A key element is achieving a sustainable, stable level of human population. Without that, if we budget ourselves to a finite, sustainable level of resource throughput, then continued growth in the human population will reduce the average standard of living that humans can enjoy, and, as Hayek warned, democracy doesn't flourish when the standard of living is in decline. Worldwide, education of women and girls has a strong effect in depressing birth rates; equal access to education should be seen not just as a civil right for women but as a necessary step toward ecological sustainability and hence toward the preservation of civil liberty for us all. (The problem is not hopelessly large or complex. Annual growth in world population is roughly equal to the number of unplanned pregnancies worldwide, which holds out the promise that worldwide access to family planning will go a long way toward stabilizing the human population.)

There are other policies that would work to halt population growth, policies that use the power of the market rather than draconian command-and-control measures like the one taken by China, limiting each couple to one child. Subsidies to families larger than is needed for population replacement — two per pair of reproducing adults — could be eliminated. Incentives for large families could be reduced. One such incentive is the fact that humans seek the security of support by children in their old age. In countries where infant and child mortality rates are high, the number of children needed to accomplish that is higher. The development and maintenance of health policies and programs, and of a social safety net for the elderly, reduces this motivation to have larger-than-sustainable families; it, too, is part of a coherent movement toward establishing a sustainable society. (Whatever its other merits and demerits, privatization of social security — having every worker fend for him- or herself in old age, relying on resources saved and on resources provided by one's offspring — is very likely to be a stimulus to population growth, and therefore a step on the other road to serfdom.)

Education of girls and young women, worldwide; providing incentives for family planning and smaller families; and removing incentives for larger families are all ways to begin using market mechanisms to rein in population growth. Given the finite capacity of the planet to carry the human population, anything we do now to reduce the growth in human population means a better material standard of living for all of us, now and into the future. Any policy that aims at and achieves zero net population growth is a step off the other road to serfdom.

It's possible that in the modern world, the human experience of freedom achieved a maximum in the middle of the petroleum era, before Garden Planet developed fully into the Factory Planet we have today. Access to cheap, liquid solar energy put enormous wealth and power at our command, and that power to work our will and to create wealth without end could be enjoyed without any thought of encountering macrolimits. Infinite expansion of the human estate looked to be the physical foundation of our freedom — until, gradually, we had to face the sad realization that there is no costless benefit and that we cannot treat the planet as though it were infinite. Hayek's warning, that democracy and planning are irreducibly in conflict, is a reminder of what we've lost as economic growth forced us from Garden Planet, with its apparently infinite possibilities and robust freedoms, and brought us to Factory Planet, a world in which both freedom and economic possibility are constrained. In the world we have made, it's not planning but the absence of planning that is the road to serfdom.

what "sustainability" is

Even some enthusiastic supporters of sustainability have begun to shun use of the term because it has grown "buzzy," has become a term that signals not careful thought but the absence of thought. You find just about any activity described as "sustainable." The word lends a gloss of moral imperative, a sense of inevitability, the cachet of environmental enlightenment to all manner of acts and works. "Politically feasible," "economically feasible," "not part of a pyramid or bubble," "socially enlightened," "consistent with neoconservative small-government dogma," "consistent with widely accepted principles of justice and fairness," "unlikely to be reversed by somebody somewhere else," "morally desirable," and, at its most diffuse, "sensibly far-sighted" — the word has been used to mean all of these.

But to paraphrase Hegel, "Humans propose; nature disposes." Like Humpty Dumpty in *Alice in Wonderland*, we can use a word any way we want, but when we exercise that prerogative there's no guarantee that our use of a word is an accurate reflection of anything more than our desire to use it. No matter what we think we signify with the term, Nature will decide what is sustainable; it always has and always will.

From the cloud of linguistic confusion over the term comes one reassuring thought: the reflexive invocation of "sustainable" as cover for all manner of human acts and wants shows that the ideal of sustainability has gained wide acceptance as a longed-for, if imperfectly understood, ideal. That counts as progress. Given the confusions behind the term, it would be good to clarify just what it means.

There are several distinct kinds of sustainability. An act, process, or state of affairs can be said to be economically sustainable, ecologically sustainable, or socially sustainable. To these three some would add a fourth: culturally sustainable.

The lack of ecological sustainability is what threatens to bring our civilization, with its civil liberties and enormous capacity for wealth generation, to a crashing halt. When its constituent systems are healthy, nature is malleable and enormously resilient, and its resilience gives it a dynamic equilibrium: always changing, always moving toward and never far from balance. This movement-and-balance is sustained against the depredations of time and chance — the assaults of entropy, that law of "rust, ravage, rot and decay," in Herman Daly's phrase — by throughput of solar energy. But the resiliency of nature has limits. To transgress them is to act unsustainably.

Thus, "sensibly far-sighted," though vague, manages to capture the strict but simple ecological definition of the term: a thing is ecologically sustainable if it doesn't destroy the environmental preconditions for its own existence.

One way of talking about the maintenance of those environmental preconditions is to speak in terms of capital. Just as a commercial enterprise can't be economically sustainable if it doesn't conserve the capital stock on which its productivity depends, a thing can't be ecologically sustainable if it draws down the stock of natural capital on which its existence depends.

This definition of sustainability finds no place in strictly economic uses of the term. "Economic sustainability" is often used to describe the point at which an enterprise makes enough money to keep going. (As part of that: an economically sustainable enterprise doesn't engage in "deferred maintenance," doesn't try to balance the books by consuming its capital as income.) On a larger scale, the term "sustainability" is used in economics to describe the point at which a less-developed economy no longer needs help from outside, doesn't need infusions of capital to generate wealth or infusions of aid to feed its people. These uses of the term are misleading. For many who use it this way (including traditional economists and many economic aid agencies), "economically sustainable" means "financially sustainable within the general industrial program of using fossil fuels to generate wealth, food, and economic growth" — a program that is, of course, not sustainable.

Social sustainability can be described in at least two ways. One: a society is socially sustainable if it doesn't contain any dynamics or forces that would pull it apart. Such a society has sufficient cohesion to bridge the animosities that arise from (for instance) differences of race, gender, income, wealth, ethnicity, or political or religious belief, or from differential and discriminatory access to such boons as education, opportunity, the fair and effective administration of justice. Social sustainability can be achieved by strengthening social cohesion (war and the demonization of out-groups are favorite devices), through widespread indoctrination of citizens in a belief system that justifies the disparities that strain that cohesion (here such notions as the divine right of kings and conservative free-market ideology have filled the bill), or by diminishing the disparities themselves. (Or all three.)

A second way to describe social sustainability: as with an economically sustainable activity (which doesn't draw down the built capital on which it depends) and an ecologically sustainable activity (which doesn't draw down the natural capital on which it depends), a socially sustainable activity doesn't drawn down the social capital on which it depends. The few economists who talk about such things define social capital as "the stock of trust, mutual understanding, shared values, and socially held knowledge that facilitates the social coordination of economic activity." But economic activity is only one category of social activity, and social capital has benefits that extend beyond our specifically economic lives. A larger, more accurate definition of social capital: the stock of trust, mutual understanding, shared values, and socially held knowledge that facilitates our ability to live a satisfying, commodious life with others.

As the United States is discovering from its difficult experience in trying to export democratic forms to other nations, democracy presumes a foundation in strong, healthy social capital of a particular sort. For democracy to work, citizens need to have some degree of trust in each other and in their forms of governance; some degree of respect and empathy for those whose views, lives, and life choices differ from their own; and some shared understanding of and appreciation for the benefits and responsibilities they have within a democratic form of government. The United States may yet learn that it shouldn't take its own social capital for granted — as it did in developing a built environment characterized by suburban sprawl, a pattern of development that makes the maintenance and retention of social capital more difficult. In an unfortunate parallel, just as individuals seeking private gain can profit by degrading natural capital, cashing it out and imposing real, sizable, but diffuse costs and harms on the population as a whole, advocates of one or another political ideology can gain partisan advantage by degrading social capital, cashing it out and pocketing the result as the coin of greater influence. This is done, for instance, when partisan voices insist that a duly elected president holds office illegally because he isn't really an American citizen. (To the extent that that message is believed, it undercuts citizen confidence in the probity of the individual who is president and the integrity of the process that put him in office. That will render his agenda more difficult to enact: partisan gain at the expense of loss of confidence in the legitimacy of public institutions.) Conversely, a politician who accepts and affirms the value of legitimate political and legal processes even when those processes go against his or her party interests, as Al Gore did in accepting *Bush v. Gore*, the Supreme Court decision that denied him election to office, can be said to build, or at least not degrade, the stock of civically relevant social capital. As with other forms of capital, so with this one: social sustainability means that whatever forces acting on social capital are in rough balance and cause no net loss of it.

What anthropologists and others call "culture" offers its members a ready-made pattern of values and socially held understandings, through shared experience of such things as foodways, habits of dress, ritual, religious observance, language, art, history, hopes, and expectations. This means that social sustainability blends, at its margin, into cultural sustainability. Some count this as a fourth form of sustainability because it asks very particularly that we preserve the opportunity for all cultures, including nonmarket and nonindustrial cultures, to maintain themselves as they choose and to have the opportunity to pass their culture undiminished to their offspring.

Ecological sustainability must be seen in historical context, on a timescale that transcends the temporal flow of old-fashioned kings-and-battles history (and even the larger dynamics of social history) to look at the unfolding tale of the relationship of human culture to the planet. Among the many possible story lines in that history, one of the most fundamental has to do with human use of energy. Human civilization has been built on the exploitation of the stored solar energy found in five distinct carbon pools: soil, wood, coal, petroleum, natural gas. The latter three pools represent antique, stored solar energy, and their stock is finite. Hunters and gatherers harvested the carbon energy of the first two, soil and wood. Since agriculture and forestry exploit current solar income, civilizations built on the first two pools have the opportunity to be sustainable. Many were not.

In 1987 the UN's Brundtland Report offered one widely accepted definition of sustainability: "meet[ing] the needs of the present without compromising the ability of future generations to meet their own needs." This is more properly a description than a definition. It rests on two key concepts. One is the presumption of a distinction between needs and wants, a distinction that comes into sharp relief when we compare the consumption patterns of people in rich and poor nations: rich nations satisfy many of their members' wants — indeed, tens of billions of dollars are spent on advertising to stimulate those wants — even as poor nations struggle to satisfy human needs. Two: we face "limitations imposed by the state of technology and social organization on the environment's ability to meet present and future needs."

That a distinction can usefully be drawn between wants and needs seems obvious. Every child — every well-parented child — learns that there is a difference. Mainstream economics, however, refuses to countenance the distinction. (Marxist economics does, which, from the viewpoint of an ecologically enlightened economics, is one of the few ways in which it is distinguishable from its neoclassical alternative.) The work of Wilfred Pareto was crucial to this development. His contribution to economic theory here marks a crucial moment in the evolution (some would say devolution) of nineteenth-century political economy into the highly mathematized discipline of economics as we know it today. Pareto's novel idea: because satisfactions and pleasures are subjective — because no one among us can say with the authority of certainty, "I like ice cream more than you do" — there is no rational way to compare the degree of pleasure that different people will gain by satisfying desires. All we can do is assert that if an economic arrangement satisfies *more* human wants, it is objectively better than an arrangement that satisfies *fewer* human wants. This seems commonsensical until we unpack that caveat "all we can do." An economic arrangement achieves Pareto Optimality if, within it, no one can be made better off (in their own estimation) without making someone else worse off (in their own estimation). Economic science, in its desire to be grounded on rational, objective principles, thus concludes that if we take a dollar from a billionaire and give it to a starving man to buy food, we can't know for certain that we have improved the sum total of human satisfaction in the world. That's because for all we can know, the billionaire might derive as much pleasure from spending his billionth dollar as a starving man would from spending that dollar on food. Marginal utility analysis, one of the fundamental insights that economics offers, suggests that if you have a billion of a thing you will of course value it less than if you have only one of that thing. But Pareto Optimality enjoins us from applying marginal utility analysis to matters of income distribution, because to do so we'd have to assume that people are, in some economically relevant respects, pretty much alike — that the human "preference structure" for food, clean air, potable water, health, and so forth are, at bottom, intersubjective, trans-subjective, objective, universal. If we're concerned that some members of our nation, neighborhood, or community are suffering from want of these "consumables," all we can do — all! — is promote the growth of income. If we care about that starving man, we must work to produce two dollars' worth of goods where before there was only one, so that both the billionaire and the starving man can satisfy their wants.

And so it was that neoclassical economic theory, putatively value-free and scientific, became structurally dependent on a commitment to infinite economic growth — a value-laden, unscientific, demonstrably unsustainable commitment if ever there was one.

The Brundtland assertion that we face "limitations imposed by the state of technology and social organization on the environment's ability to meet present and future needs" can be read as both acknowledging ecological limits to human activity and sidestepping the major issue that those ecological limits force us to confront. Yes, the existing state of technology sets limits to the amount of wealth we can create from a given throughput of matter and energy. But can technology improve forever, indefinitely? Can humans, through technological development, solve any problem brought on by resource scarcity and the limited capacity of ecosystems to absorb our acts and works? When all is said and done, can technological development allow us to enlarge the economy's ecological footprint forever in order to create wealth? The Brundtland description of sustainability doesn't tell us. Gradually, we are coming to recognize that the answer is no.

That answer becomes clearer when we model an economy as an open thermodynamic system, a system that exchanges matter and energy across its border (that mostly conceptual, sometimes physically apparent line that separates culture from its home in nature). An economy sucks up valuable low-entropy matter and energy from its environment, uses these to produce products and services, and emits degraded matter and energy back into the environment in the form of a high-entropy wake. (Emissions include waste heat and waste matter of all sorts — not just "pollution," but the matter embodied in products that have reached the end of their useful lives: yesterday's newspaper, last year's running shoes, last decade's dilapidated automobile.) Thus, an economy has ecological impact on both the uptake and emission side. The laws of thermodynamics dictate that this be so. "You can't make something from nothing; nor can you make nothing from something," says the first law — the law of conservation of matter and energy. With enough energy we could recycle all the matter that enters our economy, even the molecules that wear off the coins in our pockets. But energy is scarce: "You can't recycle energy," says the second law, the law of entropy. Or, in a colloquial analogy: the checkbook has to balance, and the bills have to be paid. Physically the inflow and outflow of the economy must be equal; to operate our economic engine we pay an energy bill, ever taking in energy anew. No matter how inventive we turn out to be, our technology won't ever give us perpetual motion. We'll never invent a way around the first and second laws.

This means that to establish an ecologically sustainable economy we must accept limits on the amount of scarce low entropy that we take up from the planet and on the amount of degraded matter and energy that we emit back into it. An effective approach would be to use market mechanisms, such as would occur if we had an economy-wide tax on low-entropy uptake — the green tax mentioned earlier. This approach adheres to the principle "Tax bads, not goods": work is good, while continually increasing the footprints of the economy — taking in and emitting more and more matter and energy — is bad.

For decades environmentalism has been primarily a *moral* vision, with principles susceptible to being reduced to fundamentalist absolutes, and this has led many environmentalists to oppose Pigouvian taxes and the market-based approach to dealing with the problem — the crisis — of our unsustainable economy. In the moral vision that has grounded environmentalism, pollution is wrong; it is profanation. A Pigouvian tax lets a transgressor pay for committing a moral wrong. *We have no right*, environmentalism has said, to cause species extinction, to destroy habitat, to expand the dominion of culture across the face of nature.

True enough, and so granted. But even Dick Cheney agreed that environmentalism is essentially, merely, a moral vision. ("Conservation," he said, on his way to giving oil companies everything they wanted in the Bush administration's energy policy, "may be a personal virtue, but it is not a sufficient basis for a sound, comprehensive energy policy.") The time has long since passed for the achievement of sustainability to be left to a hoped-for Great Awakening, to moral admonition, to finger wagging in its various forms. It's time to use the power of the market — the power of self-interest, regulated and channeled by wise policy (and Pigouvian taxes) — to do good, to bring about the socially useful end of establishing our society as an ecologically sustainable society. Environmentalism must become an economic vision.

Accepting a limit on the economy's uptake of matter and energy from the planet does not mean that we have to accept that history is over, that civilization will stagnate, or that we cannot make continual improvements in the human condition. This point was made early and well by John Stuart Mill in his *Principles of Political Economy*, published in 1848, in the same section I quoted earlier:

> It is scarcely necessary to remark that a stationary condition of capital . . . implies no stationary state of human improvement. There would be as much scope as ever for all kinds of mental culture, and moral and social progress; as much room for improving the Art of Living, and much more likelihood of its being improved, when minds ceased to be engrossed by the art of getting on.

A no-footprint-growth economy is not a no-progress economy; there would still be invention, innovation, even fads and fashions. An economy operating within ecological limits will be in dynamic equilibrium (like nature, its model): just as ecosystems evolve, so would the economy. The quality of life as it is lived (and as it is measured by alternative measures like the Genuine Progress Indicator, an ecologically minded replacement for GDP) would still improve. If a sustainable economy dedicated to development rather than growth is achieved through market mechanisms, consumers would still reign supreme over economic decision making, would be free to pursue satisfactions—and fads and fashions—as they choose. Entrepreneurs would still be free to innovate and initiate, would be free to bid against others in an open market for the use of part of a sustainably sized matter- and energy-throughput stream, would still be free to take on the risk that their proposed use of that stream won't find favor with consumers.

Environmentalists have long been criticized for offering shrill warnings, for offering up visions of doom and gloom. Nic Marks, developer of the Happy Planet Index, has pointed out that humans are hardwired to flee from or fight with fearsome things, and that visions of ecological catastrophe are certainly frightening; no wonder denial or aggressive challenges to disturbing facts are such common responses. These responses lead environmentalists to redouble their efforts, to amp up the warnings. I've offered criticism of that apocalyptic streak myself in previous work, not because I think the dire warnings are wrong but because they have proven ineffective. (And apocalyptic thinking doesn't help restore the sense of continuity through history that needs to be a foundation of sustainable thinking.) Nature's rhythms are longer than ours, longer than our news cycles and election campaigns, and when dire environmental predictions don't come true right away the general public tends to think the predictions are wrong.

Humans are motivated by fright and flight in the face of danger, but they have other motivations as well. Two of them could be engaged by environmentalism: most of us want to bring to fruition one or another appealing vision of our own future, and most of us are familiar with the satisfaction that comes from meeting a meaningful challenge. Our culture's lack of sustainability can be cast in dire, frightening terms but also as an occasion demanding that we envision an attractive future and rise to the challenge of making that vision real.

The challenge is clear and historically unprecedented. We who are alive today have it in our power to create something never before seen on this planet: an ecologically sustainable civilization that offers a high standard of living widely shared among its citizens, a civilization that respects the inherent dignity and political rights of every one of its members, a civilization that does not maintain itself through more or less hidden subsidies from antique solar income or from the unsustainable exploitation of ecosystems and peoples held in slavery or penury, domestically or in remote regions of the globe.

There has never been such a civilization in our quarter-million-year history as a species. Most hunting and gathering tribes achieved a sustainable balance with their environments, living off current solar income in many of its forms rather than on the drawdown of irreplaceable stocks, but we can't say that any of them achieved a high standard of material well-being. And they were cultures, not "civilizations"—they neither pursued nor achieved the agricultural surplus that allowed the development of life in cities. Pharaonic Egypt achieved a remarkable run as a civilization, lasting thousands of years, thanks in no small measure to the annual replenishment of its stock of soil-bound carbon energy by the flooding of the Nile (a boon it no longer gets, now that the Aswan Dam limits the deposition of sediment downstream). The culture that built the pyramids achieved great wealth and material comfort for the ruling class, but it was a slave society, dependent on the agriculturally fueled muscle power of unfree workers: not the model we need. Medieval western Europe lived in balance with its soil community, achieving a form of sustainable agriculture that lasted until the invention of coal- and steam-propelled agriculture a few centuries ago; but few of us would trade the comforts and freedoms we enjoy today for life as a serf on a baronial estate, or even for the pre-electricity, pre-petroleum life of a mid-nineteenth-century farmer.

No, there is no precedent for what we are struggling to create. We'll have to make it up ourselves.

oil, economic theory, and the
moral culpability of a discipline

n unsustainable system, by definition, cannot last.

Our society is not sustainable.

Difficult truths, these.

It isn't pleasant facing difficult truths, and our tendency to avoid them is made all the easier when authoritative voices tell us that the unpleasant truths we want to avoid are, in fact, not true at all — that we only think they're true because bad and devious people have been lying to us. This describes the current wrangle in America over climate change, which is one of the more obvious and clearly established proofs that our present system is unsustainable. The physical and chemical principles involved in climate change have been known for a century and a half. By 1908 a Swedish scientist had applied them to atmospheric science and predicted planetary warming, and by the mid-1950s a pair of researchers — Roger Revelle at the Scripps Institute of Oceanography and Hans E. Suess, a chemist at the University of California, San Diego — had seen enough to warn that by emitting ever-increasing amounts of carbon exhaust, "humans are now carrying out a large-scale geophysical experiment of a kind that could not have happened in the past nor be repeated in the future." Over the next half century scientists in a variety of disciplines worked to prove or disprove Revelle and Suess. Evidence accumulated, and gradually a near-unanimous consensus among scientists emerged: the climate is changing, and humans are driving that change. By the turn of the twenty-first century, scientific organizations were issuing position statements like this one from the American Meteorological Association in 2003: "Human activities have become a major source of environmental change. Of great urgency are the climate consequences of the increasing atmospheric abundance of greenhouse gases." In 2004, the Pentagon gave President George W.

Bush a report (which his administration suppressed) warning that "climate change and its follow-on effects pose a severe risk to political, economic, and social stability," with consequences for US national security that "should be considered immediately." "Disruption and conflict," the report warned, "will be endemic features of life" as climate change progresses. ("This is depressing stuff," one of the coauthors told reporters in Britain covering the story. "It's a national security threat that is unique because there is no enemy to point your guns at and we have no control over the threat.")

In any impartial and dispassionate analysis, the evidence supporting humanly caused climate change has to be convincing. Yet there are plenty of supposedly authoritative voices telling us that the phenomenon isn't real because the science isn't settled or is simply and persistently mistaken. To maintain that position, climate change deniers have had to do two things: deny the existence of a scientific consensus, and explain how and why so many scientists could be so wrong.

The first part of that project was outlined in a Republican strategy memo written in 2004 by pollster Frank Luntz. "The scientific debate is closing but not closed yet," the memo asserts. "There is still a window of opportunity to challenge the science." (You have to wonder about the motives behind the challenge: if the direction of the science is clear, why resist it?) Carefully staged hearings, chaired by Republicans, placed one climate change scientist next to one climate change skeptic—generally a scientist from a field not directly related to climate change, someone whose acceptance of evidence lagged well behind the median among scientists. The tactic wordlessly communicated a blatantly false impression that there is a fifty-fifty split on this issue in the scientific community. Efforts to portray the science as uncertain have been amply funded by right-wing billionaires like Art Pope and the Koch brothers, with money spent on political campaigns, public relations efforts, and "astroturfing"—giving a false sense of populist roots to the denial movement.

That still leaves another problem for climate change deniers: a vast majority of scientists agree that the evidence says beyond any reasonable doubt that climate change is real and humanly caused. How could so many scientists be so wrong? Few climate change deniers have been more pathetically creative in their work to obscure or discredit this consensus than Republican Senator James Inhofe of Oklahoma, who has said repeatedly from the floor of the Senate that climate change is a hoax cooked up by Al Gore and an international cabal of scientists. (Their motive? Fame, adulation, anti-American malevolence, grant money.) The charge is remarkably sturdy and well-traveled; it became a Republican trope during the 2010 campaigns, and I've heard it from conservative economics students in Europe, who presumably absorbed it from their equally conservative professors.

Conservative efforts to reverse the effect of the arguments and evidence reported in Gore's influential book and documentary, both titled *An Inconvenient Truth*, seem to be working. A Pew Research Center poll done in October 2009 found that the number of Americans who believe that there is solid evidence the Earth is warming dropped from 71 percent to 57 percent between 2008 and 2009. Given the size and scope of the corporate interests that profit from unregulated emissions of greenhouse gases, the United States is unlikely to take action to limit them unless corporate money is removed from politics — not very likely just now, thanks to the Supreme Court decision in *Citizens United* — or until and unless there is an overwhelming public clamor for the change. While 57 percent is a substantial majority, it looks to be insufficient to get policy changed in the face of corporate lobbying.

Why this collective ignorance on the part of the American people? Does 43 percent of the American public accept something like Inhofe's conservative conspiracy theory? Not necessarily. While extremists among the deniers are easily confounded, and while it's easy to see why conservative politicians, with major financial support from corporations and billionaires, are interested in telling us that business-as-usual creates no environmental problems, there remains a sizable proportion of reputedly intelligent people — people who would be surprised to hear themselves described as mystics and true believers, people who think of themselves as rational beings dedicated to making judgments based on good evidence and sound logic — who continue to influence public opinion by counseling us to ignore even the most obvious manifestations of our culture's transgression of ecological limits. Among them, the ones who don't simply deny the scientific evidence insist that the problem is exaggerated and will, in any event, self-correct.

No group of credentialed, supposedly intelligent people has been more sanguine in this latter faith than academic economists.

The dogmas that support their faith are clearly visible in the texts they write and assign in their classrooms. Take, for instance, the 2004 edition of *Principles of Economics* by Robert H. Frank and Ben S. Bernanke (yes, *that* Ben Bernanke — the one who left the academy to become chair of the Federal Reserve Board), in which the subject of limits to economic growth is taken up and put back down in two and a half pages that come 528 pages into the text. There's a dutiful mention of 1972's *The Limits to Growth*, by Donella Meadows et al., which offered a careful, fact-studded argument that there are, in fact, ecological limits to what we can do economically on this planet. But Frank and Bernanke mention the book only by way of inoculating students against the point of view it carries; limits-to-growth arguments are, they tell their readers, "misleading." Why? Because those arguments overlook three basic economic facts: one, growth can take the form of different and better (rather than simply more) goods and services, and it's possible that in the future the different and better goods and services will use fewer resources. Two, economic growth produces wealth, and increased wealth "frees resources" to fight pollution. And three, "political and economic mechanisms" — like the free market, with its power to find and exploit alternatives in the face of scarcity — "exist to address many of the problems associated with growth."

There's plenty of cautious hedging in the presentation. Growth in GDP *can* come from resource-saving innovation; clean air and water *may* be viewed as a luxury that's purchased only after other needs are satisfied; *in general* shortages trigger price changes that induce solutions to the problem; existing institutions can handle *many* of the problems that come with growth. Given the cautious wording, each of those statements is technically unexceptionable; they're bland and cautious enough to be true, but in sum they effectively camouflage anomalous facts that they don't directly deny. By far the largest part of growth in GDP comes from unsustainable increase in the economy's ecological footprint. Clean air and water can be viewed as flow services provided to humans by a commons we took for granted — until self-interested actors in an unregulated free market appropriated them from us, fouling them, making environmental quality a scarce good for which we have to pay. If prices solve scarcity issues "in general," and if institutions can handle "many" of the problems of growth, what are the exceptional cases? Are they minor, or crucial?

The authorial caution evident in this passage disappears when the assumptions behind these careful statements are embedded as fundamental principles of economic theory, the principles that Frank and Bernanke expounded for more than five hundred pages before misleading their readers about the prospects for infinite growth. Among those fundamental assumptions are two that are absolutely necessary if a faith in infinite growth is to be maintained. The first is that environmental degradation, as represented by pollution (including more greenhouse gases than the planet can absorb and recycle), is an unfortunate by-product (an "externality") of production that can be reduced to whatever level we like through the expenditure of money. The second is that the power of self-interest unleashed by free markets will find substitutes for any resource that becomes scarce.

The first of these assertions is embodied in a bit of neoclassical theory called the Environmental Kuznets Curve, a subject taken up later in this volume. The second of these infinite-planet premises is elaborated by Frank and Bernanke in their discussion of the oil-supply "disruptions" of the 1970s. Here our authors abandon scholarly caution to conclude unambiguously: "In short, market forces solved the energy crisis." The evidence: we have no shortage of gasoline today. (There is, of course, no mention of climate change as an aspect of the energy crisis; the book's index doesn't even contain an entry for the subject.) Their young readers — novitiates into the discipline — are thus led to accept this basic economic dogma: because high prices stimulate production and the search for alternatives, shortage of energy is not and never will be a constraint on economic growth. We'll always find more.

That message hasn't changed in the years since I was an undergraduate economics student during the gas crisis of 1973. A few blocks from the classroom, Americans waited in long lines to buy a rationed quantity of gas, and in some states drivers were further constrained by odd-and-even purchasing (you could buy gas only every other day, according to license plate number). The professor in my advanced microeconomics course used this real-world phenomenon to illustrate a fundamental point about the operation of markets: rationing (including rationing by limiting sales to those who are willing to spend time waiting in line) is made necessary whenever we don't let prices rise to clear the market.

My professor might have used the gas crisis to illustrate other fundamental economic and social truths about energy. One: in the short run, neither the supply nor the demand for fuel (and, more generally, for energy of any sort) can change much with price. This is because our use of energy is structurally embedded in life habits and in the material circumstances of our lives — the commute we make to work, the car we drive, the amount of insulation in our attic — and we can't change these on short notice. Supply, too, is inelastic with regard to price: an increase in price doesn't bring more oil to market immediately, because there's a long temporal pipeline from prospecting through discovery, drilling, refining, transport, delivery. (Inventory storage adds some resilience to the supply line, reducing price inelasticity, but storage is expensive and therefore tends to be limited. In 2005, the inventory wasn't sufficient to stabilize the price of gas when Hurricane Katrina disrupted extraction, refining, and pipeline shipping in the Gulf of Mexico. In some areas on the Gulf Coast, gas doubled in price, to five dollars a gallon.)

If price changes don't do much to affect either supply or demand in the short run, the converse is also true: in the short run, small shifts in either supply or demand have an amplified effect on price, driving it up quickly when there's a shortfall and driving it down precipitously when there's a glut.

The gas lines of 1973 also illustrated another little-appreciated fact, one that economists are, by disciplinary limit, disinclined to recognize or discuss: when US domestic oil production peaked in 1971, a fundamental power shifted from a relatively obscure state regulatory agency, the Texas Railway Commission, to an international group of oil ministers meeting as the Organization of Petroleum Exporting Countries. The Railway Commission used to set oil production quotas and thereby set the price Americans paid for oil; now that price is set by OPEC.

In 1973 OPEC was certainly a topic of discussion and analysis in economics classrooms, where it was subsumed under familiar categories: OPEC is a cartel, our professor told us, and most cartels decay over time as one or another renegade member breaks ranks — sells beyond quota — to pursue their own self-interest. (To mention the parallel with the Texas Railway Commission would have undercut the point, for the Texas Railway Commission is a government regulatory body with legitimate authority and a socially useful purpose; it's no cartel, and it didn't fall apart.) The implication we students were left with: the problem of US dependence on foreign oil, vividly illustrated by the OPEC embargo, would eventually take care of itself.

Neither my economics professor then, nor any introductory textbook I have ever found since, explained the functional equivalence of OPEC and the Texas Railway Commission. To see it you have to talk about market failures and bring political analysis into the discussion. The first runs counter to prevailing free-market ideology; the second — talk of power relations and their effect on markets — is forbidden to economists if they are thinking and speaking as proper economists. So too with another subject, the social control of capital, which after all is what the Texas Railway Commission did: exert political control over the productive resources of an industry for the common good. Then as now, the need for social control of capital — for socialism — was not a subject that mainstream economists were willing to entertain.

What the Texas Railway Commission did then, and what OPEC has done since, is called *market demand prorationing.* As long as most of the oil we consumed was produced domestically, the Texas Railway Commission could stabilize the national price of fuel by setting production quotas in Texas, prorating production among individual producers according to the proportion of demand that their production capacity represented. (If you owned 10 percent of the proven reserves in Texas, then your market share of total Texan production was set at 10 percent.) Taking the production from other states as a given (easy to do, since, compared to that of Texas, production from other states was both relatively small and stable), the commission expanded or contracted the supply of oil shipped from Texas in order to match national production to national demand. They increased supply to keep pace with economic and population growth, and raised and lowered production quotas with seasonal variation in demand (more gasoline for driving in the summer, more heating oil for the Northeast in the winter).

This social control of capital evolved because of the economically costly and socially disruptive boom-and-bust cycles that plagued the industry. Each discovery of a new field brought added production, sending the price plummeting in the face of relatively fixed demand. Several factors contributed to this. Property laws allowed anyone with the mineral rights to one sixty-fourth of an acre of land — the footprint of a drilling rig—to pump oil from the reservoir below. Since oil in its natural habitat is a migratory resource, it wasn't "economic" for the owner of mineral rights to leave oil in the ground, in its time-tested, natural storage. To avoid losing oil—and income—to a neighboring producer, you had to pump the oil under your piece of property out of the ground as fast as your neighbors pumped theirs. Newly discovered fields were exploited in a frenzy; unregulated production produced regular gluts. It's complete understatement to say that the system was inefficient. Some landscapes above reservoirs were dense-packed forests of drilling and pumping rigs—an enormous duplication of capital investment, since maximally efficient extraction could have been accomplished with a tenth, a twentieth, a fiftieth of that number. Overproduction meant that at some points in the early twentieth century, oil was worth less than the barrels it was stored in. This being the case, in some places vast quantities of oil were pumped out of the ground and stored in open-air earthen sumps, where it poisoned wildlife, seeped into soil and groundwater, fouled the air through the evaporation of volatiles, and constituted a fire and health hazard. Overproduction led inevitably to market collapse, and when that happened companies folded, workers were put out of work, and the economic life of nearby towns, juiced by the boom, ground to a halt. The unregulated use of capital in the oil industry had obvious and negative consequences for all involved: producers, consumers, workers, owners, citizens, ecosystems.

In the early decades of the twentieth century and for a good while afterward Texas was by far the largest domestic producer, a size that gave it power to influence the national market. Eventually the Texas Railway Commission stumbled on a solution to the boom-and-bust cycles that were socially disruptive, ecologically unwise, and economically inefficient: limit production to something like the quantity demanded. Having been given the authority to regulate pipelines by analogy to railroads (both are public utilities because they are "natural monopolies"— to have a dozen competing railroads side by side serving the same routes would be a waste of capital investment, so one line is established and regulated to prevent monopoly price-gouging), in 1932 the commission was given the authority to regulate not just the rates pipelines could charge but also the quantity of oil they could ship from Texas.

The commission exercised that power until market forces—and

geological and physical reality—took it away from them. Once American domestic oil production peaked in 1971, production couldn't be increased to match fluctuations in demand; the taps were already open all the way and couldn't be opened further. To maintain and increase our use of oil, we had to import an increasing proportion of it from abroad. Cause and effect: import oil, export the power to set the price of oil. Short of redesigning a complex industrial economy to run on something other than oil, there was nothing that anyone, least of all the three Texas Railroad commissioners sitting in their offices in Austin, could do to keep the power to set prices out of the hands of OPEC. My economics teacher might have used the gas lines to illustrate these points about energy, the geology and physics of oil production, and the history of its political control. But the academy, then, had no taste for interdisciplinary approaches, and economics is by inclination generally ahistorical; economists want to be scientific, and scientific truths are supposed to be timeless. For the same reason, traditional economics willingly slices off political issues, which are messy and not readily reducible to vector analyses and formulas built on simplifying assumptions.

Even acting as an economist, my professor might have offered up the fundamental observation that energy is not just another commodity within the mix of commodities an economy offers, but a key factor of production whose cost and supply affect everything else. Instead he used the real-world events outside the classroom to support a different point, one of the fundamental dogmas of infinite-planet economics: although its supply is finite, he said, "we'll never run out of oil." No: as it becomes scarcer and scarcer, the price will go up, making it so valuable that "the last barrel will be put in a museum somewhere. But by then," he reassured us, "the market will have found alternatives." In saying this he fell in line with his colleagues in the discipline, who were at that moment busily retreating from the Myth of Infinite Factor Supply and regrouping behind the Myth of Infinite Factor Substitutability.

There's no problem, this myth reassures us, if there are limits to any one commodity, like oil. The market has always found substitutes in the past, and there's no reason to think it won't do the same thing in the future.

Even though they are congenitally ahistorical, traditional economists will appeal to history on occasion when it can be made to support their fundamental assumptions—but they rarely adduce historical support from further back than the start of the "economic miracle," the sudden sharp rise in wealth creation brought about by the industrial era. (Everything before Adam Smith, in 1776, is darkness.) In support of the Myth of Infinite Factor Substitutability, traditional economists point out that when wood and therefore charcoal got scarce in eighteenth-century England, we turned to coal; in the mid-nineteenth century, when all of the easily extracted coal had been mined, we invented machinery and techniques to dig deeper; and then, as the cost of coal rose with depth of excavation, and as smog began blanketing major cities, we turned to oil. In each case, problem solved.

Whatever reassurance this argument offers comes from the fact that it takes a narrow slice of history as its base. When human energy use is seen in larger perspective, it becomes clear that humans, as noted earlier, have systematically made use of the energy stored in several distinct kinds of carbon pools: soil, wood, coal, petroleum, natural gas. Only two of those pools—soil and wood—have the capacity to be renewed on any timescale meaningful to us, because they're readily replenished from current solar income. The others represent stored solar income, locked away as fossil fuel. From a thermodynamic perspective, our exploitation of antique solar energy is the one true engine of the sudden explosion of wealth creation that defines the modern era—the development that historians of economic life, generally ignorant of thermodynamics, have had such difficulty explaining. To argue from the experience of the past few hundred years that we've handled energy crises in the past—the "so far, so good" approach—is rather like jumping from a twenty-story building and thinking, for a little more than nineteen stories, that you've been successful at learning how to fly.

In proclaiming unambiguously that the market solved the energy crisis, Frank and Bernanke reassure us that we can, indeed, fly.

How could such a perverse, counterfactual faith emerge as the foundational premise of an academic discipline? Historians of economic thought have taken up this question. In 1992 Robert Repetto offered one account in *Scientific American*: while classical economists (from the eighteenth century to the mid-nineteenth) regarded wealth creation as the product of using three kinds of assets—natural resources, labor, and invested capital—by the late nineteenth century the classical view had been supplanted by neoclassicism, whose practitioners "virtually dropped natural resources from their model and concentrated on labor and invested capital." Then, "when these theories were applied after World War II to problems of economic development in the Third World, human resources were also left out on the grounds that labor was always 'surplus.'" The result: "Development was seen almost entirely as a matter of savings and investment in physical capital." Natural resources were relatively easy for the neoclassical model to ignore, Repetto says, because there was a surfeit of them: "Food grains and raw materials were flooding in from America, Australia, Russia and the colonies, while steamships and railroads were lowering transportation costs." Economists' devaluation of natural inputs and the role of labor resulted from an all-too-typical cognitive blindness: when we have considerably more of something than we need or want, we tend to take it for granted, tend to think we don't even need it.

This is a good explanation, but it could be improved by adding this fundamental point: that glut of food grains and raw materials that made natural resources easier to ignore represents wealth created by drawdown of carbon pools; similarly, the growth of population that made labor "surplus" (chilling thought, that) was made possible by drawdown of the planet's stock of stored carbon energy. In the case of grains and foodstuffs, the drawdown is the unsustainable practice of soil mining (taking carbon energy stored as soil fertility out of the soil faster than it can be replaced). The places Repetto mentions had relatively fresh, undegraded soils, rich with stored energy. Once the geographically expanding reach of market society, with its commodification of agricultural produce, had reached these unexploited lands, that energy could be dredged out of the ground and sold for cash. In the case of other natural resources, the drawdown of carbon energy was from the fossil fuels used to extract, process, and transport them. Adding this element to Repetto's analysis, we can say that by ignoring the fundamental contribution to wealth generation made by energy, economists could, by the close of the nineteenth century, see the task of increasing the human standard of living as being essentially the problem of promoting the accumulation and development of capital.

That single-minded focus on increasing production through growth in capital has led us to where we are today — to a world economy whose two ecological footprints (uptake, output) have outgrown the planet that is its home. The engines of growth have enormous cultural momentum, to which the discipline of economics has contributed by promulgating the idea that environmental problems brought on by growth-at-all-costs can best be met only through additional economic growth. Don't worry, standard economic theory tells us: it will be easier to buy our way into sustainability when we become wealthy enough.

But in their enthusiasm for the admittedly impressive ability of free-market capitalism to generate wealth and thereby raise human society to heights of material comfort, mainstream economists have ignored this fundamental physical truth: economic activity takes in valuable matter and energy from its environment and discharges degraded matter and energy back into it. Because the planet itself is finite, its capacity to sustain either flow without ecological degradation is finite.

When theory abstracts too far from reality, then in theory anything is possible — including infinite growth on a finite planet. In the real world, though, some things are impossible. There is no process, on Earth or beyond, that can turn heat and motion back into gasoline. It's a one-way flow, from more valuable (concentrated, available) to less valuable (dissipated, unavailable) forms. Together the first and second laws forbid perpetual motion — schemes in which energy is created, or used over and over. An economy is like a living thing, or for that matter a machine: both kinds of entities take in a flow of scarce low entropy and excrete a high-entropy wake. Neither can operate by consuming their outputs as inputs.

Because we have too long ignored these truths, our inevitable transition to a sustainable economy — one that lives on a stable, sustainably sourced flow of matter and energy throughput; one whose outputs of degraded matter and energy are readily absorbable by its host ecosystems — will be accompanied by dramatic and painful changes. Much of the pain will come from one disturbing fact: for half a century we've been using an increasing amount of fossil fuels to augment agricultural production. Absent manufactured fertilizers and pesticides, agriculture reverts to the organic practice it was a century ago. To put it in thermodynamic terms: when the current subsidy from past solar income comes to an end, as it must, we'll be forced to live on, and eat from, current solar income.

The last time the planet had a current-solar-income, organic agriculture, we fed about a billion people. Even if we could double or triple that output with today's increased acreage and more detailed knowledge of botany and physics and chemistry, we are still left far short of what is needed to feed 7 billion of us. Unless we manage the transition to a post-petroleum agriculture carefully, there's little prospect of avoiding the enormous pain and suffering of a fairly rapid die-off. It has happened before in the history of civilizations, as Jared Diamond shows us in *Collapse: How Civilizations Choose to Fail or Succeed.* There's no reason to think we're exempt from the commonsense conclusion that emerges from Diamond's series of case studies: a civilization that fails to establish itself on an ecologically sustainable foundation will cease to exist.

The fall of a civilization is attended by all the human sorrows you are capable of imagining: the cruel choice between mass migration from ecologically degraded land and starvation in place; a dissolution of the rule of law; increased violence in pursuit of resources and food — violence that often comes as a moral or holy war against enemies without or scapegoated minorities within; genocide; death by starvation, disease, war, civil disturbance; death by cannibalism.

Mainstream economists, as a group, have consistently taught and counseled that infinite growth is possible on a finite planet. They have, with a rigor enforced by their discipline's precepts and boundaries, ignored the foundation that an economy has and must have in nature, and the effects of economic processes on natural systems. That ignorance put us where we are today, on the brink of an absolutely unavoidable and enormously painful transition, a transition that will come whether we plan for it or not.

Which leads to this conclusion: when and if the history of our transition to a post-petroleum society is written, a special chapter might be dedicated to the role that mainstream economists played, through their counsel of principled inaction, in producing an unconscionably excessive amount of avoidable human woe.

the economics textbook that
just might save civilization

n 2004, the same year that Frank and Bernanke published the second edition of their *Principles of Economics*, Herman Daly and Joshua Farley published the first edition of a dramatically different introductory economics textbook: *Ecological Economics: Principles and Applications*. Ecological economics is an emergent school of economic thought that stands in contrast to the neoclassical model, the model that prevails in policy circles and the overwhelming majority of academic departments. The new school is an outgrowth of the steady-state or no-growth economics that arose in the 1970s, as resource scarcity and pollution had begun to be recognized as problems that couldn't be addressed by free markets and principled inaction. (On the whole, "ecological economics" represents better branding than "no-growth" or "steady-state" economics.) The book is a classic illustration of a moment in intellectual revolutions outlined by Thomas Kuhn: if an emergent paradigm is to succeed, it must at some point be codified into introductory texts; its ideas, insights, and theoretical apparatus must be brought out of the technical journals (most of which are start-ups created by the new paradigm's advocates, who find themselves shut out of the established organs of disciplinary communication) and be laid in a coherent way in front of the discipline's next generation of practitioners. By seeking adherents among students, the new paradigm submits itself to the discipline of free and informed choice in the marketplace of ideas; without a paradigm-setting textbook, the new ideas remain on the margin, known to few, influential to even fewer.

In another classic illustration of the Kuhnian scheme, the new paradigm contained in this book can be represented as elegantly reversing some of the fundamental elements of the old. In mainstream, neoclassical economics, environmental values are treated as a subset of economic values. How does a neoclassical economist know that nature has value? Because some people will pay money to experience it. Some will also spend money on clean air, clean water, on environmental quality in general; obviously, then (says the old paradigm), environmental goods and services have economic value and can be subsumed into economic thinking as a subcategory of all goods and services. In the new paradigm offered by ecological economics, that backward relationship between the economy and the planet is reversed and set right. Economic activity is one kind of human social activity, which itself is just one kind of activity within a larger environment. That environment, not the economy, is the containing whole.

Crucial to this new paradigm is the recognition that traffic across the border of culture and nature obeys the laws of thermodynamics. The laws apply equally to both and are a definitive and controlling element in the relations between and within them; they are the fundamental truths that show how ecology and economics must be integrated. Biology was transformed by the integration of thermodynamics in the 1920s, giving us our contemporary understanding of ecological systems as energy systems. It was this understanding that Nicholas Georgescu-Roegen, a founding intellect of this view, had in mind when he admonished his fellow economists, "Biology, not mechanics, is our Mecca."

When once you become acquainted with the laws of thermodynamics, the neoclassical model looks like a never-was and never-will-be perpetual motion machine. If you model an economy as a closed system — one capable of sucking up low entropy from itself and discharging high entropy into itself forever — it's no wonder that policy and practice built on your model run into ecological difficulties. Ecological economics models the economy as nature might. To the environment, the high-entropy output of the economy is more than heat and motion from burning fuel, is more than that plus all the waste matter discharged by the processes that produce the products we buy; as nature sees it, the waste stream includes those products themselves. Everything we value ages, rusts, rots, wears out, breaks, and is eventually discarded. Even our buildings and roads become, someday, a waste-disposal problem. As Georgescu-Roegen put it: seen strictly in material terms, an economy consists of nothing other than a set of institutions and processes for converting valuable, low-entropy matter and energy into degraded, high-entropy waste.

Producing waste is not, of course, the point of an economy. When we buy something, we may think that what we want is the physical matter and energy it embodies; but what we actually want is the *service* that comes from the use of it, a service that satisfies one or another of our desires (including the desire to feel the pride or security of ownership). With those services we seek to augment what Georgescu-Roegen called "an immaterial flux: the enjoyment of life." Increasing this, and not the sheer quantity of matter-and-energy throughput, is the ultimate purpose of the economy.

The neoclassical model begins to encode its thermodynamic and ecological ignorance at the very foundation of its theory: the circular flow diagram you can find in any standard introductory text. In such diagrams the economy is represented as a closed cycle of exchange between firms and households. Households own factors of production and sell them to firms, which use them to manufacture goods and services, which they then sell to people in households. Real stuff — factors of production and goods and services — flows in one direction, and compensatory money — wages, rent, profit, and salaries, which become disposable income and consumer spending — circulates in the other. This model of the economy is so abstract that it has lost its feet — the ecological footprint on both the uptake and exhaust side. None of the standard economics texts openly profess a faith in perpetual motion, but it's there in the circular flow diagram. Few texts are as explicit as the one that Daly and Farley cite on the subject, Lester Thurow and Robert Heilbroner's *The Economic Problem*: "The flow of output is circular, self-renewing and self-feeding," because "outputs of the system are returned as fresh inputs." Anything that can take as input what it excretes as output is a perpetual motion machine.

This fundamental flaw in the circular flow model wouldn't be so consequential if the environment from which inputs are drawn, and into which outputs are exhausted and excreted, were infinite. An infinite planet offers an infinite supply of inputs and has an infinite capacity to absorb effluents and outputs; each, then, could be safely ignored in the model. No doubt when the discipline of economics was formed — when this circular flow model was first postulated — that ignorance seemed reasonable. In 1776, the year of Adam Smith's *Wealth of Nations*, there were only about 800 million people on the planet, and their acts and works had not yet been dramatically amplified by human use of the carbon energy stored in fossil fuels. Today, after the energy and population revolutions of the late nineteenth and twentieth centuries, we live in a different world—a full world, Daly and Farley say; Factory Planet, I've called it here, in contrast to the spacious Garden Planet that Smith knew. (I prefer Factory Planet and Garden Planet to Daly and Farley's terms. Their "empty planet" suggests that before humans built out to and beyond the limits of what the planet could sustainably support, it was empty, but that's not true: once life evolved on our formerly abiotic world, it expanded rapidly to fill available niches. Before humans, and long before our industrial society, the planet was already quite full of life.)

The neoclassical model's understanding of the traffic across the border of culture and nature is misconceived in another large way. Not only does it mistake the subset—the economy—for the whole, and not only does it ignore the fact that physical changes wrought by the economy must conform to the first and second laws of thermodynamics, but it also sees value only in traffic across the nature-culture boundary that moves through markets. Clean air and water and other environmental goods have value only when they are purchased: people will spend money to visit a national park, therefore wilderness has economic value. Ecological economics, in contrast, identifies a category of economic good that does not typically move through a market: ecosystem services. These civilization-sustaining services have economic value even when they have no price. Sunshine falling on rich and poor alike; the recycling of nutrients; the creation of soil fertility through natural processes; the desalination of seawater, and the purification and distribution of freshwater through the solar-powered hydrological cycle: we could not live without these services from nature. Ecological economics, drawing a parallel between the services offered by humanly built capital, has advanced the concept of natural capital: healthy ecosystems understood in their capacity as providers of ecosystem services to humans. Like built capital, natural capital is not consumed in the act of production the way that raw materials are. (The machine that stamps a steel plate into the shape of a fender works on a pile of plates, each of which is used up in the process; but the machine that does the stamping is relatively unchanged by its work, wearing only slightly with each iteration. It isn't completely consumed in production the way the steel — the through-put — is.) Capital *facilitates* an act of production without being *consumed* by it. Natural capital works the same way — with one big difference: healthy ecosystems have the capacity to use solar power to self-generate and self-repair, something no machine can do. Mechanical systems, including factories, wear out with use, eventually succumbing to entropy, the law of wear and tear. This is why owners of built capital are allowed to depreciate it — to deduct, for tax purposes, an incremental part of the value of their productive equipment for every year it's in use. Properly treated, natural capital does not depreciate.

Some environmentalists object to thinking of nature in such crass, instrumental terms. To do so, they hold, is to fail to appreciate nature as pure *other*, larger and more majestic than any of our works; nature is properly seen not as a form of capital but as sacred, ineffable, transcendent, beauteous, humbling. To cast the net of economic theory over it in this way diminishes it. The issue, here, is one of valuation: should we value nature in spiritual and aesthetic terms, or in anthropocentric economic terms? But this is a false dichotomy: the correct answer is "Both." If we conceive the question to be a practical one — if the "should" is unpacked to mean not a moral imperative but an instrumental one, something like "How should we think about nature in order to preserve enough healthy ecosystems to support human civilization?" — the answer is easier to see. The proposition that we should treat our relationship to nature as a moral issue has not been sufficient to prevent us from bringing nature (and, through it, our civilization) to the brink of collapse. For a variety of reasons economic valuations have superseded moral valuations in our culture. In suggesting that healthy ecosystems can be conceived of as a form of capital, providing us with useful flows of services, ecological economics proposes that the language of practical, economic valuation can be used to achieve a crucially important end that moral valuation has failed to achieve. And ecological economics does not claim that nature is nothing more than its usefulness to us; it offers the concept of natural capital as one among many possible lenses through which nature can be seen, a lens that brings into focus its enormous economic value.

One way, then, of succinctly describing the difference between ecological economics and the neoclassical model it seeks to supplant is this: ecological economics is the neoclassical model plus the laws of thermodynamics and the concept of ecosystem services from natural capital.

This makes the difference between the two sound like a minor tinker, the addition of a few large ideas; but the introduction of either of these ideas forces changes on the neoclassical model that completely alter the character, scope, fundamental assumptions, and policy prescriptions of the discipline. Make no mistake: it's a radical change, as radical as the transition in physics from the Newtonian to the Einsteinian paradigm, which it emulates. (It's fair to say that Einstein changed just a few of the fundamental principles of the Newtonian system; it's also true to say that in changing them, Einstein accomplished a thoroughgoing revolution in physics.)

One sweeping change suggested by ecological economics: if we admit the existence of ecosystem services, then we must also admit that our current system of market allocation is radically inefficient and completely irrational because within it prices lie to us, boldly and badly. Those prices systematically fail to account for the large environmental and social externalities of production and consumption. If markets are to be rational allocators of resources, those prices have to tell the truth.

To accomplish this, we have to find out what that truth might be. This ecological economics begins to do by placing monetary value on ecosystem services. A burgeoning literature has developed in this field, reporting valuations for services provided by all manner of ecosystems in all manner of regions and climates. In 1994 Robert Costanza and an international group of economists and biologists drew on that literature to publish their estimate of the monetary value of world ecosystem services, pegging them, conservatively, at three times the value of world economic output. In that study they organized ecosystem services into seventeen distinct categories, including water purification and transport; storm protection; flood control; pollination services; soil fertility creation; nutrient recycling; waste absorption; provision of a library of genetic information; micro- and macroclimate moderation; pest control; habitat for economically valuable species; recreational uses; and spiritual, educational, and aesthetic services. Their study reported some original computation, but mostly their numbers were derived from existing studies.

On an infinite planet, economic activity that diminishes the ability of an ecosystem to provide these services — the cutting of a forest, say, or the loss of wetlands to development — might be locally problematic but wouldn't affect the ability of the planet as a whole to sustain civilization. By definition, on an infinite planet, destruction of one part of the service flow leaves an infinite amount of the service still available for use. It's time to admit — with ecological economists — that the ever-expanding footprint of economic activity diminishes the ability of the planet to maintain delivery of an uninterrupted, undiminished flow of ecosystem services, services that are crucial to civilization.

The circular flow diagram you find in textbooks can be made any size you like; all you have to do is change the scale. In theory it could expand forever. But once an economy is placed in its home in nature, it's clear that when economic activity expands, it expands into something — and, because the size of the whole is fixed, the expansion of the economy must mean the diminution of something else.

"There's no such thing as a free lunch," as neoclassical economists are proud to proclaim. Ecological economics applies that bit of wisdom to the economy as a whole. There is no costless benefit to growing our ecological footprint, because as we do so we diminish nature's ability to provide us with ecosystem services.

In *Ecological Economics* you find many of the traditional tools and concepts of standard economic analysis: supply and demand curves, acknowledgment of the efficiency of market relations, acceptance of the overall project of economics as the effort to allocate scarce productive resources rationally in order to promote the efficient satisfaction of human want. Sometimes standard tools are applied in novel ways; for instance, the authors apply the principle of diminishing marginal returns (the idea that your tenth slice of pizza is not as satisfying as your first) to a new object: economic growth as a whole. (Why didn't the neoclassical model do this? There's no good explanation.) The result is a concept that is, within the mainstream, a heresy, an oxymoron: uneconomic growth. In the neoclassical model, economic growth is always good. In the model elaborated and codified by Daly and Farley, growth becomes uneconomic when it costs more in "disamenities," including loss of ecosystem services, than it brings in the form of increased wealth and well-being.

With a nod to John Stuart Mill's exposition of the matter in "On the Stationary State," Daly and Farley make a useful distinction between economic development and economic growth and tell us clearly that a no-growth economy is not a no-development economy. Growth comes by increasing the size of an economy's rate of throughput. It increases the economy's output, and its ecological footprint, by getting the economy to do what it does more quickly and on a larger scale. Economic development comes through increased efficiency, and other changes and improvements, in the use of a constant rate of throughput. (More efficient use of energy, for instance, allows for development without growth: fewer losses to entropy.) A sustainable society will be limited to a constant, sustainably sized level of throughput.

Recall that Frank and Bernanke dangled a change in product mix in front of their readers as support for the idea that the economy could grow forever: new products, they said, might use fewer resources to accomplish the same purposes as the old. This is development, not growth. A rhetorician would charge that Frank and Bernanke are guilty of the Fallacy of the Definitional Slide: allowing one term to encompass two ideas, they drew a conclusion about one by offering evidence in support of the other. Here, Daly and Farley clearly distinguish two concepts that need to be distinguished.

In the text you also find much that is neither novel nor part of current practice but has simply been underappreciated in recent decades. There's a very cogent explanation, for instance, of when and how markets fail—a subject that hasn't been in the forefront of economic attention during the past half-dozen decades. Daly and Farley's analysis here begins with a classification of economic goods according to six characteristics: rival and nonrival, exclusive and nonexclusive, and, for nonrival goods, congestible and noncongestible. A rival good is one for which one person's consumption precludes another's. (My dinner is my dinner, and when I eat it, you can't.) A nonrival good is one for which my consumption has an insignificant impact on your ability to derive benefit from it (streetlights, information, radio broadcasts, beautiful views, climate stability). A good or service is rival or nonrival by its very nature; this aspect of it can't be affected by human institutions. Excludability, though, is a human construct, a product of legal institutions. Ownership of an excludable good entails sole right to use it, and public authority will support that right. (If I find you trying to enjoy the housing services I purchase with my mortgage or rent, I can get the sheriff to turn you out.) Some goods are nonexcludable by their very nature: street lighting and national defense. Some goods could be made excludable, but aren't: unregulated ocean fisheries, radio broadcasts, public beaches, non-toll roads.

Roads and beaches are also examples of congestible goods. When usage rates are low, use by others doesn't diminish the benefit I get from use; but at some point increasing usage deteriorates the benefit for all.

The resulting six-panel grid allows for clear characterization of types of goods and some clear conclusions about them. Goods that are non-rival and nonexcludable, like national defense and street lighting, are pure public goods and can be provided only by public authority. (A private company could provide street lighting, but only under contract to a public authority with the power to tax; payment-for-use can't work because it's impossible to limit the benefit of streetlights to paying customers.) Only rival, excludable goods are efficiently allocated by markets. Other categories of goods can most efficiently be allocated by markets in which governments intervene to adjust price signals, or, in the parlance of economists, to internalize (bring into the price) externalities (the costs and benefits not paid or enjoyed by the user), through Pigouvian subsidies and taxes. We all benefit from having neighbors and fellow citizens who are well educated — benefits that come in the form of increased economic productivity and reduced costs for social welfare and health care. (Venturing beyond economics and into political theory, we can see that we all benefit if our fellow citizens are educated to be sophisticated in their political understandings: an educated citizenry resists encroachment on the civil liberties we enjoy and is less susceptible to demoguery and emotional manipulation by those seeking to represent our interests.) Thus, while education is not a "pure" public good — much of the benefit accrues to the individual who is educated — it has enough of a public character that its allocation by market mechanisms will not produce the socially optimal amount. (This is basic stuff, but it needs mentioning; it's underappreciated in the rush to privatize public education.) Nonrival congestible goods, like roads, might have time-variable usage fees pegged to degree of congestion: the highway might be free at night and midday, but users would be charged an access fee during rush hours. Many ecosystem services are nonexcludable (an up-land forest protects all downstream residents from flooding) and can be either rival (the fish I net is one you won't catch) or nonrival (my being protected from harmful uv rays by the ozone layer is not diminished a whit by your being protected also).

The origin of the boom-and-bust cycle in domestic oilfields in the early part of the twentieth century can now be easily categorized: one part of the problem was that under existing property law, oil extraction was rival but nonexcludable. Goods in this category are prey to what Garrett Hardin called "the tragedy of the commons," and what Daly and Farley propose should more accurately be called "the tragedy of open access regimes." Establishing property rights—closing the open access, making the rival, nonexcludable good a rival, excludable good—is the traditional solution, because it gives the owner of the new property right a vested interest in protecting the resource. Hardin's example was overgrazing on publicly held, open-access pasture land; historically the solution was enclosure and the management of the former commons as a private holding, whose owner could be supposed to have an incentive to pursue long-range management goals. Similarly, in the oil fields of Texas, unitary reservoir management was instituted, prorating the amount of oil that could be pumped by any one extractor to a share equivalent to their percentage ownership of the mineral rights to the reservoir; the overall production could then be limited to the reservoir's Maximum Efficient Rate of extraction (the rate that maximizes the long-term extraction).

Daly and Farley call for closing open-access regimes with property rights where it will work. But privatizing access to ecosystem services won't work in a substantial number of cases. "It's pretty much impossible to conceive," they say, "of a workable institution that could give someone exclusive ownership of the ozone layer, [or] climate regulation, [or] water regulation, [or] pollination (by wild pollinators)." Daly and Farley point out that natural capital exists as a *stock* or *fund* that provides a *flow*, and they caution that while all stocks and some flows can be privatized, some flows cannot.

It is often possible to establish exclusive property rights to an ecosystem fund (e.g., a forest) while at the same time impossible to establish such rights to the services the fund provides (e.g., regional climate regulation). If, like a forest, the fund is simultaneously a stock that can supply a flow (e.g., of timber), market allocation will only account for the stock-flow benefits of the resource.

In short: establishing and enforcing property rights won't solve all our ecological problems.

The distinction between stock and flow illuminates another aspect of oil economics. "If oil is so scarce," naive questioners have asked, "why isn't it more expensive?" The answer: the stock of oil is finite, and therefore it is scarce in absolute terms. It is becoming scarcer and scarcer in relative terms, as the stock of oil (however we measure it—as "known and recoverable reserves" or, in the abstract, as the unknown but certainly finite stock of all oil, discovered or as yet undiscovered) grows smaller with use. But the rate at which we exploit that stock—the flow of oil into the economy—is something we have the power to determine, and it is the rate of the flow that determines price. We could, if we wanted, pump existing stocks of oil out of the ground faster and faster and make the price decline as it becomes relatively less scarce in the economy—although this would increase the rate at which oil becomes absolutely scarce on the planet.

Like justice, wise policy treats similar things similarly and different things differently. The difficulty is in knowing what is similar to and what is different from what. The typologies offered by Daly and Farley (including others: biotic and abiotic resources, source and sink services) allow for meaningful and appropriate classification of goods and services, including ecosystem goods and services, and illuminate the policy problems that stem from our use of them. Climate stability is, like many other ecosystem services, nonexcludable, nonrival, and noncongestible: it's a flow service that is a pure public good. As such, it cannot be successfully allocated by market mechanisms (by itself, the market gives us too little of it). Policy has to intervene. You don't need to be an ecological economist to advocate putting a price on carbon emissions, through a carbon tax or a less efficient but apparently more acceptable system of cap-and-trade; but the analysis offered by Daly and Farley shows that climate stability, while a major problem, is not the only ecosystem service on which we rely—and not the only one whose continued supply is threatened by the market's failure to allocate resources efficiently in pursuit of maximum benefit.

In producing this introductory text, Daly and Farley have collated existing contributions from current and recent practitioners of the emergent paradigm, particularly Georgescu-Roegen's work on entropy; Daly and Cobb's critique of GDP as a deeply foolish measure, in which costs (like medical care, insurance, repair work, and so forth) are counted as benefits; Robert Costanza's work mentioned earlier; and the work of Frederick Soddy in providing a thermodynamically astute analysis of money. That's the function of a paradigm-changing textbook: it assimilates the subject matter that's been presented in the technical journals and makes it into a coherent whole for presentation to novitiates.

But the text also makes remarkable and novel contributions to the analytic tool kit of economic understanding, sometimes by importing concepts from other fields. One of these, from wildlife population biology, is the "sustainable yield curve," which plots the amount of a renewable resource that can be harvested without reducing the size of the stock from which it is drawn. Each year, the annual growth of such a population can be culled or harvested without changing the physical biomass of the population. This amount varies with the size of the stock and isn't a straight-on, linear progression. Picture a graph in which the vertical axis, the x-axis, plots a number of units and the horizontal one, the y-axis, plots the size of the population. Sinusoidal in shape, the curve that marks the sustainable yield starts at the origin, dips below the y-axis as it moves to the right, then curves above it in an arc that descends back to the y-axis farther out, at a higher level of population. The two points of intersection mark population levels at which there is no amount of harvest—an extracted flow—that will leave the size of the population—the stock—unchanged. At the innermost, lowest-population intersection, the species is at its minimum viable population—it barely has enough members or territory to reproduce itself. Any harvest here will send the species into extinction (unless—as is represented in the part of the curve below the y-axis—there is a "negative harvest," a purposeful seeding of new members of the species). At the upper intersection with the y-axis, the sustainable yield curve marks a population at the carrying capacity of its niche. From year to year, the population doesn't grow but does reproduces itself, because it is already at a maximum. Here, any harvest will reduce the size of the population stock, and—perhaps counterintuitively—increase the sustainable harvest from zero to some positive number. It does this by giving members of the population room to grow. Thinning trees in a climax forest will change the forest in many ways, including allowing it to increase its annual growth, as more trees have more access to sun and water and nutrients. Management of a climax forest can move it from a point at which the maximum sustainable harvest is zero to a point at which a positive harvest can be sustained.

The curve can be used to illustrate graphically and analytically how and why it is that some species that we might harvest sustainably, forever, instead go extinct. In an open-access regime (like, say, unregulated ocean fisheries), standard, self-interested economic behavior by humans will drive the renewable resource below the point at which it can renew itself, the point at which the harvestable resource becomes so scarce that its population can't maintain itself, often because individuals simply can't find each other to reproduce. The curve clearly illustrates that there is, conceptually, a point of maximum sustainable yield, which holds out the hope that with the right kind of data we might be able to discover that point and manage our resources in order to achieve it. (The authors make a point about this, and all other curves in economics, that is worth remembering: the curve itself should probably be drawn as a wide and fuzzy band, to indicate that our knowledge of such technical detail is uncertain, at best.) The curve can also be transected with various rays and other curves to illustrate the effects of quotas, taxes, technical advances, and outright prohibitions on harvest. It's an enormously useful conceptual tool.

Reality, economic reality included, is sufficiently complex that diametrically opposed idea-systems can serve as lenses through which to interpret it, with both systems claiming to be confirmed by what it is that is seen. I'm confident that my long-ago economics professor—the one who said that we'd never run out of oil because as the price rose we'd discover alternatives—would no doubt take the ongoing development of the renewable energy industry as evidence that his prediction was correct. We are turning to alternatives; and we will, in fact, never "run out" of oil (mostly because, when it costs us a barrel's worth of energy to extract a barrel of oil, further extraction of oil will cost us more than we get. Lots of oil will be left underground, thermodynamically inaccessible to us.) Here too, though, there has been a definitional slide: "We'll never run out of oil" is easily mistaken to mean "Declining production of oil is not a problem for our economy or civilization," or even that (as Frank and Bernanke strongly imply) we haven't got and will never really have an energy scarcity problem. The first assertion is, technically, true; the latter two are not. On this point the neoclassical model and the ecological economics model clearly diverge.

We will, sooner or later, learn to live on solar income, most probably by exploiting forms of it, like wind and wave power, whose flow is so generous that their exploitation even at significant levels looks (to our eyes in the present, at least) to have few negative ecological consequences that can't be absorbed, avoided, or ameliorated. (As we exploit solar, we should keep in mind that there truly is no such thing as a free lunch. One consequence of harvesting wind energy: the velocity of the air is reduced, reducing volume of air that sweeps across the ground, reducing the ability of the wind to transport ground heat away. Ground temperatures below wind farms are measurably higher than ground temperatures outside the farm, and that change in temperature may yet prove to have consequences.)

While not infinite, the flow of solar income is sizable, and currently we simply throw much of it away (as we do when our buildings and built spaces deny sunlight to ecosystems but fail to capture it for our use). If we steer clear of increasing our appropriation of photosynthetic products, we may be able to maintain a high level of energy input into the economy without destroying ecosystem services. With enough energy, we could recycle a significant amount of the matter we've extracted from nature, keeping scarce and valuable materials in the economic loop.

The same optimism isn't possible for our other footprint, which lands squarely on the absorptive and recycling, or sink, services supplied by the environment. As Daly and Farley caution, "It would appear that the global sink is becoming full more rapidly than the global sources of natural resources are being emptied. This is understandable in view of the fact that sinks are frequently freely available for anyone to use—that is, they are rival and nonexcludable. In contrast, sources are more often rival and excludable resources that are under the discipline of property, either privately or publicly owned and managed" (121). Human engineering can do little to alter the sink services — the cycling capacity of ecosystems — like the ability of a marsh to filter toxins from water, the ability of trees to capture carbon. (We can plant more trees and rehabilitate and nurture marshland, but we can't alter by much the fundamental capacities of the systems each contain. And converting land to the production of sink services in this way deprives us of using that land for other production. Here, too, there's no free lunch.) For this reason, "the most binding constraint on economic growth may be the waste absorption capacity of the environment, the sink."

Classical economic theory used to, and Marxist economic theory still does, emphasize human labor as the ultimate source of economic value. Of course capital contributes to production; but in the labor theory of value, capital is seen as being nothing more than embodied labor — scarce human effort mingled with materials that are, by definition in both traditions, so plentiful as to verge on infinite and therefore are valueless — "like air," my undergraduate professor explained. "Absolutely essential but no price." Daly and Farley aren't looking to replace the labor theory of value (or the neoclassical model's elaborate but mistaken treatment of value) with a thermodynamic theory of value. While everything we value is, in physical terms, organized matter or energy — a bit of low entropy — not all low entropy has immediate economic value for humans (poisonous mushrooms, for instance, aren't of much use). Low entropy is a necessary but not a sufficient or definitive condition of economic value. Thus: "We do *not* advocate an 'entropy theory of value.' Value has psychic roots in want satisfaction, as well as physical roots in [low] entropy. To propose an 'entropy theory of value' would be to focus on the supply side only and neglect demand. And even on the supply side, entropy does not reflect many qualitative differences in materials that are economically important." To this Daly and Farley add a large and important qualification: "Any theory of value that ignores entropy is dangerously deficient" (70).

This new paradigm in economic theory offers a different conceptual slicing of productive activity, yielding a new and promising set of categories of factors of production. Neoclassical theory is capable of assimilating the idea that land is a factor of production; as Repetto noted, classical economists divided factors of production into land, labor, and capital, though the neoclassical synthesis has historically ignored both land and labor and focused nearly exclusive on capital as the dominant, most important factor of production. The neoclassical model could revert to including resources—land—as a factor of production. But a thermodynamically enlightened economics suggests a different cut, one that slices across those three categories at right angles with a different tripartite division: matter, energy, and intelligence. Capital—the tools and equipment we use to increase the productivity of our labor—is matter embodying both energy (the energy used to extract, refine, shape, and assemble the materials from which it's made) and intelligence (the accumulated inventions and innovations that have gone into its design). Labor is discretionary intelligent energy that participates in production. Land—nature—is the source of all matter and energy—and it also embodies billions of years of design intelligence encoded into genes, evolution's information storage system. All economic value is produced by intelligence operating on matter using energy.

In this model, it's easy to see that under conditions of maximum sustainable uptake of matter and energy from the environment, any further increase in production has to come from the development of intelligence—through innovation; through the application of what we know and can learn about wringing greater efficiency from matter and energy throughput; through development, not footprint-expanding growth.

Besides encompassing thermodynamic truth and ecological reality, Daly and Farley's book is also an implicit call for a return to the disciplinary unity of yore, before economics decamped from political economy in search of a promised land of analytical rigor, leaving behind any question suffused with valuation, moral judgment, or "political" content. That departure was facilitated by Wilfred Pareto's notion of optimal distribution, discussed earlier, which comes in for deserved criticism here. If infinite economic growth is not possible, economics must abandon Pareto Optimality as its exclusive standard of economic improvement. Because Pareto's work sliced off nonquantifiable aspects of well-being, casting them out of the discipline, the movement beyond Pareto Optimality might then also be a movement beyond the discipline's absolute commitment to what Georgescu-Roegen called "arithmomorphism" and a recovery of subjects less amenable to mathematical analysis: the comparison of satisfactions between people, along with questions of equity and justice in distribution. Justice, fairness, equity — these are the classic concerns of political theory and philosophy, and they take on crucial importance in a world that can no longer convincingly avoid these problems by reaffirming a faith in infinite growth. This text reminds us that economists have resisted integrating political theory and economics for too long.

If, as some of us passionately hope, we are to minimize the amount of human pain and suffering by building an ecologically sustainable civilization with a high degree of material well-being, economics will first have to undergo a revolutionary change to incorporate the reality of a finite planet into its structures and systems. Through that incorporation, it will also have to admit that political and economic reality are neither as easily nor as beneficially divisible from each other as economists have long assumed. Daly and Farley's text is one important harbinger of, and impetus in furtherance of, that change.

As anyone who has read an economic textbook is likely to attest, the experience doesn't usually bring to mind adjectives like "pleasurable" and "exciting." But, having endured my share of economic textbooks, I found myself reading this one with a pleasure that verged on excitement. Here, finally, is common sense about economics; a body of theory and understanding that starts from realistic premises about nature and energy and ecosystems and humans; and a rigorous approach to the study of human productive life that doesn't achieve that rigor by slicing off crucial elements of the reality it is supposed to help us understand.

If you've ever had a traditional economics course, I recommend you read Daly and Farley's *Ecological Economics* as an antidote. If you've never had an economics course, read this book for the light it sheds on how we have committed ourselves to infinite growth, and how we have to start thinking if we are to learn to live within limits. And, after reading, recommend it to your friends. The ideas in it just might save civilization.

getting over GDP

A s currently organized, our economy creates wealth by drawing down natural and social capital, a process that can't go on forever. One positive result of an economic slowdown is that it slows this rate of ecological and social degradation, giving our system a little more time and breathing room to make the transition we need to make from our infinite-planet ways.

And, lest you think that in pointing this out progressives and environmentalists are uniquely indifferent to the human sorrows and difficulties wrought by recession, keep in mind that infinite-planet economists have long found a considerable amount of silver lining in the dark clouds of economic woe. High unemployment reduces "upward pressure" on wages and constrains the nonwage claims of labor, like the desire for safer working conditions; both are taken to be positive developments by corporations and those identified with them, including conservatives who have taken to heart the slogan once offered by a president of GM, "What's good for General Motors is good for the country." To some of these infinite-planet thinkers, recession is also an opportunity to release the economy from unwanted environmental regulation. Thus the remarkable avowal by Ryanair chief executive Michael O'Leary: "We would welcome a good, bloody, deep recession for 12 to 18 months. . . . [It would bring a halt to the] environmental bullshit . . . that has allowed [Prime Minister] Gordon Brown to double air passenger duty. We need a recession if we are going to see off some of this environmental nonsense."

With less particularly partisan sympathies, mainstream economists acknowledge that with recession comes what Joseph Schumpeter called "creative destruction," the failure of outmoded economic structures and their replacement by new, more suitable structures. Downturns have often given a last, fatality-inducing nudge to dying industries and technologies. (Very few buggy manufacturers made it through the Great Depression.) With a good portion of 2009's deficit-financed stimulus money being directed toward building renewable energy infrastructure, recovery from the worldwide Great Recession — the downturn that started with the collapse of the subprime lending market in the United States in 2008 — may leave us with an economy several steps closer to being sustainable, an economy better prepared to deal with the waning of the petroleum era.

Creative destruction can apply to concepts as well. The current downturn offers an excellent opportunity to get rid of one economic concept that has long outlived its usefulness: gross domestic product, or GDP. It's one measure of national income, of how much wealth Americans make, and it's a deeply foolish indicator of how the economy is doing.

Every mainstream economics textbook that covers GDP in any depth at all offers cautions about using it as a measure of economic well-being — and then most of those books go on to offer reams of analysis and theory that take GDP to be a measure of economic well-being. None of them take good account of the fact that human well-being is, in total, much broader than material well-being and that GDP is a deeply flawed measure even of that. In its very structure GDP lies to us, telling us that infinite expansion of the economy's ecological footprint is possible. It's an infinite planet statistic, unsuited for our economic life on Factory Planet. It ought to join buggy whips and cassette recorders on the dustheap of history.

The first official attempt to determine our national income was made in 1934, while the country was in the Great Depression. How bad was the economic pain? No one knew, because there were no national data. "We had no comprehensive measures," says economist William Nordhaus, speaking in the first-person plural on behalf of economists back then, "so we looked at things like boxcar loadings." The goal of GNP was to measure, by dollar value, all economic production involving Americans whether they were at home or abroad. In 1991, the US Bureau of Economic Analysis switched from gross national product to gross domestic product to reflect a changed economic reality — as trade increased, and as foreign companies built factories in the United States, it became apparent that the United States ought to measure what gets made in-country, no matter who makes it or where it goes after it's made.

Since then GDP has become our most commonly cited economic indicator, the basic number that we take as a measure of how well we're doing economically from year to year and quarter to quarter. It's written into thousands of laws and contracts and is the defining element in the widely accepted, if unofficial, definition of a recession: GDP decline for two successive quarters. But it's the product of a time when the sheer amount of economic activity could be mistaken for a good indicator of our level of economic well-being, and it ignores important contributors to human well-being that aren't bought and sold in markets: the satisfactions and contributions of volunteer work, nonremunerated domestic production, strong social and family relations, and the ready availability of natural capital services like clean air and water. From the vantage point of the Great Depression, "having more stuff"—and getting people back to work—looked to be the end-all of economic and social progress, and GDP seemed to be a good measure of that.

It isn't. Not only does GDP not include unpriced goods like volunteer work, housework, child rearing, and do-it-yourself home improvement; it also completely ignores the huge economic benefit that we get directly, outside any market, from nature. A mundane example: If you let the sun dry your clothes, that natural capital service is free and doesn't show up in our domestic product; if you throw your laundry in the dryer, you burn fossil fuel, increase your carbon footprint, make the economy more unsustainable—and give GDP a bit of a bump.

Very often, the replacement of natural-capital services (like sun-drying clothes, or the propagation of fish, or flood control and water purification) with built-capital services (like those from a clothes dryer, or an industrial fish farm, or from levees, dams, and treatment plants) is a bad trade—the capital we build for ourselves is costly, doesn't maintain itself, and in many cases provides an inferior, less-certain service. But in gross domestic product, every instance of replacement of a natural-capital service with a built-capital service shows up as a good thing, an increase in national economic activity. One result of GDP's use as our basic indicator of economic well-being is the current global crisis in natural capital services, as their civilization-sustaining flow has been dramatically diminished. It's no accident that we haven't held on to a source of well-being that our basic economic indicator fails to value.

This points to the larger, deeper flaw in using a measurement of national income as an indicator of economic well-being. In summing all economic activity in the economy, gross domestic product makes no distinction between items that are costs and items that are benefits. If you lose your access to free clean water, as some communities have as a result of fracking and mountaintop-removal coal mining, that doesn't show up in GDP as a cost; but the bottled water you now have to buy is included and shows up as increased economic activity, a supposed benefit. GDP is thus literally perverse: if you get into a fender-bender and have your car fixed, GDP goes up.

A similarly counterintuitive result comes from other kinds of defensive and remedial spending. Health care, pollution abatement, flood control, and costs associated with population growth and increasing urbanization—crime prevention, water treatment, school expansion, wider roads to handle increased traffic—all increase GDP when we buy them, even though what we mostly aim to buy isn't an improved standard of living but the restoration or protection of the quality of life we already had.

The amounts involved are not nickel-and-dime stuff. Hurricane Katrina produced something like $82 billion in damages in New Orleans, and as the destruction there is remedied, GDP goes up. One economist to whom I spoke pooh-poohed this flaw in GDP by pointing out that some of this remedial spending on the Gulf Coast represents a positive change to economic well-being: old appliances and carpets and cars and housing are being replaced by new and presumably improved versions; flood victims who rebuild are getting new stuff. But that is, frankly, a foolish observation. The vast majority of the expense of recovering from the flood leaves the community no better off—indeed, leaves it mostly worse off—than before. The failure of economists to call for subtracting such remedial expenditures from GDP is, at bottom, a disciplinary stamp of approval to a host of stupid, obviously uneconomic exchanges: no sane person would pay the full cost of demolishing a perfectly useful house and rebuilding it in order to get new carpet and a new refrigerator.

The damage done by Katrina to the Gulf Coast illustrates one kind of natural capital service in particular, and the consequences of failing to value it. Between New Orleans and the Gulf Coast there once lay a band of wetlands fifty miles wide. A marsh is a sponge; a strip of it a mile wide can absorb four inches of storm surge. When the bayous south of New

Orleans were lost to development — sliced to death by channels to move oil rigs, mostly — gross domestic product went up, even as these "improvements" destroyed the city's natural defenses and wiped out crucial spawning ground for the Gulf Coast shrimp fishery. The bayous were a form of natural capital, and their loss was a cost that never entered into any account — not GDP or anything else. Had those bayous been in place, they would have absorbed seventeen feet of Katrina's twenty-two-foot surge. In all likelihood the city's built-capital defenses would have held against a storm surge diminished by bayou absorption.

Wise decisions depend on accurate assessments of the costs and benefits of different courses of action. If we don't count ecosystem services as a benefit in our basic measure of well-being, their loss can't be counted as a cost — and then economic decision making can't help but lead us to undesirable and perversely uneconomic outcomes.

The basic problem is that gross domestic product measures economic activity, not benefit, and it doesn't distinguish remedial and preventive activity from the beneficial kind. If you kept your checkbook the way GDP measures the national accounts, you'd record all the money deposited into your account and make entries for every check you write — and then add all the numbers together. The resulting bottom line might tell you something useful about the total cash flow of your household, but it's not going to tell you whether you're better off this month than last or, indeed, whether you're solvent or going broke. That's GDP: it measures the commotion of money in the economy, not the physical production that may (or may not) improve our general standard of living. We ought to rename it "gross domestic transactions" — a statistic that fewer of us would mistake for a measure of well-being.

Because GDP is such a flawed measure of economic well-being, it's foolish to pursue policies whose primary purpose is to raise it. Doing so is an instance of the fallacy of misplaced concreteness — mistaking a map for the terrain, mistaking an instrument reading for the reality it represents. When you're feeling a little chilly in your living room, you don't hold a match to a thermometer and then think, "Problem solved." But that's what we do when we seek to improve economic well-being by prodding GDP.

This is readily illustrated by the events in Egypt and Tunisia during the Arab Spring of 2011. The regime changes there were widely hailed as victories for democracy, as proof of the liberalizing power of social networking media, as testimony to the power of nonviolent political action. All of that they may indeed have been, but they were also something else: a cautionary lesson in mistaking GDP for a measure of economic well-being. Despite significant gains in per capita GDP in both Egypt and Tunisia in the past decade, the level of well-being of their citizens had been falling, and that decline played a very large role in putting people into the streets in protest.

The details: in Egypt, per capita annual GDP rose from $4,762 to $6,367 between 2005 and 2010. In Tunisia it rose from $7,182 to $9,489. But both countries saw a significant decline in the percentage of the population that is classified as thriving according to a standard, well-established measure.

That measure is the Cantril Self-Anchoring Striving Scale, developed by a researcher named Hadley Cantril. It's a survey research tool and asks respondents to answer a few simple questions:

> Please imagine a ladder with steps numbered from zero at the bottom to ten at the top. The top of the ladder represents the best possible life for you and the bottom represents the worst possible life for you. On which step of the ladder would you say you personally feel you are standing at the present time? On which step of the ladder do you think you will stand about five years from now?

To rank as "thriving," respondents have to have positive views of their current place on the ladder (seven or higher) and positive expectations about the future (eight or higher). Below that, respondents are ranked as "struggling" — their "ladder-future" expectation is lower than the present, or both values fall below the thriving range. Below struggling is "suffering," people who report their place on the ladder at four or below.

The Cantril Scale correlates with objective and subjective markers of well-being. Thrivers have fewer health problems and fewer sick days, while reporting less worry, stress, and anxiety and more enjoyment, happiness, and respect. Those in the struggling category report more daily stress and worry about money than the "thriving" respondents and take more than double the amount of sick days. Those in the "suffering" category are more likely to report that they lack basics like food and shelter, more likely to report physical pain, and more likely to experience higher levels of stress, worry, sadness, and anger. They have more than double the rate of diseases compared to "thriving" respondents.

In both countries, as GDP rose steadily, the number of citizens categorized as "thriving" fell. In Egypt in 2005, 29 percent of people reported themselves as thriving, but that number fell to just 11 percent five years later. In Tunisia, Cantril Scale data are unavailable prior to 2008, when 24 percent of the population could be classified as thriving; that number fell to 14 percent—a 40 percent decline—in just two years.

The nonviolent revolutions in both countries may have been motivated less by abstract commitment to democratic freedom than by widespread experience of a declining standard of living and increased economic insecurity, even in the face of rising GDP. As Hayek had warned half a century ago, "The one thing modern democracy will not bear without cracking is the necessity of a substantial lowering of the standards of living in peacetime." In the modern world—and perhaps because of new media, which make it much harder for totalitarian states to control public and civic discourse—the warning needs to be made more general: not just democracies but even repressive regimes don't fare well when there's a substantial lowering of standards of living in peacetime. Within the standard model, a rising GDP and a declining standard of living amount to a paradoxical result. Two factors contributed to this paradox: increasing inequality in income and increasing food prices.

Thanks in part to the Soviet-built Aswan Dam, which interrupted the regular cycle by which Nile delta farmlands were renourished by annual flooding, Egypt has in past decades been the world's single largest importer of Russian grain. When Russia announced an embargo on grain exports (the result of unprecedented, climate-change-driven weather that scorched into ruin a quarter of Russia's usual annual harvest), the price of food shot up. Before the embargo, the average Egyptian family spent 38 percent of its income on food (for comparison: that figure is 7 percent in the United States). Most simply couldn't afford the post-embargo higher prices, and hunger and food insecurity spread through the middle class. Perversely, GDP counted higher food prices as a positive contribution to well-being.

Because of that basic flaw, a rising GDP, even a rising per capita GDP, did not mean a rising standard of living. And even if GDP were a more accurate measure of material well-being, it would still be mathematically possible for a very large number of people to become worse off economically as per capita GDP rises. This can occur when there is growing income inequality (i.e., the benefits of increasing GDP aren't widely shared).

In Egypt and Tunisia, one or both of these factors shaped history. Rising per capita GDP and falling well-being became an economic fact — and a politically charged social condition. Declining standards of well-being are politically destabilizing and can lead, expectably enough, to widespread support for sweeping change.

In Egypt and Tunisia the regimes happened to be repressive, and the call for change came as a commitment to democracy, an end to corruption, and demands for civil liberties. But within democracies, declining standards of living can have the opposite effect. Open and institutionalized systems of regime change — voting — will absorb the discontent for a time, but if the decline lasts too long, and if it can't be blamed (successfully) on a particular party in power, pressure grows for stepping outside established parties and systems for new, radical, revolutionary approaches. Democratic forms are no certain proof against a slide into repressive forms. No system of government — despotic or democratic — fares well when the majority of its citizens experiences a declining standard of living.

Thus the changes wrought by the Arab Spring are not only worth celebrating, but also offer us a cautionary lesson. Sustained or rising well-being is what is economically and politically desirable, and we should measure it directly, instead of counting on GDP to do the job. And because well-being includes non-economic factors (like enjoyment of a healthy environment, enjoyment of rich and rewarding leisure time, enjoyment of family and social relations), it is possible to have a rising standard of well-being while per capita GDP remains constant or even decreases.

A host of alternatives to gross domestic product have been proposed, and most of them tackle the difficult problem of placing a value on goods and services, and of assessing aspects of human well-being, that never had a dollar price. The alternatives are controversial, because that kind of valuation creates room for subjectivity — for the expression of values that are not as cut-and-dried as market price.

How, after all, do we judge the exact value of the services provided by those bayous in Louisiana? Was it $82 billion? But what about the value of the shrimp fishery that was already lost before the hurricane? Or the insurance value of the protection the bayous would be offering against another $82 billion loss? And, at a broader and even more difficult level: what about the security and sense of continuity of life enjoyed by the thousands of people who lived and made their livelihoods in relation to those bayous before they disappeared? It's admittedly difficult to set a dollar price on such things — but this is no reason to set their value at zero, as gross domestic product currently does.

Robert Zoellick, president of the World Bank, is a recent convert to this line of thinking. He's not exactly a poster child for progressive causes — nominated to the bank by Bush Junior, he was Bush Senior's deputy secretary of state and signed the infamous letter from the Project for a New American Century calling on Bush Junior to invade Iraq and oust Saddam Hussein. He's got some credentials as a practicing conservative. But he's also on the board of the World Wildlife Federation; he seems to have a particular interest in the plight of panda bears. And perhaps for him, as for many others, a totemic attachment to one symbolic species unfolded into a larger sense of care and concern for the web of life within which that species, and every other, finds a home. In October 2010 Zoellick spoke to a conference convened in Japan to find ways to halt the destruction of ecosystem diversity, saying, "We need to assist . . . economic agencies to measure 'natural wealth.' . . . The value of services we derive from ecosystems shouldn't be assumed to be zero." As he explained: "In clearing mangroves for shrimp farming, the calculation will no longer simply be the revenue from profit on shrimp farming minus the farming cost. It would now deduct the loss of coastal protection from cyclones, and the loss of fish and other products provided by the mangroves."

Zoellick's call to measure natural wealth is an admission that our economic accounting systems don't capture all costs and benefits — and that the standard, market-based model that led us to rely on GDP as an indicator of well-being is fundamentally flawed. To state the problem in the most abstract, most theoretical terms: if everything that contributes to human well-being had to be bought through a market, and if everything bought in markets was a positive contribution to well-being (instead of being a defensive or remedial expenditure), and if the price of everything accurately reflected all the costs involved in its production (including ecosystem losses and social costs imposed on individuals and communities by production), then and only then would GDP begin to be an accurate indicator of our level of well-being. Under those completely unrealistic conditions, the cost-benefit calculations that Zoellick wants to modify would not need to be modified.

The problem with GDP isn't just our use of it; the problem with our use of it signals a deeper problem whose roots lie in the nature of market activity itself. Left to themselves, markets can't produce socially optimal amounts of some goods—pure public goods, goods whose benefits are neither completely rival nor completely excludable. In general, markets can't produce socially optimal amounts of anything, not unless prices tell the truth—and for a long time our prices have been lying to us about the economy's root in nature. Changing that is no minor tinker but a wholesale transformation of standard economic theory.

As noted earlier, before we can count decline of ecosystem services as a loss in our accounting system, we have to know their value. Ecological economists have been working to define those values for decades. Some ecosystem services seem to have a clear market value, as when beekeepers are paid to place their hives in orchards needing pollination services. A clear dollar price is attached to the provision of the service. But it's the bees that actually do the work, and they aren't paid. No bees, no crop; by that measure, the value of bee labor is the value of the total harvest.

That's just one possible method of inferring a value for ecosystem services. Others have names like "avoided cost," "replacement cost," "factor-income," "travel cost," and "hedonic" pricing. Avoided cost gives a solid number for the value to New Yorkers of the water purification services of their watershed. New York City has been buying and preserving land that drains into the Hudson and Delaware Rivers, looking to save the $6 billion that a water filtration plant would cost the city; that can be taken as the value, to New Yorkers, of the water purification services of the watersheds that supply the city. And the value of the storm protection services of Louisiana bayou is, in retrospect, fairly easy to calculate. (So is the value of that service into the future: until climate change started depriving insurance companies of the usefulness of historical weather data, they were expert at this sort of risk-to-benefit calculation, because their profit margins depend on them.) Replacement cost is similar to avoided cost and can be similarly clear. Pollination services can be valued at what it would take to do the job by (human) hand: $6 billion to replace us honeybee pollination alone, according to one study.

The factor income approach tries to quantify something else — the increase in human incomes that comes from ecosystem services. When cleaner water boosts marine life, the quantity of fish that can be sustainably harvested increases, which increases the income of fishermen. Travel cost and hedonic pricing are familiar to mainstream economists, who have long been using them to estimate some aspects of consumer benefit. If people will pay money to travel to a national park, or pay extra for a house on the beach, then parkland and oceanfront property must provide services with a measurable dollar value.

None of these methods is completely satisfactory for all services, and some services have no clearly appropriate method. Different methods give different results.

Beyond these problems lie others. The attempt to parse the value of individual ecosystem services to particular recipients doesn't fully capture the complex interactions of ecosystems and the fact that they exist on the planet as wholes, not as bundles of discrete multitasking service providers. The ocean that provides a beautiful view is also home to fish, host to 70 percent of planetary photosynthesis, and a major element in the planet's climate control. Upland forest that purifies New York's water also moderates flooding, yields forest products, holds recreational and aesthetic opportunities, and provides refuge to species that perform other services, like population control of prey and pest species, and so on. Interactions and synergies — the ones we know about — have to be mapped, to avoid undervaluing or double counting. And some ecosystem services have no replacements: the ozone layer that protects us, and all life, from radiation damage is crucial to the existence of life on the planet, and no human engineering could ever work as fully or as well. That suggests that the value of the ozone layer is the value of a habitable planet — which many of us would say is infinite. There's no conceptually elegant way to put a dollar price on incremental damage to something infinitely valuable.

And there are deeper, philosophical issues. The selection of the valuation method is in part the selection of the result. Within the results of any one valuation method, the results that are obtained can be internally consistent — they can have reasonable, rational relationships that can serve as the foundation of economically rational decision making. If, for instance, all other variables are equal, then we can logically assume that a certain amount of forest *here* would provide the same amount of ecosystem services as the same amount of an identical forest *there.* And we can identify formulas and algorithms that tell us at what rate the quantity of those services change as the forest area is increased or decreased (because of synergies between the elements of ecosystems, the relationship isn't linear — when you halve the size of a forest sometimes you reduce ecosystem services by more than half). But the choice between methods can seem arbitrary, hence subjective. Rational choice theory doesn't take kindly to arbitrary decision making rooted in subjectivity — not unless the subjectivity is consumer choice that's been laundered first by being cumulated across an impersonal market; which is to say, economics has never been totally free of subjective valuation.

Another problem: what is the present value of a cost, or the risk of a cost, that is avoided in the future? What might future generations pay us today, if they could, to stop the destruction of ecosystems whose services they'll want in the future? The only correct answer is "We can't know." We need some kind of answer if we're to be economically rational about valuing ecosystem services; but any useful answer is as philosophical as it is technical.

Ultimately, putting a cash value on ecosystem services is like putting a cash value on a human life. Romantics protest that both efforts are impossible, morally suspect, and pretty certain to be wrong. All of these are reasonable objections. But we place a monetary value on human life, implicitly, all the time. Is it worth putting airbags in cars to save 2,788 lives a year? Collectively we've said yes, and a bit of information on cost and a little arithmetic will tell you the implied value of a human life. Would an additional MRI machine in a city hospital be a wise investment? If we're going to make a rational decision, we have to equalize lives-saved-per-dollar-spent among competing choices and decide how much to spend. Unless we're willing to spend, literally, an infinite amount on health care technology, the amount we spend implicitly sets a value on individual human life. Such economic cost-benefit analysis aside, justice (and tort law) sometimes demand that we make an explicit calculation of the value of a human life, as when compensation is awarded to family survivors of a wrongful death.

Valuing ecosystem services is just as difficult, and just as necessary. The default is to continue to value them at nothing, and even the World Bank sees that that's wrong.

If in politics "Follow the money" is apt advice, in economics and ecology "Follow the energy" proves equally useful. An economy subsists on intake of matter and energy. With enough energy, all the matter that moves in the economy could be recycled. Energy is ultimately what's scarce, and its flow defines the relations within ecosystems and economies. One of the most promising approaches to valuing ecosystem services looks to the energy embodied in ecosystems and their products. As developed by ecological economist Robert Costanza and others, this energy approach to the problem may yet produce a nonsubjective, non-anthropocentric, intergenerational system of valuation — one that can encompass ecosystem services.

Given all the problems, the task of putting a monetary value on ecosystem services begins to look like rocket science. Would that it were that easy. With rocket science, at least you get a ready indicator of success: the rocket either does or doesn't do what you intend. With valuing ecosystem services there's no experimental feedback, no chance to return to the drawing board. Generations to come will be the ones who know whether we got the numbers right. It's a daunting, difficult task, filled with potential for contentious disagreement, and the result will have to be implemented within political systems that are vulnerable to influence by entrenched interests.

Still, it's better than the alternative, which is to leave these critical services unpriced and watch them disappear. That's not just economically irrational, it's collective suicide.

We can't manage what we can't measure, and the obvious problems and dire consequences of GDP's flaws have led to a strong international movement to abandon it and start using something else — an indicator or group of indicators that is more accurate and useful. In calling for the valuation of natural wealth, World Bank president Zoellick joined an international chorus that had been singing for a few years before he picked up the tune. Europe has been in the forefront of the movement. Since 2002, Germany has been using an environmental economic accounting system that deducts ecosystem service losses as Zoellick advocates. In November 2007, the European Commission convened an international conference dedicated to looking "Beyond GDP"—a conference meant to serve as "the launching pad for the political debate on the need to move beyond the principles of Gross Domestic Product." It brought together 650 policy planners, academics, and civic leaders in Brussels to articulate what a new indicator or indicators should look like and to plot paths forward toward implementation. In early 2008 French president Nicolas Sarkozy convened an international commission, led by Nobel laureate economists Joseph Stiglitz and Amartya Sen, to devise an indicator or set of indicators to serve as an alternative to GDP. Their report, issued in the fall of 2009, called for fixing GDP by subtracting costs from it and adding unpriced goods to it and retaining the result as a measure of material well-being—which would be just one element in a "dashboard" of indicators that would also measure quality of life in seven other areas: health, education, environment, employment, interpersonal connectedness, political engagement, and equity of income distribution. By 2009, the year the Stiglitz Commission report was issued, the Environmental and Sustainability Management and Accounting Network of Europe had held its twelfth annual conference on developing and refining indicators to measure sustainable development. Typically the participants and presenters include directors and staff members from Bureaus of Economic Statistics from most European and many other nations. When I attended the conference in 2007, I was the only American there.

Proposed alternatives to GDP—and there are dozens—fall into three broad categories. Some seek to fix GDP by deducting costs and adding benefits that are not presently taken into account. Others, like the Stiglitz Commission, propose that we fix GDP and keep it, but supplement it with other indicators. In the third category fall proposals that would start with a clean slate and build an indicator or a set of indicators that measure directly what Georgescu-Roegen called the true purpose of the economy: the increase of "an immaterial flux, the enjoyment of life."

Behind those three categories is another strong division in the field, a straightforward dichotomy: should we measure material well-being alone, or develop some broader gauge of overall well-being? Doing the latter involves a greater deal of subjectivity and invites easy criticism: "You want the government to be in the business of measuring psychological states?" and "Life satisfactions are too personal, too individual, to be aggregated by any useful measure." There are, however, answers to each criticism.

The strongest criticism is this: if the point of the economy isn't simply to increase throughput infinitely, but to augment that "immaterial flux: the enjoyment of life," then clearly it's beside the point (and, on a finite planet, self-defeating) to measure anything else.

While life satisfactions are indeed subjectively experienced, there is a great deal of research showing that its foundations are remarkably similar across cultures, time, and social groupings. For instance: no matter where or how people live, for the vast majority of them the number and quality of their social connections are an important contributor to their well-being, as subjectively reported and as measured by objective markers (like physical health, which is easily quantifiable as health care expenses or doctor visits or disease rates or life expectancy). It's clear: for humans in any culture, stronger and deeper social connections conduce to health and happiness. The level of social connection can be derived from survey data with answers to a few simple questions like "In the past week, how many meals did you eat in the company of friends or family?" or "How many people do you feel you could turn to in time of desperate need?" Social isolation has demonstrable negative effects on psychological and physical health; if we care about smoking as a public health problem, why not also care about social isolation? To fail to register these aspects of well-being in an indicator is to invite their continued degradation by processes (like the mobility of labor, the increase in hours worked per week, the outsourcing and commercialization of family-building domestic work like cooking and childcare) that augment material well-being at their expense. At some point, the loss of life satisfaction from the loss of social connection outweighs, in both subjective and objective measurements, the gains to be made by pursuing more work and more income; as with ecosystem services, a rational decision about maximizing benefits can't be made unless we put a value on what it is that is decreased when material well-being is increased. The default, again, is to value social connectedness at zero — and to continue policies and approaches that heedlessly degrade this contributor to individual well-being.

It's true that an indicator built solely on subjective reporting is vulnerable to being gamed or corrupted by policies that provide citizens with superficial satisfactions — the "bread and circuses" policy of ancient Rome (which, updated, looks a lot like "cheap beer and professional sports"). Two responses: one, surveys that measure self-reported happiness or degree of life satisfaction consistently show that humans in a variety of nations and cultures don't consistently and persistently mistake distraction and numbing for genuine life satisfaction. Two, any indicator that measures whether or not we're getting better at providing ourselves with that "immaterial flux, the enjoyment of life" is going to be built on both subjective and objective measures.

Do we want a government that, in its policies, purposely aims to promote individual and general well-being? To that question I'd respond the way realpolitik theorist Hans Morgenthau did to the question "Do the ends justify the means?" His answer: "Of course. What else could?" He went on to add, though, that people mistake the slogan "The end justifies the means" to mean "A desirable end justifies *any* means," and that assertion, he said, is one he most emphatically disagrees with. Should government actively promote the well-being of its citizens? Of course; it should do nothing but. That doesn't mean that the government is or should be the sole agent of our well-being. It does mean that in order to be effective in its duties — in order to serve the ends for which it is constituted — a government needs to assess the well-being of the citizenry. The promotion of sustainable, delivered well-being justifies a variety of means; but in our pursuit of that end, some means are forbidden to us, because (like distraction and chemical numbing) they conflict with other ends that we value. (Besides, they're dysfunctional: ultimately they don't serve but conflict with the goal of improving well-being.) Getting clearer about the ends we seek, including the end-in-view of economic life, is not an automatic decision to achieve those ends with means that are odious or problematic. Nor is deciding to pursue well-being a slippery slope to employing the worst possible means of achieving it. Under any good, broad-gauged measure of well-being, movement toward authoritarian government or toward a bread-and-circuses society will not register as improvement. Policies aimed at numbing and distraction might produce progress in a few narrow areas but will fail to boost the overall measure as long as that measure accurately reflects the full panoply of human satisfactions. Many elements of human well-being, such as a feeling of personal efficacy or satisfaction in achieving meaningful life goals, are not achievable by people who are numb and distracted. To argue that we shouldn't measure the economy's delivered well-being because if we do some politicians will be tempted to use unpalatable means to raise it is thus not a telling argument against a well-constructed indicator.

In the age of popular sovereignty, we came to understand that governments are instituted not to satisfy the wants and urges of those in power but for the common good—"to promote the general welfare," as the US Constitution puts it. The various pursuits of government, from national defense to energy policy, from road and school construction to the provision of a social safety net, are justifiable only in pursuit of this end. We should not let ourselves be forced into a false either/or choice between freedom or government, between measuring material well-being (and nothing but material well-being) or descending a slippery slope to serfdom. If promoting the general welfare—our collective well-being—is the end-in-view of government, it is only reasonable (and, ultimately, reasonable only) to measure progress toward fulfillment of that end. Even a minimalist government ought to monitor the progress of society toward the ultimate end for which it is instituted, rather than commit the fallacy of treating a poorly chosen instrumental end—the promotion of the sheer volume of commercial exchange—as the one and only measure of how well it fulfills its legitimate purpose.

One of the strongest entrants in the clean-sweep, measure-total-well-being category is Gross National Happiness (GNH), an indicator developed in the small mountainous kingdom of Bhutan. In 1972, the young, Western-educated and newly crowned king of Bhutan, Jigme Singye Wangchuck, used the phrase in a speech to his people signaling his intention to retain core Bhutanese values even as the country modernized: "Gross National Happiness is more important than Gross National Product." Whether an unstudied remark or a calculated policy choice, it eventually became the latter. After years of work, by 2006 the Centre for Bhutan Studies in Thimphu had developed a sophisticated survey instrument to gauge the well-being of Bhutanese citizens in nine different domains: Psychological Well-being; Health; Time Use; Education; Cultural Diversity and Resilience; Good Governance; Community Vitality; Ecological Diversity and Resilience; and Living Standards. (A comparison to the Stiglitz Commission's proposed dashboard shows broad agreement and some divergence. Both seek to measure health, education, and environmental values. GNH collapses material well-being and employment into living standards; enlarges interpersonal connectedness into community vitality, and political engagement into good governance; and takes up time use, psychological well-being, and cultural diversity and resilience while dropping equity).

The survey is long — "too long," says Michael Pennock, the Canadian health care epidemiologist who was one of its codevelopers — and can be criticized for cumulating subjective perceptions and reports rather than objective data. This, in itself, is not the completely devastating criticism that some economists take it to be. Most economists acknowledge the worth and utility of US unemployment statistics — which are generated in the same way, through interviews with a randomized, statistically significant sampling of Americans: "How many hours last week did you engage in paid employment?" The whole point of survey research is to turn subjectively reported experience into objective data.

Some information that the Bhutanese collect by survey — about, for instance, geographical access to health care, with the question "How long does it take you to walk to the nearest doctor?" — could, with greater effort, be answered objectively through analysis of the physical distribution of population, transportation routes, and health care service locations. More troubling is that the GNH survey instrument uses subjective reports to gauge some aspects of well-being that are better assessed with objective data. For instance, the GNH instrument gauges ecological diversity and resilience by asking, among other questions, "Are the following environmental issues of concern in your area? Pollution of rivers and streams; air pollution; absence of proper waste disposal facilities; decreasing wildlife species . . ." This substitutes the judgment of individual citizens, who may be misinformed or ignorant, for hard data about pollution and ecosystem degradation. Bhutan remains a largely agricultural society, and its lower level of urbanization means that its citizens may have retained the direct contact with natural systems that would let them be decent judges of ecosystem health.

Even so, the health of ecosystems is an objective quality that is better assessed with data than with survey research. Pennock allows that this is a valid concern that will be addressed in future development of the instrument. It's true, though, that as GNH's other primary codeveloper, Karma Ura of the Centre for Bhutan Studies, has said, "Self reporting of . . . experience along with objective statistics will provide a more accurate picture" of well-being.

In Bhutan, the government has implemented a GNH Impact Statement process—proposals for major policy changes have to be evaluated for the impact the change would have on GNH. If the impact is unpredictable or would lower GNH, the policy is not undertaken. (Note the conservative premise built into this: in the absence of good information, the default is "no action.") This process led Bhutan to reject membership in the World Trade Organization; in the judgment of the cabinet-level ministers asked to make the review, membership would have increased some elements of well-being (material welfare, perhaps employment), but only at the cost of greater losses in other elements of well-being that the Bhutanese value. Confident that their nine domains measure the elements of a gratifying life, Bhutan has undertaken a revision of national standards in education to support "education for GNH." Thus, the index is being thoroughly integrated into policy and the life of the nation.

Gross National Happiness has gained ground outside of Bhutan, in large measure because of that country's generous support, in time and money, for the export of the idea to other places. Between 2005 and 2009, Bhutan cosponsored a series of annual conferences—in Nova Scotia, Brazil, and Thailand—and these conferences have had noticeable effect in encouraging movement away from GDP and toward GNH or GNH-like measures.

But GNH may prove a difficult sell in the United States. "Happiness" and "the economy" strike the American ear as disparate categories; the one doesn't seem to have anything to do with the other. After decades of commercial advertising premised on the idea that our satisfactions are each our own, we have grown accustomed to thinking of happiness as a private rather than a civically relevant matter—even though our Declaration of Independence proclaims that the pursuit of happiness is one of the fundamental rights on which our nation is founded. Another alternative to GDP has made more headway in the United States: the Genuine Progress Indicator.

The GPI traces to work done in the 1980s by Herman Daly and John Cobb to create an Index of Sustainable Economic Welfare. The idea: subtract all relevant costs from GDP, and add uncounted benefits, to derive a single number—a monetary figure for positive economic change—that can be compared across time within an economy and across different economies. It takes as its starting point personal consumption expenditures as reported in US government statistics, then adjusts them by adding unpriced services and deducting remedial and defensive expenditures. It does not try to measure psychological well-being (as does GNH) or social connectedness and political engagement (as the Stiglitz Commission suggested)—though it does deduct "loss of leisure time" from the account, and this loss tracks social connectedness fairly well. (If you're going to maintain friendships and family connections, you need time.) A nonprofit organization, Redefining Progress, has been calculating the GPI for the United States since the early 1990s and has run the number back in time to the 1960s; it shows that while GDP had steady growth in that period, genuine well-being, as measured by the GPI, peaked in the early 1970s and has been relatively flat or declining since then. This reflects the experience of many Americans, who realize that even though GDP has increased exponentially in the past forty years, they are scarcely better off and in many cases are worse off than people in their parents' generation.

In February 2010, Maryland became the first US state officially to endorse the GPI and begin compiling it at state expense, describing it as "an educational tool" for Marylanders and "a complement" to gross state product. The GPI figures are generated primarily from data already on hand, which are assembled in the Department of Natural Resources. The numbers are placed in front of—and, one hopes, are used by—policy planners and legislators as they make decisions about economic development. That same function has been performed by the GPI indicator in Nova Scotia, where Atlantic GPI, a nongovernmental think tank and research center, has compiled it for the province since 1997. The number is respected and used by policy makers and legislators and has influenced the development of the quasi-official Canadian Index of Well-Being.

Between Nova Scotia and Maryland we can triangulate a classic moment in revolutionary change: having built alternative institutions that would supplant those of the system in power, partisans of the new way work, war, or wait to have those institutions replace the ones that are legitimate and official. Maryland has made the generation of its GPI official, but its use is not (yet) the law of the land; in Nova Scotia, neither the generation nor use of GPI is official, but it has gained considerable de facto authority through official use.

These signs of change are encouraging—much more encouraging than when the administration of Bush Junior put a halt to efforts begun in his father's administration, and advanced under Clinton, to have the Bureau of Economic Analysis add environmental "Satellite Accounts" to the national income accounts and thereby create a measure of "Green GDP."

Even more encouraging: the developing edge of thinking in this field points to a synthesis of the objective and subjective approaches represented by GPI and GNH. The GPI measures objective markers of sustainable well-being, using data (about such matters as net change in forest cover, net change in soil fertility, net depletion of nonrenewable resources, and net change in leisure time) that are, to a large degree, already collected by various governmental and nongovernmental groups. It aims to measure a variety of objective conditions that are judged to be important to, or are known to correlate with, sustainable well-being. GNH is based on survey research: the data-collection instrument asks people what they are experiencing, and thus aims at measuring directly the delivered well-being of the social, political, and economic system. The two approaches are not incompatible. They complement each other: the results from one approach provide a back-check, a test, of the results of the other. This may, at first glance, seem redundant, and hence an unnecessary expense. But in language and in data transmission, a bit of redundancy is necessary in order to isolate and fix errors and ensure that the communication is accurate. In the crucial effort to assess well-being, a similar approach is warranted. Without it, a new indicator set may perpetuate the problem that makes GDP so unsatisfactory. Any indicator set makes assumptions: "It would be good for this to go up" or "for this to go down." During the Depression it seemed that increasing the sheer volume of monetary transactions was a worthy goal, but now, seventy years later, we've outgrown it. Today, reduction of pollution is a worthy goal. It's likely to be sturdy, but we can't gauge that goal's continuing role in promoting health and well-being unless we measure those values. It seems the most desirable approach would be the construction of a dashboard of indicators that draw on both GPI and GNH, using both objective criteria and subjective reports. The two in combination not only allow assessment of a broader range of well-being than either measure gets when used singly, but their joint use offers an area of overlap that improves the validity of the result.

At the Gund Institute for Ecological Economics, students and Fellows have been working to articulate "GPI Plus," an expanded indicator set that aims to integrate the standard GPI indicator set with additional measures that assess well-being, some of which are derivable from objective data (for instance, the percentage of Vermonters who have access to affordable housing, which is federally defined as housing that costs less than 30 percent of income) and some of which are generated through survey research.

Another promising development: this movement to develop macroindicators of the overall performance of the economy in a variety of areas integrates nicely with the movement to assess governmental and NGO programs according to the results they produce per dollar of expenditure. Policy makers have always faced constrained choices; no governmental budget has ever been infinite. But for the past century humans have benefited from the historically unprecedented opportunity to turn past solar income, stored as fossil fuel, into wealth in the present. As civilization passes Hubbert's Peak and enters an era in which the current subsidy to the economy from past solar income must necessarily decline, additional pressure is being placed on governments to provide their services in the least-cost, most efficient manner. That pressure is being met, in part, by outcomes-based budgeting: the effort to identify, for each policy or program that a government or nonprofit agency may choose to pursue, the expected costs and the expected benefits.

In 2005 Mark Friedman published *Trying Hard Is Not Good Enough*, in which he made the case for "results-based accountability": governments and social service organizations should be given or should establish for themselves benchmarks or indicators for what they intend to accomplish, and assess their performance in achieving them. This sort of information on program achievement, when combined with information on program cost, allows us to assess the dollars-to-results efficiency of those programs. That, in turn, allows for economically rational policy making—policy making that gets the most bang for the buck by shifting funds from programs with low payoffs to programs with high payoffs. In the technical language of economists, results-based accountability lets policy makers and social service providers equalize the marginal returns of each unit of money they spend.

The approach is being promoted by the Pew Foundation's Results First initiative, which assists states in implementing "outcomes-based budgeting." That program has developed a core expertise in corrections, where data show very clearly that a dollar spent on providing training to foster parents of juveniles at risk of becoming offenders pays off at a 16:1 ratio in terms of savings on crime and corrections expense down the road, while spending money on enlarging juvenile detention centers has a negative total payoff. "Evidently, when you house juvenile offenders together, they teach each other things you'd rather they didn't learn," says Gary Vanlandingham, director of the Pew program. The Results First initiative is being "built out" into other areas of health and human services policy. If it were also built out into environmental policy, it would make use of the kind of ecosystem service valuation discussed above and would also begin to provide a foundation for the broad-ranging indicator set we need in order to assess the sustainable delivered well-being of the economy.

That is precisely what GPI Plus aims to do. At this point GPI Plus is more concept than established fact; the Gund Institute is seeking funding to support the further articulation of the appropriate indicator set in a process that brings together the international community of alternative-indicator practice with government officials and nonprofit managers in the state of Vermont. (All have shown interest in the development.) When fully articulated, such a measure would, over time, provide the information that is necessary for macroefficiency in state budgetary allocation. It's one thing to see that money spent on training foster parents has a higher payoff than expanding juvenile detention facilities, and quite another to be able to tell whether a tax dollar spent on corrections has more payoff in terms of citizen well-being than a dollar spent on, say, a program to improve water quality. Clear assessment of costs and benefits across a range of well-being indicators is necessary to accomplish that. As Vanlandingham noted about the Pew program, possession of such data doesn't turn all budget decisions into technical ones, doesn't eliminate the need for judgments rooted in political processes. But good data will enlighten the process and make the terms of necessary trade-offs a great deal clearer for all involved.

In the Depression, the economist Simon Kuznets led the development of national income accounting in the United States and hence the world. The United States has lost the opportunity to be a world leader in developing a better, more accurate measure to replace it—but that doesn't mean we shouldn't join the movement. In his very first report of national income to Congress in 1934, Kuznets listed GNP's shortcomings, warning that "the welfare of a nation can scarcely be inferred from a measure of national income." For lack of a better measure, and because GDP seemed to suffice when the planet seemed infinite and growth in economic activity seemed always and everywhere a good thing, we nevertheless have taken it as our primary indicator of economic well-being. Just as the Great Recession that began in 2008 gives us the opportunity to begin recasting the nature-be-damned, more-is-always-better economy that flourished when oil was cheap and plentiful, it also gives us the opportunity to act on Kuznets's wise warning. We're in an economic hole, and as we climb out, what we need is not simply a measurement of how much money passes through our hands each quarter, but an indicator set that will tell us whether we are really and truly gaining ground in the perennial struggle to improve the material conditions of our lives. That indicator set will have to measure the quality of the sustainable well-being delivered by the economy across the broad range of the human social and economic experience.

industrial civilization as
a pyramid scheme

f I said to you, "Give me a thousand bucks today, and in forty-five days I'll give you fifteen hundred bucks," you'd think I was stupid or crooked or both. That kind of interest rate works out to a phenomenal 2,466 percent per year, and it's what Carlo Ponzi offered investors in Boston in 1920.

If I said to you, "Give me a barrel of oil today, and in a month and a half I'll give you a barrel and a half back," I'd be making the same deal — but, thanks to the generous energy return on investment (EROI) of oil back in the 1920s, I could have made good my promise. I could have used the energy in your barrel of oil to help drill a well, which would have returned to me one hundred barrels of oil for every barrel I invested in the effort of extraction. (The EROI of US oil back then was about 100:1.)

Too bad Ponzi wasn't an oilman. He went to jail for what he did — as have some others, like Bernie Madoff, who imitated his basic business model. Ponzi's spirit lives on, though, not just in the pyramid schemers who defraud investors but in economists who assure us that infinite economic growth is possible on a finite planet — and that resolution of the problems created by growth can only come from continued exponential expansion of the economy's extractive base. The pyramided structure of our industrial economy becomes clearer when you use EROI to think about what Ponzi did. Before we turn to that, let's first review the life and work of this man who lent his name to unsustainable, infinite-growth investment schemes.

Ponzi came to Boston from Italy in the early years of the twentieth century, and after a few decades of knocking about at the edges of the law, he figured out a sure-fire way to make money. The International Postal Union (IPU) had been set up to facilitate the exchange of mail between countries and was authorized to print and sell International

Postal Coupons for use as postage (which it still does, since one country's postal system doesn't accept stamps issued by another's). In the wake of the First World War, the values of different national currencies were in flux, but exchange rates were fixed and the IPU hadn't adjusted the various national costs of their coupons to reflect the underlying economic reality. Ponzi noticed that by arbitraging these coupons — buying them where they were cheap (like in Italy) and exchanging them for currency where they were expensive (like in the United States) — he could make a profit. Quite a tidy profit: 400 percent, by his reckoning.

Arbitrage isn't illegal. Many of its practitioners provide a valuable service: their actions tend to equalize the cost of investment and commodities across borders, which promotes efficiency (by equalizing marginal returns and costs, less transaction costs). Ponzi explained his scheme to a few associates and friends, and they gave him some money and received in return promissory notes that said very clearly: in exchange for one thousand dollars, Ponzi would pay 50 percent interest in forty-five days, when the note came due.

In theory, the plan could have worked — the changes in exchange rates had created a significant disparity — but it would have been stymied by transaction costs. Though the potential gains were large on a percentage basis, a 400 percent gain on a three-cent stamp doesn't net a whole lot of money in absolute terms.

Still, word of the good deal spread, and Ponzi had eager investors — friends of friends, friends of friends of friends. He wrote his first promissory note in February 1920; within a month he had taken in half a million dollars; by the early summer, he was taking in a quarter of a million dollars a day. Some newspapers celebrated the immigrant's egalitarian dream of sharing financial wealth more equitably; didn't bankers get rich by depriving little guys of their fair share of returns? Others — including Charles Barron, founder of the financial journal that bears his name — smelled a rat. To invest with Ponzi you had to ignore warnings that for his company to make good on the claims against it, it would have to be holding 160 million IPCs — and only 27,000 were actually in circulation. (Barron's skepticism offers a lesson: there are benefits to be had from taking a whole-systems view of economic matters once in a while.)

It's not clear that Ponzi ever bought any International Postal Coupons. Apparently, from his microeconomic, self-interested view of the matter, he didn't have to. Thousands of people wanted to invest with him, and it seemed a simple matter to pay his old customers out of the proceeds of the incredible cash flow he got from his exponentially increasing base of new customers. And that's how Ponzi's business model became fraudulent; the exponential increase of his customer base — the geometric expansion of his financial footprint — allowed him to start treating investment capital as current income.

As any accountant can tell you, treating capital as income is a no-no. Any company that cashes out its capital stock (sells off its productive assets, like factories and infrastructure) and treats the result as income is going to go broke.

And here's the connection with oil. The fossil fuels of the planet are a capital stock: they represent past solar income the planet received in its 4-billion-year history that wasn't consumed at the time but was "saved" — locked away as fossil energy. We're drawing down our capital stock and treating the inflow of money as income.

Does this make our economy a pyramid scheme? Consider: anyone who offers you interest in exchange for a loan of money is betting that the economy will grow. Suppose I borrow the price of a gallon of milk today and promise to pay you a gallon and a pint next year. Multiply by billions: for all those promises to be kept, the economy has got to grow, has got to produce a gallon and a pint next year for every gallon it produced this year. If it doesn't, some lenders are going to be left holding worthless claims.

There are only two ways an economy can grow. It can suck up a larger flow of matter and energy, or it can achieve internal efficiencies — keep the rate of uptake of matter and energy stable, but lose less to waste and entropy within the productive cycle. That's it; there are no other ways. And there are limits to both of these avenues. When we increase the rate at which the economy sucks matter and energy out of nature, we increase the economy's ecological footprint — which has already exceeded a sustainable size. And while there is still plenty of room for additional efficiencies in how we use that matter and energy, we achieve those efficiencies within physical limits. Many of the things we make we could make using less matter and energy. We cannot make things — cannot create real wealth of any sort — using no matter and energy.

When debt — a claim on the future productivity of an economy —

grows faster than that productivity grows, then somebody who holds a claim is going to have to have that claim go unfulfilled. There are some basic ways this happens in an economy: inflation, bankruptcy, defaults on loans and bonds, stock market crashes, loss of pension promises or paper assets of any kind. You could, with some effort, correlate the amount of debt that is erased by these mechanisms every year to the difference between claims on future income and actual increases in productivity. It would be interesting to examine the recurring inflationary episodes and bankruptcy crises of the American system in this light—from the savings and loan scandals of a few decades ago, through Enron, on up into the subprime mortgage crisis. It seems that the system is always shedding claims on future income, because it systematically allows those claims on income to grow faster than the income itself can grow. (As ought to be clear, this structural need for spasms of debt repudiation is a fundamental driver behind the economy's cyclical swings, the boom-and-bust cycles that have characterized market capitalism from its inception. Note that sometimes developed nations can insulate themselves from the phenomenon by outsourcing the necessary debt repudiation, forcing it abroad, as when the World Bank forgives loans to developing nations, or those nations experience high rates of inflation.)

Ecological economics models the economy as a physical system rather than a textbook abstraction. From its thermodynamically enlightened perspective, it's clear that compounding interest is a wager that says we will continue to increase our economy's capacity exponentially—which usually comes down to increasing the economy's ecological footprint exponentially. Or, to see it from another angle: one of the strong drivers of our economy's rapacious drawdown of natural capital in all its forms (including our loss of ecosystems that provide crucial ecosystem services) is the practice of compounding interest on loans.

So, a hypothesis: for much of the twentieth century, this essential element of the relationship between money and physical reality was obscured by the increasing exploitation of fossil fuel with a high energy return on investment. Just as word of Ponzi's great investment opportunity swept like wildfire through the immigrant neighborhoods of Boston and beyond, postponing his inevitable day of reckoning, we've raced through the hydrocarbon endowment of the planet, spending capital as income, obscuring financial reality as effectively as Ponzi and Madoff did. Petroleum allowed us to build a financial pyramid that must eventually crumble.

Energy return on investment is a fundamental measurement that we're all going to learn more about as we face the end of the oil era. A particular energy source may or may not be economically viable, but that's an accident of the market, which is a human construct: economic viability is determined by market prices, which (as previously discussed) are influenced by rates of extraction, human thinking, government subsidies, and the degree to which an energy source's negative and positive externalities either are or aren't reflected in its monetary price.

A sturdier measure of an energy source's viability is its EROI ratio. How much energy does it take to get a unit of usable energy into the economy? When it takes a barrel of oil to get a barrel of oil out of the ground, refined, and transported to market, the oil era will be over, no matter what its monetary price happens to be. Actually, because we are economically rational, the oil era will end *before* the EROI of oil declines to 1:1; it will end when the EROI of oil is smaller than that of the next-best system (though we may find it economical to keep pumping some quantity of oil even when it's a net energy loss, with an EROI below 1:1, because some current uses — lubrication, perhaps — might not be fully and satisfactorily met by sustainable alternatives).

In the 1920s the EROI for US oil averaged something like 100:1. This fact makes several things clear:

If you could invest one valuable unit (like, say, a dollar) and get a 10,000 percent return, you'd have to be a fool not to make money. And look at the history of the United States in the twentieth century: quite an impressive record of wealth creation. From one perspective, the creation of that wealth was the result of a long, hard struggle, which neoclassical economists and others attribute to the virtues of our free-market system, with its impetus to innovation, invention, and entrepreneurship. Sure, no doubt it was a struggle, and no doubt free-market institutions and the quality of American character played a role. But if you were party to a deal in which someone regularly gave you a hundred dollars for every dollar you invested, well, you'd have to be stupid or crazy not to end up with quite a pile of money. With the EROI of oil, the United States could hardly lose.

Certainly the people who trusted Ponzi were naive, but maybe they weren't completely stupid. Oil was giving stunning returns; why shouldn't some other form of investment do the same? Ponzi and his scheme need to be seen in this broader socioeconomic/historical context. It seems that in Ponzi's day, as in Bernie Madoff's, people's expectations of large returns were encouraged by the vast quantity of income being achieved through drawdown of natural capital.

When you think of the economic history of the United States this way, you're led to wonder: What did all that energy wealth buy? What do we have to show for it?

It's no accident that oil barons—John D. Rockefeller, J. Paul Getty—became some of the richest people on Earth. Some of that wealth went into millionaire extravagance: mansions, yachts, Adirondack lodges, balls, parties, other forms of material self-indulgence. Some went to philanthropy: it built museums and libraries and universities. Some "trickled down," establishing America as a middle-class nation in which the benefits of our EROI-fueled prosperity were widely shared. Eventually, through taxes, some of that went to creating our country's impressive infrastructure: bridges, railways, water systems, schools, parks, public buildings. As we watch our infrastructure age, as we begin calculating what it might cost to replace it, as we struggle to find the wherewithal to pay for an educational system that keeps the United States competitive in a globalized world, we're led to this sobering thought: we'll never have that oil wealth again. Everything we accomplish we will now have to accomplish on the EROI that renewable energy can give us. The ongoing decline in EROI is an underappreciated root of the "new austerity" in public finance, the sense that is sweeping Europe and the United States that government expenditures need to be cut and should no longer be financed by borrowing against future growth. With the 100:1 engine of the economy having declined to 20:1, there's simply less money to spend on anything else.

From an EROI perspective, it seems that perhaps too much of the wealth created by oil was spent on current consumption: on Gilded Age excess, on mansions and armaments and war, and, in some degree of trickle-down, on the development of a middle-class consumer society in which people measure their happiness by how much they can buy, how many material belongings they have, how fast they can cycle through the irreplaceable resources of the planet.

Oil has given us a once-in-the-history-of-the-planet chance to build a sustainable industrial infrastructure, one that can provide a high standard of living by running on current solar income rather than by drawing down the planetary stock of capital, and so far, we've blown it. We've been like Ponzi, meeting current expenses out of capital rather than true income. Like him, we've built a system that has to grow to keep from crashing, and like him, we've built a system that cannot grow forever, so it must crash.

Ponzi went to jail, and when he got out he moved around the world; eventually he died in poverty in South America. He survived the crash of his eponymous scheme—not well, but he survived. It remains to be seen whether industrial civilization can do the same.

the financial crisis is the
environmental crisis

tandard, neoclassical economic theory offers several explanations
of the origin of the 2008 financial crisis that led to our collective
slide into the Great Recession, and these explanations are wrong.
They're wrong because they're incomplete, and that means that
implementing changes in the economy based on them — even
deep-reaching, structural changes — will do little to prevent another
crisis.

One standard explanation of the origin of the financial crisis was offered by Lawrence (Larry) Summers in March 2009, when he was director of the White House National Economic Council. At a talk at the
Brookings Institution, he laid out the dynamic that led to the Great
Recession. Two or three times a century, he said, citing Keynes, "the
self-equilibrating properties of markets break down as stabilizing mechanisms are overwhelmed by vicious cycles." He went on to describe those
cycles: "Declining asset prices lead to margin calls and de-leveraging
which leads to selling and further declines in asset prices, perpetuating
the cycle. Lower asset prices mean banks hold less capital. Less capital
means less lending. Less lending means lower asset prices, and the cycle
perpetuates." According to classic supply-and-demand theory, markets
tend naturally to move toward equilibrium. When there's an oversupply of cars or computers their prices fall, leading people to buy more of
them and producers to make less of them, until a new, market-clearing
price obtains. But that dynamic doesn't operate in some markets, as
Summers noted. He listed other key markets that have this tendency
to "disequilibrate" or spiral out of control: falling home prices lead to
foreclosures, which further depress prices, which produces more foreclosures. Unemployment leads to less spending, which leads to more
unemployment, which leads to less spending. He sketched out a couple

more. "And I could go on," he said. The whole downturn started, he said, when

> an abundance of greed and an absence of fear led some [people] to make investments not based on the real value of assets, but on the faith that there would be another who would pay more for those assets. At the same time, the government turned a blind eye to these practices and the potential consequences for the economy as a whole. Bubbles were born.

And what happens to bubbles? Eventually, they pop — "the process stops and reverses," Summers said, as prices fall, greed "gives way to fear and this fear begets fear" and more fear, and the disequilibrating mechanism that ran things up runs them back down — but much more rapidly.

A different version of the standard interpretation — one that makes no mention of that conservative bête noir, John Maynard Keynes — was offered in testimony delivered to the bipartisan Financial Crisis Inquiry Commission by economist Pierre-Olivier Gourinchas: "Cheap and poorly documented mortgages" fueled a run-up in housing prices — an "unsustainable boom" — that halted in 2006. (When he says "boom," we should hear "bubble.") And when it collapsed, it triggered "severe markdowns on high-risk mortgage products" — the subprime mortgages at the center of the crisis. Three factors, Gourinchas told the committee, ensured that this collapse in "a minor segment of the U.S. financial markets" became a global crisis:

> First, profound structural changes in the banking system, . . . coupled with an increased securitization of credit instruments, led to a decline in lending standards and a general inability to re-price [such] complex financial products when liquidity dried-up.

In plain speak: deregulation and the resulting invention of complicated investment instruments (in which original investments, like mortgages, were bundled together and then divided up into shares and resold) created such a demand for risky, high-payoff investments that lending standards declined; and these investments — derivatives and derivatives of derivatives and futures contracts on derivatives — were so complicated that players in the market couldn't judge their worth accurately. And then, Gourinchas says, "This [dramatically] lowered . . . [the degree of] confidence between financial intermediaries, severely disrupting interbank markets and the flow of credit." The players in these markets got scared and ran for cover—lending stopped, crashing the economy. Second, he said,

> banks relied increasingly on short-term financing—either directly or through off-balance-sheet vehicles—exposing themselves to significant funding risk. [And third] . . . increased financial globalization and the strong appetite of foreign—especially European—financial institutions for U.S. structured credit instruments quickly propagated the crisis to Europe and the rest of the World.

It's clear from context that this description is offered as the standard, consensus view of events. Gourinchas went on to propose that an underappreciated aspect of those events was the origin of the crisis in "the imbalance between the global demand for safe and liquid debt instruments—both within and outside the U.S.—and the limited supply of this asset." As he sees it, investors, seeking more safe debt than there was to be had, took risks, bidding up the prices of safe debt and inviting the creation of unsafe debt (falsely labeled as safe), creating an international bubble:

> The excess demand for safe debt instruments [denominated in dollars] created conditions under which it became profitable for the U.S. financial sector to 'manufacture' pseudo triple-A assets that turned out to be extremely vulnerable in case of systemic distress.

This description-and-diagnosis ignores a seedy and telling detail: much of the demand for repackaged subprime mortgage instruments— the demand that drove the housing bubble—wasn't foreign demand for supposedly safe US debt, but domestic demand for debt that was specifically *unsafe*. Newly created hedge funds allowed investors to bet against bad debt by the carload, and this bet was so attractive that demand for bad debt soon outstripped the supply. Ever aiming to please and profit, financiers set about creating bad debt, asking for and repackaging cheap and risky (and "poorly documented") subprime mortgages specifically to fulfill this demand. "Go ahead. Just sign here. There's no reason you can't live in a $250,000 house just because you don't have a job or a credit rating. Isn't America great?" Some banks, fully aware of what they were doing, did both: bet against bad debt and created bad debt to bet against.

Gourinchas goes on to assert that it was "the unique position of the U.S. as a global provider of liquidity, and the important role of the dollar as a reserve currency," that "played an important role in generating excess demand for safe dollar assets." Worldwide, investors know that the US economy is the world's largest, and it has always been too big to fail. So investments held in dollars seem very sound.

In yet another variation in the standard description of the problem, Randall Kroszner, in his testimony to the commission, allowed that the "length and complexity" of "intermediation chains"—the routes by which money gets from lender to borrower—give them a "fragility" that needs to be "mitigated." Mitigation consists, in his opinion, of making "market structures more robust" and dealing with the problem of a cascading series of bankruptcies by moderating some of the uncertainty that propels it—the fear that Summers cites as a contributory cause. Kroszner's solution: "pre-packaged bankruptcy" procedures—what he called "living wills" for financial institutions—which would reduce fear and uncertainty because they'd "give greater clarity about how a troubled institution will operate as it winds down operations."

Accurate diagnosis is the first step in rational problem solving, and all diagnosis begins with description. There is a great deal of merit in the descriptions just quoted. Each of them identifies key parts of the problem, and no doubt each of the parts played a contributory role in bringing about the collapse that put 50 million people out of work and destroyed the financial security of many hundreds of millions more. You can easily tick off the solution that's implied by each element of these problem-statements: If the problem is cyclical swings between greed and fear, we need somehow to dampen the effects of one and assuage the other. If the problem is self-reinforcing market dynamics, as sketched out by Summers, then those dynamics ought to be identified and brought under control—through law, regulation, intervention, or pronouncement. If "cheap and poorly documented mortgage financing" created an unsustainable boom, then mortgage financing shouldn't be cheap and poorly documented. If there's a problem in confidence between financial intermediaries, confidence should be restored—perhaps through regulation that constrains the risky behavior that undermines confidence, or perhaps through insurance schemes modeled on the Federal Deposit Insurance Corporation (the FDIC, which secured consumer confidence in what, in retrospect, looks like tame and ordinary banking practice). Financing should never be off-balance-sheet and should be long term, to temper the effects of the sort of crowd-think that can stampede the economy off a cliff. The international flow of debt, sold as assets, could be limited to ensure that various national economies are not completely structurally integrated. Or the debt instruments that move in international commerce could be subject to international minimum quality standards. (The free-market solution is bolder: let investors in other nations learn the hard way that just because debt carries a "Grade A, made in America" stamp, they shouldn't assume it's high quality. This may in fact be the lesson that Europeans draw from recent experience.) Government's "blind eye" should be healed and regulatory failures fixed, and of course assets should be appraised accurately. Financial instruments that appear to transform sure-to-fail loans into sure-to-pay investments should be prohibited.

While Gourinchas would certainly not endorse it, one element in his diagnosis — that the bubble grew because the world was clamoring for debt denominated in dollars — points to another possible solution. We could tackle the source of that excess of demand for US debt by destroying the dollars' status as the default world reserve currency. That project would take some time, but it would be relatively easy: we could display fecklessness as a world power, running up huge deficits by using our military might for narrowly self-interested operations with flimsy cause, hazy goals, and morally objectionable practice; we could flirt with suspending government operations and government payments while the ceiling on the federal deficit is negotiated, transforming the prospect of governmental default on obligations (to employees, to investors holding government bonds) from unthinkable into very thinkable, perhaps even likely; we could let other economies outpace us in the movement toward a post-petroleum economy so that when the oil is gone (as it surely must be someday), American economic preeminence will give way to that of China, or India, or the European Union; and in general we could see to it that investors who trust our economy come to regret that choice.

To make the point clearly and without irony: if we were intending to implement this solution, US policy could scarcely be better designed to that end. Achieving it will have a profound and profoundly negative effect on the quality of life of us citizens. When and if the United States is no longer a preeminent world power and the owner-operator of the world's preeminent national economy, dollars will no longer be used as the world's default reserve currency, and a bursting bubble in relatively small sector of our economy would no longer be exported as a world financial crisis. Problem solved.

All of these solutions would, if implemented, reduce the chances that we'll see a repeat of the particular problematic chain of events that sent the global financial and economic system to the brink of collapse. Many of these solutions are worth implementing on their own merits: who could be against seeing assets appraised accurately, who could be in favor of suckering citizens into signing on to mortgages they can't afford, and who could defend the continuation of the two-card monte game in which bankers create bad debt specifically in order to bet against it? But all of these solutions address intermediate causes, not the root cause, because they proceed from a faulty and incomplete description of the problem.

The American philosopher John Dewey cautioned that the movement from *experiencing* a problem to *describing* it to *diagnosing* it can appear seamless but in fact consists of distinct (if often unconscious) steps; make a mistake in one of those steps and it's likely (though not guaranteed) that your efforts will not have a satisfactory result. Being human, we tend to offer descriptions and diagnoses that are consistent with the theories, principles, rules of thumb, and habits of perception that have served us well—or have *seemed* to serve us well—in the past. But there is not and never can be a guarantee that what we've taken from past experience will allow us to be successful in our dealing with future experience. New experience might be unprecedented.

It might seem that Dewey's warning doesn't apply here, to our attempts to understand the chain of events that led to the Great Recession, because the financial crisis that led to this recession had plenty of precedent. We've had crises like this one before, and we've gotten through them acceptably well; employment recovered, some losses were made good, the engines of wealth generation were restarted, life continued for both winners and losers. (There are studies, though, that tell us that some people never recover, even after returning to work;

there are long-lasting personal, social, and economic costs of economic insecurity and involuntary joblessness.) We might therefore infer that the lessons we've learned — including our habitual ways of perceiving and defining the problem — have been serving us well.

But from the phenomena of our economic experience we can draw the exactly opposite conclusion with equal justification: the market crisis that cascaded into the Great Recession is but the latest and worst in a series of similar crises that have beset our economy, and we are unlikely to solve the problems they create until we learn to see and to define these crises in different terms. Whatever lessons we draw from previous experience, we must be wary: our experience (as Dewey also cautioned) may not have been sufficiently sharp and pointed — lawyers would say "dispositive" — to offer sturdy lessons that will serve in similar-but-different circumstances in the future. Despite our apparent successes, in the uncontrolled laboratory of the world a variety of factors can mask fundamental and essential causal relations, leading to misperception and false conclusions — ideas and interpretations that seem to serve us in the moment but fail us in the face of continued experience. As previously noted, through most of the twentieth century the historically unprecedented energy return on energy invested of oil — which stood at 100:1 in 1930 — obscured some fundamental flaws in our economic theories. If you've got an economic engine cranking out a 10,000 percent rate of return as the motor driving your economy, you can hold on to just about any economic theory you want and still see the economy generate a whole lot of wealth.

In order to solve the problem of the recurring financial crises that beset our industrial economies — and that have become more severe and more widespread in our era of global economic integration on Factory Planet — we need to begin with a different and broader description of the origin of such crises. In this latest one, two facts stand out: the world came to the brink of global economic collapse, and the world remains on the brink of widespread ecosystem collapse. The fact that the economy is humanity's primary instrument for interacting with its environment suggests that these two facts are somehow related, yet none of the descriptions reviewed above come anywhere close to connecting them. They can't, because standard theory can't even acknowledge that an economy involves the movement and transformation of real things drawn from a real (and finite) planet. The standard descriptions, and the diagnoses that emerge from them, are as bloodless, lifeless, and abstract as the textbook theory from which they are drawn.

One thing is striking about all of the standard diagnoses and variants mentioned here (which have been culled from, among other sources, testimony heard by the US Congress's Financial Crisis Inquiry Commission): living, breathing people are absent. The economy is a great abstraction that operates without them. They're alluded to as the holders of financial instruments, the signatories to various kinds of agreements, the (presumable) subjects of employment and unemployment figures, perpetrators of this or that transaction, carriers of this or that expectation or motivation, but they aren't present as live beings who derive sustenance and wealth from their engagement with the planet. There is absolutely no mention of the larger environment in which the economy operates; in the index to the Financial Crisis Inquiry Commission's 500-plus-page report, you won't find such key terms as *ecology, environment, energy, entropy, thermodynamics, energy return on energy invested,* no entry for *Earth* or *ecosystem* or even for *natural resources.* No people, no planet: it's as if the financial crisis befell an economy that consists solely of formalized systems of relations between financial entities, systems which are only tenuously connected to people and which have absolutely no connection to the larger worlds — social, ecological — in which economic relations operate. Systems that don't connect with reality like that give us an absolutely free hand: because they are imaginary creations, we can adapt, modify, or tinker with them as we choose.

Put plainly and simply: that vision is wrong. The financial crisis is, at bottom, the environmental crisis. It's a consequence of the deeply flawed relationship that we have developed between culture and nature, between humans in society and the ecosystems that support them. It's just the latest iteration of what happens when an infinite-growth economy runs into the reality of a finite planet.

The spasm of debt repudiation with which the crisis began — the collapse of the subprime lending market — is not a pathological rarity in the world economy but a structural necessity within our ecologically unsustainable economy. That insight comes from the reference frame suggested by the work of Frederick Soddy, a little-regarded British chemist-turned-economist who wrote before and during the Great

Depression. A 1921 Nobel laureate in chemistry for his work on radioactive decay, during the First World War Soddy became disgusted at his discipline's complicity in the mass death made possible by mustard gas and turned to thinking and writing about economics — the fundamental institutions of the world that science gives its gifts to. In a series of books published from 1921 to 1934, he carried on a quixotic campaign for a radical restructuring of global monetary relationships. He was roundly dismissed as a crank, but we'd do well to resurrect his perspective and analysis.

Soddy offered a vision of economics as rooted in physics — particularly in the laws of thermodynamics. An economy is often likened to a machine, though few economists follow the parallel to its logical conclusion: like any machine, the economy must draw energy from outside itself. The first and second laws of thermodynamics forbid perpetual motion, schemes in which machines create energy out of nothing or recycle it forever. Soddy criticized the prevailing belief in the economy as a perpetual motion machine, capable of generating infinite wealth — a criticism echoed by his intellectual heirs in ecological economics.

Soddy argued that all wealth has an irreducibly physical dimension. Even the apparently nonphysical goods and services that move in our economy — burger flipping and economic theorizing, information processing and manipulating pixels on a screen — rely on physical intake of matter and energy: food for the workers, matter and energy embodied in the tools and physical plant they use, and of course the energy that operates this capital equipment. Real wealth, even the provision of services, is irreducibly rooted in physical reality.

The money we use to represent this wealth is not real wealth, but virtual wealth — a symbol representing the bearer's claim on an economy's ability to generate real wealth. When money meant gold or silver (or the paper notes that represented it when it was safely locked away in Fort Knox), money was a physical thing. Because the mining, refining, casting, and stamping of valuable metals used productive resources that couldn't be used to do something else (like make steel), money represented an amount of real wealth that a community voluntarily denied itself in order to have the convenience of a medium of exchange. (Now that money is fiat money, and most of it isn't even printed on paper, the quantity of virtual wealth in the economy is less significant;

we don't forgo much of anything by increasing a number in a bank account database.)

Debt, for its part, is a claim on the economy's ability to generate wealth in the future. "The ruling passion of the age," Soddy said, "is to convert wealth into debt"—to exchange a thing with present-day real value (a thing that could be stolen or broken, or could rust or rot, before you can manage to use it) for something immutable and unchanging, a claim on wealth that has yet to be made. Money facilitates the exchange; it is, Soddy said, "the nothing you get for something before you can get anything."

Problems arise when wealth and debt are not kept in proper relation. The amount of wealth that an economy can create is limited by the amount of low entropy that it can sustainably suck from its environment—and by the amount of high-entropy effluent that natural systems can sustainably absorb. (We can exceed those limits, but only temporarily; that is the definition of "unsustainable.") As noted, there are only two ways that an economy can increase the rate at which it creates wealth: it can process a larger and larger flow of matter and energy throughput, increasing its ecological footprint on both the uptake and the effluent side; or it can achieve efficiencies in its use of a constant rate of throughput. Both means of growth have limits. Increasing an economy's ecological footprint decreases the ability of healthy ecosystems to provide us with a civilization-sustaining flow of ecosystem services (like climate stability, a service currently in critically short supply). Efficiency gains in the use of a constant flow of throughput offer large returns today and into the future, but will become harder and harder to achieve as we run into diminishing returns. Technological advances will allow us to make more with less, especially in places where we've been profligate in our use of low-entropy inputs; but no technical advance will get us around the first law of thermodynamics, which tells us, "You can't make something from nothing, nor can you make nothing from something." Creation of wealth is irreducibly physical, and all physical phenomena obey the laws of thermodynamics.

Thus, the creation of wealth has physical constraints, set by ecosystem limits, physical law, and the limits of the technology we currently employ. But debt, being imaginary, has no such limit. It can grow infinitely, compounding at any rate we choose to let it.

These considerations from Soddy lead to this incontrovertible truth: whenever an economy allows debt — a claim on wealth — to grow faster than wealth can be created, that economy has a structural need for debt to be repudiated.

Inflation can do the job, decreasing debt gradually by eroding the purchasing power of the monetary units in which debt is denominated. But when there is no inflation, an economy with overgrown claims on future wealth will experience regular crises of debt repudiation — stock market crashes, bankruptcies and foreclosures, default on bonds or loans or pension promises, the disappearance of paper assets in any shape or form. As Larry Summers noted in that same speech quoted above, "In little more than two decades, we have seen the stock market crash of 1987, the savings and loan scandals, the decline of the real estate market, the Mexican crisis, the Asian crisis, LTCM, Enron and long-term capital. That works out to one big crisis every two and a half years." He went on to add: "We can and must do better." Each and every one of the crises he listed was, at bottom, a crisis of debt repudiation. Absent the discovery of another energy source that could return one hundred units of energy for every unit we invest in exploiting it, we are unlikely to do better until we stop allowing claims on real wealth to grow faster than real wealth can grow.

Frederick Soddy would not have been surprised at the subprime lending meltdown and its cascading impact on the global economy. The problem, he would certainly say, isn't simply opportunistic financiers exploiting the lag between innovation and regulation, isn't simply ignorance, isn't a failure of regulatory diligence, isn't a cascading lack of confidence that could be solved with some new and different version of the FDIC or "living wills" for banks. All of that is, at bottom, elaborately and pathetically beside the point. The problem is a systemic flaw in our treatment of money. Whenever and wherever growth in claims on wealth outstrips growth in wealth, our system creates a niche for entrepreneurs who are all too willing to invent instruments of debt that will someday be repudiated. There will always be a Bernie Madoff or a subprime mortgage repackager or a hedge fund innovator willing to play their part in setting us up for spasms of debt repudiation. Regulation will always be retrospective. The best solution is to eliminate that niche. To do that, we must balance claims on future production of wealth with the economy's power to produce that wealth.

Soddy distilled his heterodoxical vision into five policy prescriptions, each of which was taken at the time as evidence that his theories were unworkable:

1 Abandon the gold standard.
2 Let international exchange rates float against one another.
3 Use federal surpluses and deficits as macroeconomic policy tools, countering cyclical trends.
4 Establish bureaus of economic analysis to produce statistics (including a consumer price index) to facilitate this effort.

Obviously, these proposals—once universally dismissed by the economics profession as the work of a crank—are now firmly grounded in conventional practice. Only Soddy's fifth proposal remains outside the bounds of conventional wisdom:

5 Stop banks from creating money (and debt) out of nothing.

Soddy's work helped to inspire the short-lived "100 percent money" movement that emerged during the Depression, which offered a diagnosis that went beyond treatment of symptoms (the cascading collapse of confidence that led to bank failures, which was addressed through creation of the FDIC) to reach the underlying cause: the leveraging of debt through the practice of fractional reserve banking. Not many Americans realize that banks create money, and debt, through their normal operations (indeed, most of our $1.3 trillion money supply has been created privately in this way). Here's how it works: when you deposit $100 into your checking account, the money doesn't sit there waiting for you; the bank lends it out at interest. By law it keeps a small percentage of the money on hand against the possibility that you'll show up and ask for it back. If this reserve requirement is 10 percent, the bank wants to lend out the remaining 90 of your dollars and start getting interest on it. This they do simply by crediting the account of the borrower. That deposit looks like $90 of fresh money, and the bank can again lend out 90 percent of it, or $81. And so on, until, with a reserve requirement of 10 percent, a $100 "fresh injection" of money into the system leads to a $1,000 growth in the money supply—$900 of which was created by the banking system. Against that $900 of money it has created, it has created more than $900 of debt; the borrowers, after all, have promised to pay back both the principal and an interest charge.

In the 1930s economists Irving Fisher at Yale and Frank Knight at Chicago supported the elimination of fractional reserve banking and debt-based money as a way to prevent the recurrence of the bank runs and failures that led to the Depression. For a time the movement counted no less an economic eminence than Milton Friedman as a sympathizer. (Perhaps because he saw that the tide of history was against him, Friedman eventually dropped his call for elimination of fractional reserve banking from his policy recommendations.) The 100 percent money movement makes for an unusual alliance: long a staple of conservative, Austrian school economics (the school that includes Hayek and gave rise to the conservative Chicago monetarist school), the idea finds enthusiastic expression on conservative, "sound money" websites — and in the work of ecological economists like Herman Daly. Daly has called for the gradual institution of a 100 percent reserve requirement on demand deposits, in order to shrink what he has called "the enormous pyramid of debt that is precariously balanced atop the real economy, threatening to crash," and to remove excess debt creation as the driver of our insatiable need for the economy to grow beyond its sustainable ecological footprint. In a system with a 100 percent reserve requirement, banks would support themselves by charging fees for safekeeping, check clearing, loan intermediation, and all the other legitimate financial services they provide. They would not generate income by lending out, at interest, the money entrusted to them for safekeeping — money that does not belong to them. (There's more than a hint of moral judgment behind some of the calls for 100 percent money — a moral judgment, I hasten to add, that I am not offering here; 100 percent money can be supported on purely practical grounds.) Banks would still make loans and still be able to lend at interest "the real money of real depositors," as Daly puts it — the savings of people who forgo consumption today in order to take money out of their checking account and put it in time deposits — CDs, passbook savings, 401ks. In return these savers would still receive interest payments — a slightly larger claim on the real wealth of the community in the future.

In a 100 percent money system, every increase in spending by borrowers would have to be matched by an act of saving — abstinence — on the part of a depositor. This would reestablish a one-to-one correspondence between the real wealth of the community and the claims on that real wealth. To achieve 100 percent money, the creation of monetarized debt through other mechanisms — repackaged mortgages and securitized derivatives and the like — would also have to be brought under control.

An added benefit: eliminating fractional reserve banking would have a large and positive effect on the public treasury, because it would allow the public treasury to capture something called "seigniorage."

This is the term for the difference between the face value of money and its cost of production; it's the profit that comes from the manufacture of money. A gold doubloon with just a half a doubloon's worth of gold in it gives a tidy profit to the king's treasury. When money is fiat money, seigniorage is even larger; when money is just pixels on a screen, seigniorage is nearly the face value of the money. The US Treasury captures the seigniorage on the currency it issues (and it pays negative seigniorage when it costs more to produce a coin, like the penny, than the coin is worth). But currency is only a small percentage of the money supply; banks create the rest through lending. And they capture the seigniorage on it — which is one reason banking has always been a very profitable industry.

Under a 100 percent money regime, money would be created — spent into existence — by public authority. (This is what Friedman advocated.) The capture of seigniorage would have obvious benefits for governmental budgeting. And, when you come right down to it, to whom does seigniorage, by rights, belong? I think that despite long-standing custom to the contrary, on any disinterested examination of the question the answer has to be that the profit that comes from the issuance of money belongs to the sovereign power that guarantees that money. In our system, that's us: We, the People.

The elimination of debt-based money issued by banks would eliminate the main structural cause of spasms of debt repudiation. It would also eliminate one strong driver of *uneconomic* growth — growth that costs more in lost ecosystem services and other disamenities than it brings in the form of increased wealth. The change is thus economically and ecologically sound. It is also, obviously, politically difficult — so difficult that advocacy for it sounds hopelessly unrealistic. But consider: in the 1920s, the abolition of the gold standard and the implementation of floating exchange rates sounded absurd. If the laws of thermodynamics are sturdy, and if Soddy's analysis of their relevance to economic life is correct, we'd better expand the realm of what we think is realistic.

the battle over the environmental
kuznets curve

n November 13, 2005, an accident at a petrochemical plant in Jilin Province, north central China, sent a large but unknown quantity of benzene and nitrobenzene into the Songhua River. Downstream, the capital of neighboring Heilongjiang Province draws its drinking water from the river. Authorities there didn't alert the population to the danger but tried to dilute the toxic plume. Unsurprisingly, that didn't work, and they soon were forced to shut off the water supply to the city's 3.8 million residents—well after citizens had noticed that the water coming out of their taps was contaminated. (The explanation the provincial authorities gave for the shutdown: "to carry out repair and inspection work on the pipe network.") After the resumption of service, the governor of the Province, Zhang Zuoji, drank a ceremonial glass of water in the home of a seventy-five-year-old citizen and told the official news agency, "I took the first drink . . . to reassure the public and dispel their worries." Given the delay and dissimulation, the gesture seems unlikely to have had its full intended effect.

The previous April the *New York Times* had reported on a riot in the southeastern province of Zhejiang: as many as sixty thousand residents blockaded the entrance to the Zhuxi Industrial Function Zone, protesting the pollution that its thirteen chemical plants spewed into their lives; the demonstration turned violent when officials dispatched three thousand police officers and government workers to take down the protester's tent city. The protesters repelled the assault and held their ground, overturning police buses and cars and setting them afire. Official reports said that officers and government employees were attacked by a crowd wielding clubs and rocks and that thirty officials were hospitalized, some with serious injuries. No reports were offered of injuries or deaths to the protestors, although bloggers posted photos that included civilian bodies on the ground.

These were not isolated incidents. In March 2004, a million people lost water for twenty-five days when a chemical spill in the Tuojiang River shut down urban water systems. In July 2005 in Xinchang, an estimated 15,000 people rioted for three days protesting pollution from a recently built pharmaceutical plant. (It was, the *New York Times* reported, "a pitched battle," with the crowd "overturning police cars and throwing stones for hours, undeterred by thick clouds of tear gas.") In June 2007, in the coastal city of Xiamen, demonstrators protested the proposed construction of a chemical factory that would have undercut the city's role as the center of a lucrative ecotourism trade. May 2008, in Chengdu, saw another demonstration against a proposed petrochemical factory and oil refinery.

By 2006, the Chinese government was receiving six hundred thousand official environmental complaints per year, a number that had risen by about 20 percent per year from 2002 on. That complaints are voiced can be taken as a sign of progress: China is more open than it was. But the magnitude and number of the problems suggest that China's bureaucratic culture of secrecy and its centralized, command-and-control decision making have survived the liberalization of capital ownership and the transition to a privatized, free-market, corporatized economy — and that Chinese officials continue to take the imperative of industrial expansion as a public interest so compelling that it overrides other public interests — in free speech, in freedom of assembly, in having a nonpoisonous environment. Citizens harmed by the damages that economic development has imposed on them risk their lives in protest.

In the thirty years from 1978 and 2008, the Chinese economy, as measured by GDP, grew tenfold. (In contrast, the GDP of the world's largest and strongest economy, that of the United States, did not quite triple in the same period.) The growth has come at considerable and notorious cost in dirty air and water and other "disamenities," including environmentally caused human illness and death. A report by the Council on Foreign Relations affirms that China's "focus on economic development at breakneck speed has led to widespread environmental degradation" and catalogues the "environmental challenges" that the country faces: One-third of the population doesn't have access to clean drinking water.

Seventy percent of the country's rivers and lakes are polluted. (Roughly 200 million tons of untreated sewage and industrial waste was poured into Chinese waterways in 2004.) The country's ambitious dam-building program—at 25,000 and growing, China has more dams than any other country in the world—has a high cost in money, farmland loss, ecosystem loss, and forced migration of millions of people. An area the size of Connecticut is lost every year to desertification brought on by intensive and unsustainable farming practices the government promotes in grassland ecosystems, many of which were suddenly and severely overgrazed to satisfy China's growing taste for meat. Desertification degrades air quality: dust accounts for a third of China's considerable burden of air pollution. In 2008, China passed the United States as the world's largest emitter of greenhouse gases (two-thirds of its considerable energy consumption is coal). Acid rain falls on more than 30 percent of the country. In 2005 China's deputy minister of the environment said, "The western regions of China and the ecologically stressed regions can no longer support the people . . . living there. We will need to resettle 186 million residents from 22 provinces and cities." He calculated that China itself could "absorb" only 33 million; "that means . . . more than 150 million ecological migrants, or, if you like, environmental refugees." China has begun a systematic program of land purchases in Africa and long-term agricultural contracts in Brazil, trying to ensure food security for a population that inhabits an increasingly degraded landscape.

Was all that ecological damage necessary? Of course not. Was it necessary for economic growth, for the Chinese to achieve improvements in their material standard of living? No, not if you accept Daly and Farley's distinction, traceable to John Stuart Mill, between footprint-expanding growth and steady-state, sustainable development. So why did China pursue development at such a high environmental cost?

As with most real-world questions, there is no single answer, but one of the clearest, strongest, and saddest elements in any accurate answer has to be this: the reason that China suffered enormous environmental degradation on its path to economic growth is that China listened to the wrong economists.

Neoclassical economists are neither crazy nor blind. They can see that as a consequence of economic activities, humans often face "disamenities"—externalities that include dirty air, poisoned water, and ecosystem loss—even if their model doesn't specifically allow that low-entropy uptake and high-entropy output are physical necessities of economic activity. In the neoclassical model economic growth—more stuff—is always good, and of course pollution is recognized as a bad. Thermodynamics tells us there's a connection between the two: you can't crank more stuff out of the economy unless you either achieve internal efficiencies or increase the rate of throughput in the economy. That connection, between growth in throughput and growth in the output of pollutants, is precisely what neoclassical economics denies. At the center of that denial stands the idea of the Environmental Kuznets Curve.

This curve is named after Simon Kuznets (the same Simon Kuznets who warned us not to mistake GDP's predecessor, GNP, as a measure of economic welfare), though he had nothing to do with it. It was named after him because the curve mimics the shape of a curve he did invent, a curve describing a rise and then a decline in income inequality as countries develop. This upside-down-U-shaped curve models what Kuznets proposed, in 1954, as a historical process: as countries develop, income inequality at first increases, then reaches a peak, then declines as further increases in national income begin to be distributed more widely. The idea had a certain intuitive appeal to conservatives—it says that the creation of an enormously wealthy class is an observable, expectable, and perhaps necessary stage in the development process and that whatever social and political problems might come from a high degree of income inequality will simply take care of themselves over time.

Questions about whether or not income is divided equitably or fairly, and whether a largely unequal distribution is socially dysfunctional or politically unstable, are questions that fall outside the boundaries of the discipline as the neoclassical model draws them. But even though the Kuznets Curve deals with income distribution, it has found a place as one of the canonical ideas of the discipline. No political valuation need be attached to it (it can be treated as an elegant instance of the politically neutral task of mathematical puzzle solving), though it is easily used to support a conservative political ideology. Income inequality at first increases and then decreases with economic growth, the argument says, for several reasons in succession: Growth happens best when innovators and ambitious people are rewarded by larger incomes. That wealthy class then has sufficient income to engage in the savings that create the financial capital for the level of investment needed to produce future growth. The benefits of the ensuing growth accrue not only to the wealthy but also to others as jobs are created and the wealth "trickles down." And no doubt neoclassical economists of all political persuasions find the Kuznets Curve additionally acceptable because when this political conclusion is drawn from it, the curve supports the continued acceptance of one the fundamental premises of the standard model. To the extent that income inequality in developing nations might be perceived as a problem, the Kuznets Curve reassures us — lets economists, speaking with the authority of disinterested science, reassure us — that the problem takes care of itself. The solution to this problem of development is more development. Growth is always good.

By the 1990s the Kuznets Curve seemed to some economists to model another problem in developing countries: the environmental degradation that comes from exploitation of resources and of open-access regimes like air and water quality. At low levels of income (the model suggests), pollution levels are low; pollution increases with increase in per capita income as the country develops; but then, at some level of income, pollution-per-unit-of-income peaks and then begins to decline. And thus was born the inverted U of the Environmental Kuznets Curve.

Although the idea that environmental degradation self-corrects with increasing income had been around for decades, modeling it with an Environmental Kuznets Curve (EKC) was the innovation of two economists, Gene M. Grossman and Alan B. Krueger, in a 1991 study of the environmental impact of the North American Free Trade Agreement. The notion behind the EKC "is intuitively appealing," as one review of findings and implications has it — if your intuition is shaped by neoclassical assumptions rather than an understanding of economic life that's rooted in thermodynamics. If environmental quality is one category of good and service that we can purchase, it seems obvious that our purchase of it should at some point increase — after other needs are met and if we have sufficient money to pay for it. (In the language of economists, this supposes that environmental quality has "income elasticity": the quantity demanded per dollar of income increases as income increases.) The EKC tells us, explicitly, that environmental quality is a species of luxury good and that we'll be able to afford more of it — and will no doubt want to buy more of it — when we're wealthier.

The title of a recent newspaper opinion piece explaining the EKC is a succinct statement of its clear policy implication: "Growth Is the Key to Protecting the Environment, Not Its Enemy." The World Bank gave this concept its imprimatur—and began to encode the EKC into development policy—in its *World Development Report* in 1992: "Some problems initially worsen but then improve as incomes rise. Most forms of air and water pollution fit into this category." (The report did offer a caveat, one that is ignored by some enthusiasts for the idea: "There is nothing automatic about this improvement; it occurs only when countries deliberately introduce policies to ensure that additional resources are devoted to dealing with environmental problems.")

If economic growth actually comes mostly from increasing the matter and energy throughput of the economy, which on Factory Planet can't help but have a cost in lost ecosystem services (like clean air and water), and if those ecosystem services are necessary to sustain civilization, then continued growth of matter and energy throughput doesn't fix the problem of environmental degradation but instead threatens the foundations of civilization itself. Which means that the continued existence of our civilization depends on how we answer the question: is the EKC an accurate representation of economic and physical reality, or not?

A simple answer isn't easy to come by in the economics journals. If you want an illustration of Nicholas Georgescu-Roegen's criticism that economics as practiced in the neoclassical tradition is guilty of "arithmomorphism" and "methodolotry," you need look no further than the scholarship that has arisen around the EKC. When the topic is taken up by economists writing for economists, the literature is filled with recondite mathematical analysis, enough to draw a barricade of methodological complexity around the controversy. (An economist might say that "information costs" pose "significant barriers to entry" for those wanting to understand the discussion, let alone participate in it.) "It is very easy to do bad econometrics," warns econometrician David Stern, "and the history of the EKC exemplifies what can go wrong." It's as though a crucial decision about the fate of civilization were being made, and made badly, behind closed doors. (In this, it's similar to Vice President Dick Cheney's infamous energy summit—a closed-door policy meeting attended by representatives of coal and oil and gas companies, no environmentalists allowed.)

Some economists have broadened the conversation a bit by addressing the general public. One such economist is Don Boudreau, former chair of the Economics Department at George Mason University, who blogs regularly on environmental matters for *Café Hayek*. In a short piece titled "The Environmental Kuznets Curve," Boudreau points to two facts that, if taken together, explode (he says) the "myth"—the old, discredited, *Limits to Growth* myth—about the environmental impact of economic growth. The two facts: China's economy, despite its impressive growth, remains about one-third the size of the $14 trillion us economy. And China is now the world's largest producer of carbon dioxide and other greenhouse gases. Put these two facts together and you get this: "America's economy—nearly three times larger than China's economy—produces less pollution than does China's economy." Conclusion: "So much for the myth that economic growth inevitably and always increases pollution and environmental damage. Clearly, after some point, continued growth can *reduce* pollution and environmental harm." (In this Boudreau is not a popularizing outlier; that conclusion is offered by any number of EKC studies, in language like this: "Economic growth is likely to be accompanied by environmental degradation at low income levels, but as income grows the demand for environmental protection also tends to increase, leading to a development path characterized by both economic growth and environmental quality improvements.")

Boudreau's brief passage offers a simplistic and reductive argument that's easy to pick apart—as easy as shooting fish in a barrel, or tasting benzene when it's a few thousand parts per million in your water. But it's worth reviewing the criticisms that can be leveled against even this simple statement of the argument, for those criticisms model some of the ones that can be made against more elaborate and sophisticated presentations of the EKC. The nature of the argument doesn't change a whole lot, just the level of complexity at which it takes place.

First and most obviously, correlation is not causation. That facts about income and environmental quality can be presented as varying together does not establish any causal or necessary link between them. (Research on the EKC has repeatedly been challenged for not having successfully answered this elementary criticism.) Next, and equally obvious, the EKC purports to model a process in time within a national economy, and here Boudreau has tried to support the EKC by comparing two different countries at one moment in time. Structural differences between the two countries might account for the difference he ascribes to a necessary EKC process; such differences might include ease of access to resources, the proportion of low-emission carbon fuels available to power industrial development, the size and relative absorptive capacities of ecosystems that provide "sink" and cleansing services, GDP per unit of land area, and so on. Cross-country comparison at one moment in time does nothing to prove or disprove the relationship between economic growth and pollution that is asserted by the EKC.

Second: Boudreau's rough-cut comparison of GDP and greenhouse gas emissions between China and the United States doesn't allow for the possibility that America outsources much of its ecological footprint, including greenhouse gas generation, to poorer economies (like China's) that, reassured by the EKC, welcome the opportunity to degrade their environment in order to increase their GDP through trade.

Another issue: it may be the case that pollution per unit of GDP declines not because pollution declines in absolute terms, but because GDP has gone up thanks to GDP growth in economic activities that pollute less per dollar unit of production. Rather than signaling a shift in the entire economy away from pollution production, the curve may simply record the fact that service industries with smaller ecological footprints have been layered on top of the existing, and dirty, economic base. If this is what has happened, then the curve is not telling us that pollution decreases with rise in per capita income. Pollution per unit of GDP may decrease while the absolute level of pollution is stable or increasing. (When GDP is increased through the purchase of pollution control technologies, pollution per unit of GDP declines *even if the technology is never used*.) This is a telling point because what matters to human and ecosystem health is not the ratio of pollution per unit of GDP but the relation between the absolute amount of pollution and the maximum levels that humans and ecosystems can absorb without damage. A forest forced to deal with forty thousand tons of sulfur dioxide emissions doesn't care whether the processes that produced that pollution represent 2 or 20 percent of some region's GDP.

Another similar, but different, conceptual problem: the data used to develop an EKC track pollution at particular points in time or yearly averages. For some ecosystems, some human communities and some pollutants, the relevant figure will be the cumulative burden or a transient spike, not the average burden or the quantity present at the particular moment of sampling. A chemical spill that places deadly levels of toxins in a river for a week could kill all the aquatic life in it for years but could be missed by biweekly sampling or barely register in the yearly average if during the other fifty-one weeks the river runs clean.

These are roundhouse criticisms that flatten the EKC. (Econometricians would say that by taking them into account, the EKC tends to become "monotonic"—more of a straight line, pointing ever upward.) Even if the historical discharge of some pollutants, or some groups of pollutants, can be charted against per capita income by an inverted-U curve in one country or a group of countries, these conceptual problems completely undermine the conclusion that the EKC aims to support: that pollution decreases as wealth increases.

There are other deal-breakers as well. As the World Bank cautioned, income is not the causative and explanatory factor of measurable pollution decreases in wealthy countries. The first presentation of the EKC looked at sulfur dioxide levels in the United States and found an inverted-U-shaped relationship between per capita income and pollution levels. But the peak and decline did not result from growth in per capita income as such; the decline in measured pollutants owe a great deal to the passage of the Clean Air and Clean Water Acts in the 1970s.

To this criticism, defenders of the EKC have a ready, but only partially successful, rejoinder: rising income led to demand for cleaner air and water, a demand that couldn't be expressed in the market as such and therefore found expression in legislation. That causal chain makes sense—but it also acknowledges that the focus of classical EKC analysis is too narrow. Defending the EKC this way does not support the conclusion that increasing wealth decreases pollution, but points instead to a larger research agenda for economists—one that would have them take up subjects and variables that are less easily quantified than a ratio between per capita GDP and parts per million of this or that pollutant. Some of those subjects and variables belong to political science. "Research that links the inverted-U to actual policies would seem to be badly needed," one pair of economists noted with commendable academic diffidence and understatement. Yes, that research is badly needed, and so the EKC leads directly to the reintegration of economics and political studies, steering economists back to the pre-Pareto practice of political economy.

Some EKC researchers have recognized this. One researcher finds that the curve shifts up or down depending on "the quality of institutions related to the enforcement of contracts." Others find that improvements in political rights and civil liberties, or a movement toward greater income equality, account for the downward turn (or part of the downward turn) in the EKC. Yet other researchers find "a robust association" between democratic systems and the provision of environmental goods; others, that the movement modeled by the EKC is also and more tellingly "a movement through a well-known set of property rights stations," as open-access regimes are closed through the institution of property interests in them.

Even as these researchers follow the causal chain into political structures and systems, others are following it across political borders—overseas, to other national economies. The problem: With the passage of the Clean Air and Water Acts, US environmental quality, as measured by some key pollutants, clearly improved. Did the laws actually diminish the ecological footprint of US enjoyment of its wealth, or was most of that footprint simply exported? This was one of the concerns raised in the original article that gave the EKC its name—Grossman and Krueger had set out, after all, to investigate "environmental impacts of a North American Free Trade Agreement." Are there, in effect, "pollution havens"—countries that accept (or have forced upon them by economic necessity or trade regimes) dirty economic processes, leaving the EKC intact for the country doing the exporting? If there are, then the measurement of the EKC in any one country is close to meaningless. Grossman and Krueger's work said there weren't "pollution haven" effects; its main message was that trade and higher income levels make for a better environment. But that result and the methods that produced it have been repeatedly challenged. The data sets that were used for different countries were too dissimilar to support sturdy conclusions; like wasn't compared to like, and the researchers didn't seem to notice this. Other relevant and possibly causal variables weren't controlled. Using aggregated data obscured important trends and factors that would have undercut the conclusion. If the EKC is to have any value at all as a representation of the relationship between wealth and levels of particular pollutants (let alone serve as a representation of the relationship between economic development as a whole and a more generalized environmental degradation), then "pollution haven" effects must be small-to-vanishing. But the methods that researchers have employed to investigate the issue have a discernible bias toward producing just that finding.

Grossman and Krueger's work relied on data collected by the UN-sponsored Global Environmental Monitoring System (GEMS), a commendable effort to collect comparable information about the presence of a variety of pollutants in air and water worldwide. But the reach of the data is not yet worldwide or temporally very deep; it covers forty-two countries and forty years—and the countries included are those that perceived pollution to be enough of a problem to begin devoting resources to measuring it back in the 1970s. It's not only possible but actually very likely that most or all of the pollution-dump countries fall outside the GEMS data.

For reasons like these, no methodologically sturdy study has been able to dismiss "pollution haven" effects. Plainly and simply, the studies allow for the possibility that wealthy nations use part of their wealth to export their ecological footprints. Rarely to never is the footprint exported by force—you don't see armadas of cargo ships offloading toxins under the protective cover of naval guns. It's more common for the receiving nation to welcome the processes of ecological degradation that make it a pollution haven, which they do for the jobs and economic activity that come from hosting dirty manufacturing processes, or from reprocessing industrial products containing toxic wastes (everything from rusted ships to cell phones). Widespread acceptance of the EKC makes this export easier; whatever the costs of ecological degradation, the EKC reassures authorities in the pollution haven that the costs are temporary and will eventually be compensated. Gay culture has a word for what the EKC does: it's a beard, a companion that conveys a false impression.

The phenomenon of pollution havens should be intuitively appealing to an economist. If export of pollution is possible, and if exportation is cheaper than abatement or capture and quarantine at home, why would any benefit-maximizing self-interested actor do anything else? But, evidently, the attraction of a sturdy EKC is even stronger than the intuitive appeal of "pollution haven" effects. The EKC is not only "intuitively" appealing to a discipline that has yet to acknowledge the truths of thermodynamics, it's desperately essential if infinite growth in matter and energy throughput is to continue to appear to be a viable option.

An obvious point about the EKC is worth stating: whether or not it has an inverted U shape will depend on the two variables that are used. What goes on the bottom, horizontal axis? If development of civil liberties or democratic institutions or property law is the explanatory factor that produces the inverted U relationship between pollution and economic growth, then in order to continue to find that the EKC models a "don't worry" relationship between pollution and economic growth, you have to argue that development of such things as civil liberties, democratic institutions, and property law are a necessary and inevitable result of economic growth. That's an argument from political theory — and it's a dubious argument. If democracy were the inevitable result of economic growth, there could be no such thing as an economically developed totalitarian state — no "Evil Empire," no socialist Bad Example whose lack of democratic freedoms is a warning to us about the dangers of the road to serfdom.

It's true that the protests and riots in China can be taken as evidence that an increasing standard of living leads to political demands for democracy and environmental quality, but they can also be taken as evidence that the causal connection is not automatic, that it takes time to develop, and that it comes only at considerable cost: in violence, in citizen effort and risk, in endurance of environmental damage, in damage to human health and community vitality. Leaving aside the moral issue of economists' giving their stamp of approval to a system that requires violence, pain, and significant citizen sacrifice (including death) in order to produce the effects that the EKC models, we can note that to ask for environmental quality to be bought through the "disamenities" of civil violence and direct action, as is being done in China, is to ask many cultures to pay a price that they cannot and will not pay. Is that price the least-cost, most efficient, market-clearing price? By continuing to use the EKC to argue that improved environmental quality is correlated with increasing wealth, neoclassical economists implicitly say yes, though it's an answer that lies beyond their professional expertise — and it's an answer for which they haven't even begun to do the math.

Even if the development of democratic institutions or civil liberties or property law could be shown to be a necessary, automatic, and relatively painless consequence of an increasing material standard of living, there is no guarantee that their development will happen quickly enough to prevent irreversible ecological harm. As two EKC critics have noted, an EKC for biodiversity is "a theoretical impossibility": there can be no downward slope signaling the return of extinct species. Loss of biodiversity is the definitive dynamic in the ecological crisis that threatens the continued existence of civilization—the civilization that includes universities with departments of economics—and EKC modeling assumes the problem away.

To generalize: there's an unsupportable ontological assumption behind the idea that humans can restore ecosystem health as easily as we destroy it. In the worldview in which mathematical modeling of an EKC makes sense, humans are the master of all the physical and natural processes that happen within the host-ground of our economy. One bedrock assumption of that world-view is that environmental quality —something we might otherwise call "nature"—can be commodified, made into a good that we can purchase or refrain from purchasing at will, in any amount that we collectively "choose." In truth, the problem just isn't that easy or simple. Once the passenger pigeon was gone, no amount of growth in per capita GDP, no increase in property law or democratic institutions, could allow a society to "purchase" healthy ecosystems that continued to include it.

Given these problems, the logical end of the movement to expand what is encompassed by the EKC's vertical axis is to make a conceptual switch: to measure not the levels of substances known to cause damage, but the loss of ecosystem services that those substances cause. (First you'd have to admit that there is such a thing as an "ecosystem service," an idea that's central to the challenge ecological economics makes to the neoclassical model.) Rather than trying to specify each of the thousand cuts by which ecosystem services are lost, it would be simpler and more elegant to measure the loss itself. This would flip the curve over and—if the EKC relationship holds—make it a straight-up U, registering a movement from plentiful ecosystem services to reduced ecosystem services to plentiful again.

No one, to my knowledge, has done this. It would be interesting to see, but we're not likely to see a neoclassical economist do it. When charted against the simple variable of time on the horizontal axis, a graph of world ecosystem services will display not a U shape but a strong, undeniable, and depressing linear trend: down, down, generally and everywhere down.

Despite the methodological and conceptual problems that call into question its value, work on the EKC continues apace. An impressive amount of energy has been committed to searching for (and sometimes massaging data in order to generate) correlations between changes in income and indicators of environmental degradation. Mostly that search has been an instance of what Thomas Kuhn called the puzzle solving of normal science — the rule-bound search for an outcome that can be anticipated ("often in detail so great that what remains to be known is itself uninteresting"). Puzzle: if there is an inverted-U-shaped EKC, then what's the peak point? Various researchers have calculated the annual-income-tipping-point for various pollutants for various regions and countries. For arsenic in water, one study of countries in the Organisation for Economic Co-operation and Development (OECD) says it was US $8,000 in 2001. Fecal coliform? $13,100. Lead? $17,200. Smoke? $10,200.

It's moderately interesting to note that different pollutants have different peaks, and researchers offer explanations for the differences. If you compare water (OECD dissolved oxygen peak at per capita GDP of $2,700) to air (OECD sulfur dioxide at $4,100), you can explain that "harms from contaminated water occur much more swiftly and therefore are more clearly visible than those associated with air pollution." But it's not clear how useful these numbers are. They're mostly useful if you want to argue that if these problems persist in some regions where incomes are below those levels, income needs to go up in order to fix them. And thus you come to an absurd conclusion: the reason we have climate change is that the richest economies the world has ever seen are still not rich enough to afford the environmental good known as "climate stability."

One intriguing result of some of these empirical investigations is this: the typical EKC curve may not be an inverted U shape at all, but rather something more like a cursive N: up, then down, then back up. There is some indication that for a time pollution increases with increasing income, then peaks and declines, then increases again. This result has intuitive appeal for anyone who sees a necessary linkage between economic growth — the increase in the matter and energy throughput of an economy—and ecosystem degradation. The flowing N shape can be easily explained. The inverted U of the traditionalist's EKC holds up to some level of income, as pollution and other undesirable outputs at first increase with income and then decrease; but before that right-side tail of the inverted U comes down very far, the low-hanging fruit of pollution avoidance or capture and quarantine has been picked. Easy fixes have been implemented, and the fundamental physical relation—low entropy in, high entropy out—reasserts itself.

One survey of EKC studies—the one in the *New Palgrave Dictionary of Economics*—summarizes the empirical research in these skeptical terms: "[Efforts to model the EKC] are designed to yield inverse-U-shaped pollution-income paths, and succeed [by] using a variety of assumptions and mechanisms." If inquiry begins with the inverse-U-shaped EKC, if assumptions and data analysis are systematically massaged to confirm it, and if failure to produce the curve for a crucial greenhouse gas is no reason to stop believing in it, then the EKC can hardly be said to dwell on defensible methodological ground. If there is rationality here, it must be directed toward some other end. Efforts to find EKCs in the face of these criticisms look like a mannerist exercise undertaken by some academic economists mostly to please themselves—to solve a puzzle, to exercise the tools of their trade, to shore up confidence in the project of economic growth. The work has all the trappings of a sturdy empirical exercise, but the result depends so completely on the assumptions embedded within it that all the empirical analysis in the world is unlikely to answer the question definitively.

Recall that Daly and Farley tell us that nature's sink services are likely to be the choke point that defines the limits to our economic expansion. Because it falls at such a critical test-point for faith in the infinite-growth economy, EKC research will no doubt continue. In continuing, it may yet serve a useful function. The EKC is a prime arena of contest between two paradigms engaged in a struggle to define the discipline; to the extent that readers of economics journals retain an open mind and pay attention to the methodological and ontological criticisms that are made of EKC research, continued publication of that research and criticism of it may change the minds of individual economists. (It could happen—despite Max Planck's cynical observation that most intellectual progress comes not through reason and argument and appeal to observable data but "through funerals.") At least one mainstream environmental economist has converted, telling his colleagues that "little substance lies behind the EKC."

More likely, the debates and discussion between practitioners of the competing paradigms will have their greatest influence beyond the immediate circle of econometricians who comb through environmental quality data trying to isolate variables and find sturdy, defensible relationship among them. Mostly the relevant audience consists of students and younger faculty in the discipline, economists and economists-in-training who will either choose to accept the EKC, reject it out of hand, or see the income-and-ecology degradation curve as being, intuitively enough, N-shaped. If the laws of thermodynamics are sturdy and if their application to the material processes of economic production is valid, the EKC will not survive its problems, and rejection of it will be one doorway through which the principles and practice of ecological economics will eventually find their way into acceptance within the discipline.

Thirty years ago Chicago school monetarism was a dissenting and minority voice in the academy; many good departments of economics had a single, token monetarist. But monetarism is now the dominant school and Keynesians are marginalized. A similar transition, from neoclassicism to ecological economics, is under way today. Some of the econometric work that subverts the neoclassical understanding of the EKC — work that correlates pollution decrease to rises in civil liberties or the development of democratic institutions — appears not in neoclassical economics journals but in other places, including *Ecological Economics*, a relatively recent start-up that illustrates Kuhn's dictum: new paradigms need new professional journals. But work published there has begun to find its way into neoclassical discourse, as its articles are increasingly cited in mainstream journals, including review articles on the EKC. This crossing of the boundary between the two schools portends further change. Soon, most economics departments will have at least a token ecological economist — either through conversion of their environmental economist to the new way of thinking, or by purposive choice as faculty members realize that their commitment to free and open inquiry means they really should hire someone to represent this new way of thinking about economics. And if the new way of modeling the economy proves its value in the classroom by attracting students, departments will be motivated to hire other proponents of it.

Another part of the audience for the debate over the EKC is the group of policy makers, like those at the World Bank and in China, to whom the EKC gave reassurance that continued growth would solve the ecological problems that growth creates. Here too the tide of opinion is turning. In 2005, Pan Yue, the vice minister of China's Ministry of Environmental Protection, specifically fingered the EKC as having played a large role in the considerable ecological crisis that China is experiencing. In a listing of faulty economic ideas that had led China astray, Yue first mentions the leadership's reliance on GDP as the metric they sought to maximize; then their acceptance of the Kuznets Curve, the idea that the problems brought by income inequality would fix themselves; and then he added: "There's yet another mistake in this thinking. . . . [It's] the assumption that the economic growth [we pursued] will give us the financial resources to cope with the crises surrounding the environment, raw materials, and population growth." In February 2011 Chinese premier Wen Jiabao announced that his country's annual growth target had been lowered a percentage point out of concern for ecological damage: "We absolutely cannot again sacrifice the environment as the cost for high-speed growth. That economic development is unsustainable." While cutting growth targets, even by a full percentage point, does not guarantee that unsustainable growth has thereby been forestalled, the recognition of a trade-off between growth and environmental quality is a rejection of the EKC, which is a large conceptual step toward sustainability. And in October 2010, speaking in Japan, World Bank president Robert Zoellick signaled another major shift at that institution. To a conference convened to develop strategies to halt loss of ecosystem diversity, he said that "preserving ecosystems and saving species are not luxuries for the rich" — a similarly unequivocal rejection of the logic of the EKC. (As noted previously, he also called for finding ways to value ecosystem services, and to take account of those valuations in making decisions about economic development — a fundamental element in program advocated by ecological economics.)

That article by Grossman and Krueger that first named the EKC was published in 1991. A few years before that IBM had brought out its electronic typewriter, a machine capable of displaying one line of pixelated text in a window before it was hammered out onto the page. The machine was an improvement on the electric typewriter but not nearly as useful as the computer word processors that would soon replace it. It was an intermediate technology, not destined to last long in the marketplace. (The same year the EKC was named, IBM, seeing the handwriting on the wall, spun off its typewriter division.) I think that the EKC, too, will prove to be an intermediate technology—a conceptual tool that is the product of a brief moment in the evolution of our understanding of the relationship between economy and ecology. Like the electronic typewriter, it deserves a place on a shelf in a museum, as an interesting artifact that testifies to our ingenuity—and to the limited nature of our understanding at the time it was produced.

revisiting "the bet that ruined the world"

n 1980, *Science* magazine published an essay by an economist named Julian Simon titled "Resources, Population, Environment: An Over-supply of False Bad News." Its first line struck squarely at what its author saw as the prevailing but mistaken idea that the world faces an increasingly serious population problem: "False bad news about population growth, natural resources and the environment is published widely in the face of contrary evidence." "For example," Simon went on to say, "the world supply of arable land has actually been increasing, the scarcity of natural resources including food and energy has been decreasing, and basic measures of US environmental quality show positive trends."

Concern about overpopulation and resource scarcity, Simon said, was generated by mistaken assumptions and analysis. In contrast, "models that embody forces omitted in the past, especially the influence of population size upon productivity increase, suggest a long-run positive effect of additional people." "A long-run positive effect of additional people": literally, the more of us, the wealthier we can be. As Simon understood the matter, there are no limits to growth, because (as he put it in the title of his book published the same year), humans are "the ultimate resource," capable of technological innovation and invention, which will forever let them do more with less and find substitutes for anything that might run low.

Simon's target wasn't simply those who were concerned about the problem of increasing population, but something broader: environmental awareness, which had grown considerably during the 1970s, had led to the passage of landmark environmental protection legislation in the United States, and was developing into a growing realization — Simon thought a consensus — that economic growth could not go on forever. That had been the point of 1972's seminal *Limits to Growth*, which Simon saw as tragically mistaken: if we believed the Club of Rome Report, we would forgo economic growth that could (indeed, was the only thing that could) bring about greater human welfare.

Whether or not the idea that there are ecological limits to growth was anything like a consensus view in 1980 is open to debate, but certainly there was at that time a broad consensus among academic economists in the West that the foundation of Simon's argument was demonstrably incorrect. The idea that all value stems from human effort, that neither nature nor capital are distinct and different factors of production — also known as the labor theory of value — was no longer accepted by any serious Western economist. It had been fundamental to the work of John Locke, the democratic theorist whose *Second Treatise on Civil Government*, published in 1690, swept aside the divine right of kings as a foundation of political legitimacy and advanced in its place the notion of popular sovereignty — that legitimacy in government comes from the just consent of the governed. He did this by arguing that in the state of nature, before the formation of civil society (roughly, what I have been suggesting we call, anachronistically, Wilderness Planet), humans had the right to appropriate whatever they needed or wanted from an Earth held equally by all as a God-given commons; each person gained title to their appropriation by dint of having invested their labor power in it. A little less than a century later, Adam Smith noticed that the quantity of labor invested in an object was not a good register of its value: as we might put it today, after the invention of automobiles, carriages and buggy whips declined in value, even though they continued to embody the same amount of human labor power. Classical economic theory, as developed by Smith and those who followed, articulated a distinction between use value and exchange value and rejected "embodied labor" as a sufficiently explanatory source of either.

But the labor theory of value had a reprise in the work of Karl Marx: for him, wealth was "labour as such"; all wealth was "past, objectified labour." (Marx credits Adam Smith with inventing this revolutionary insight, but then notes, "How difficult and great this transition was may be seen from how Adam Smith himself from time to time still falls [away from it].") The labor theory of value was the foundation of Marx's theory of alienated labor and thus was central to his call for revolution (as it had been for Locke): since capital was nothing but labor objectified and embodied in physical form, it followed that the wealth, and the power to create additional wealth, that was embodied within it belonged by rights to labor, not to capitalists. From that it also followed that capital should be controlled by labor, collectively, through the seizure of state power by the working class.

Reading Marx on Malthus shows the depth of Marx's commitment to the labor theory of value. In 1798, the Reverend Thomas Malthus published his *Essay on the Principle of Population*, which observed that human population can increase geometrically, while the means of subsistence can increase only incrementally, which puts population pressure on food resources; famine and misery result. War, disease, and starvation check population growth, and—in an era with rather primitive technologies of contraception—are unavoidable unless humans voluntarily undertake the "moral restraint" of abstinence. Malthus was thus the first to warn that there are environmental limits to the growth of human population. Half a century later Marx directed his most vitriolic invective (and he penned some mightily vitriolic invective) against "this libel on the human race," authored by "the contemptible Malthus," a "plagiarist," "a shameless sycophant of the ruling class" who perpetrated "this infamous, vile doctrine, this blasphemy against nature and humanity," this "sin against science." Marx held firmly to this point: every human born into the world is born with two hands—the capacity to use their own labor power to create more economic value than they consume.

He wouldn't get an argument from Simon. Compare this, from Simon's *The Ultimate Resource*:

> Adding more people to any community causes problems, but people are also the means to solve these problems. The main fuel to speed the world's progress is our stock of knowledge, and the brake is our lack of imagination. The ultimate resource is people—skilled, spirited, and hopeful people—who will exert their wills and imaginations for their own benefit as well as in a spirit of faith and social concern. Inevitably they will benefit not only themselves but the poor and the rest of us as well.

Right along with Marx and Engels, Simon believed that increasing population didn't produce resource problems or economic problems; it was the *solution* to those problems.

The neoclassical consensus held then, as now, that returns to capital are justified as a return to the services that capitalists provide: innovation, organization, the entrepreneurial assumption of risk. (Some of that risk is a gamble on what consumers will want, a bet on what use values will be successful in the market.) These are human energies: the labor theory of value, slightly displaced. With his foundation in neoclassical theory and his emphasis on the human contribution to the production of use values, Simon's optimistic enthusiasm for the industrial project matches that of Marx, though he turned it to a very different conclusion: Marx wanted to see the capitalist system overthrown, and Simon wanted to see it celebrated, honored, extended. (The two share more than a bedrock commitment to the labor theory of value; as prose stylists they're bedfellows as well: both are by turns ungenerous, condescending, vitriolic, populist, paranoid—though Marx scores higher in intellectual honesty.) An astute neoclassical economist might have noticed that the optimism of both was rooted in an idea that the neoclassical school believes it rejects; but to my knowledge, no neoclassical economist ever called Simon out on this.

Also crucial to the neoclassical consensus is acceptance of another fundamental principle that Simon explicitly rejected: the law of diminishing returns. This idea, which defines the project of "constrained optimization" that is the economists' reason for being, holds that at some point, additional increments of something that's good stop being as good as they were when they were scarcer. (Your thirtieth piece of pizza is not as enjoyable as your first.) Because of these diminishing returns, if we are to maximize our pleasures and satisfactions we must make delicate comparisons and rational choices, must allocate our energy and income "on the margin," as economists say—the margin between what we have consumed already and what we intend to get and consume right now: a bit more of this, a bit less of that. If marginal returns did not decrease, we'd have direct and simple optimization: more of everything would always be better, and, absent diminishing marginal returns to productivity, that infinite increase would be possible. As Simon himself saw, his argument requires that the law of diminishing returns not apply—not to population growth, not to economic growth, not to our pursuit of and use of resources.

After Simon's essay appeared in *Science*, the letters column carried seven responses, along with a rejoinder from Simon; only one of the respondents was an economist. Warren Sanderson of the economics department of Stanford, writing with colleague Bruce Johnson of the Stanford Food Research Institute, led off with praise: "We applaud Simon's article for its systematic reconsideration of much of the 'false bad news' which is fed to the public in the guise of careful analysis." But Sanderson and Johnson went on to say the article left an "unwarranted" impression: that development policies need not concern themselves with rates of population growth. The two stood by the elementary and eminently defensible point that progress in improving per capita well-being is a function of total well-being divided by the number of people: rather obviously, population matters. Interestingly, the only respondent to call Simon out for his failure to apply the law of diminishing returns was a biologist (Wayne H. Davis of the University of Kentucky), who expressed wonder that an economist should so directly contradict it.

One reader of Simon's essay was the biologist Paul Ehrlich, author of the 1968 book *The Population Bomb*, which had laid out the neo-Malthusian case that Simon was contradicting. In that book Ehrlich had argued that population growth was straining at and would soon exceed the limits of the planetary carrying capacity. Ehrlich, too, had put his thesis up front: "The battle to feed humanity is over. In the course of the 1970's, the world will experience starvation of tragic proportions, [and] hundreds of millions of people will starve to death." The book went on to describe how and why unchecked growth in the human population would outstrip supplies of food and other resources, producing crisis and catastrophe. It too relied on facts and figures: "In 1966, each person on Earth had 2 percent less to eat, the reduction, of course, not being uniformly distributed. Only ten countries grew more food than they consumed: the United States, Canada, Australia, Argentina, France, New Zealand, Burma, Thailand, Rumania, and South Africa."

The Population Bomb drew a great deal of attention; it became a national best seller (3 million copies), and Ehrlich made book appearances and gave lectures and interviews. In some of them, he offered other predictions — splashy pronouncements calculated to attract attention: "If I were a gambler, I would take even money that England will not exist in the year 2000."

Ehrlich and three colleagues (John Holdren, John Harte, and Anne

Ehrlich, Paul's wife and frequent coauthor) thought the position outlined in Simon's *Science* article was hopelessly wrong-headed and dangerous. Their lengthy letter in reply charged Simon with "errors about the economics of scarcity," disputed some of the factual claims on which Simon had based his argument, and pointed out conceptual errors—that, for instance, recent and current increase in arable land was a meaningless number because obviously such increase could not go on forever; land capable of being used for agriculture was finite in supply, and so was the freshwater needed for irrigation if drier lands were to be turned to agriculture. And the letter made a new prediction: "If deforestation for agriculture proceeds on a large enough scale, the resulting pulse of carbon dioxide may combine with that of increasing fossil fuel combustion to alter global climate in a way that undermines food production to an unprecedented degree." They also corrected a factual error they found: electricity had not gotten cheaper, as Simon claimed. "The fact is real electricity prices bottomed in 1971 and were already up 18 percent . . . in 1972."

"I was taken aback," Simon recounted in his reply—not for the conceptual mistakes of thinking arable land could increase forever, or for failing to count the cost of deforestation against the benefit of increased agricultural land; no, he addressed neither point in his reply. He was taken aback by being told he had gotten a fact wrong. So he checked sources. He even went so far as to call the author of the report cited by Holdren, Harte, and the Ehrlichs. "He, too, was puzzled. Upon investigation, the 1971 number (80.2) proved to be a typographical error and should have been 93.3." With the higher base number, electricity prices showed a decrease. "So much," Simon added in his reply, "for Holdren et alia's 'fact.'"

This illustrates the strategy Simon frequently used when responding to his critics: find a minor flaw in an opponent's argument and seize upon it to discredit the opponent, rather than address the best case for the substantive argument that could be, and was being, made against him. And about that concluding fillip at the end, the snottiness of "so much for their 'fact'": ill feeling had come to characterize the relationship between Ehrlich and Simon (who never actually met; their animosity was played out publicly). Sorting it all out is as difficult as parsing responsibility between siblings squabbling in the backseat on a long car trip. Charges and countercharges passed between the two: Simon declared that thinkers of Ehrlich's persuasion "must either turn a blind eye to the scientific evidence or be blatantly dishonest intellectually," a remark not calculated to elicit dispassionate analysis of data and underlying assumptions. (While repeatedly protesting the ad hominem judgments leveled against him, Simon was quite capable of employing the tactic himself.) For his part Ehrlich was no better. He declined to debate or appear with Simon face-to-face, calling him a "fringe character" and the leader of a "space-age cargo cult" for having proposed the idea that technological progress could be infinite and could overcome any limitation to economic growth. (This belief led Simon to make bold, and newsworthy, statements that were on their face absurd—statements that even he acknowledged were difficult to credit: for example, "Natural resources are not finite.") When lecturing, later, to sympathetic audiences, Ehrlich would draw laughter by playing on the title of Simon's book: "The ultimate resource—the one thing we'll never run out of is imbeciles."

At the time he coauthored that letter to *Science,* Ehrlich was reaching a large audience. His book had been propelled onto the best-seller lists thanks in part to an appearance on the *Tonight* show tied to Earth Day 1970. His segment lasted an unprecedented forty-five minutes (a monosyllabic starlet was bombing, so the producers brought Ehrlich out earlier and had him stay on longer than had been planned). Simon recalled seeing the show: "Carson, the most unimpressable of people, had this look of stupified admiration. . . . But what could I do? Go talk to five people? Here was a guy reaching a vast audience, leading this juggernaut of environmental hysteria, and I felt utterly helpless." (The show received five thousand letters about Ehrlich's appearance, nearly all of them appreciative—and worried.)

Simon spent the next decade working tirelessly to dissuade the country from heeding the "doomsayers" in the environmental movement. Despite his efforts, the limits-to-growth perspective became increasingly influential. National speed limits were lowered to fifty-five miles per hour to save fuel; Jimmy Carter warned Americans about their use of energy, admonishing us to turn down thermostats and wear sweaters, and installed solar photovoltaic cells on the White House. Feeling very much that he was an isolated voice in the wilderness trying to call people to a world of plenty that doomsayers refused to let them see, in 1980 Simon sharpened the contest by throwing down a public gauntlet: in the pages of *Social Science Quarterly* he offered a put-up-or-shut-up wager, challenging anyone to stake one thousand dollars against his proposition that the cost of nongovernment controlled raw materials, including grain and oil, would not rise in the long run. Whoever took the bet could pick the time frame (beyond a minimum of one year) and the raw material or materials of their choice.

Ehrlich recognized that the wager was aimed at him and responded — eagerly, if we trust Ehrlich's own public statement, "before other greedy people jump in," or with reservations (knowing that market prices of a small group of resources were not a good indicator of increasing scarcity), according to his account of it later. After consultation with others, in October 1980 Ehrlich and Holdren and Harte selected a basket of five metals (chromium, copper, nickel, tin, and tungsten) that had gone up between 1950 and 1975. The deal: a contract was drawn up obligating Simon to sell to Ehrlich in 1990, at 1980 prices, the same quantities of these five metals that could be purchased in 1980 for one thousand dollars. If the combined prices rose, Simon would owe Ehrlich. If they fell, Ehrlich would owe Simon.

Time lapse, ten years (eliding much rancorous debate). In October 1990, Ehrlich mailed Simon a check for $576.07, without so much as a cover note. The prices of three of the five metals had gone down — in amounts greater, in sum, than the rise in the two others.

To some observers, the bet looked like a close thing: three-to-five are slim odds. To others, Simon's $576 return on $1,000 looked definitive. (In percentage terms, it amounts to 4.7 per year, compounded annually.) The wager played in the press as a triumph of Simon's vision over Ehrlich's. (You can find popular accounts of it that state, as supposed fact, that the price of every one of the five metals went down.)

Simon offered a rematch — a repetition of the bet, straight up, another ten years. Ehrlich declined — a widely reported demurral that was taken to mean that the environmentalist limits-to-growth mindset had been thoroughly routed. Less widely reported was the counteroffer that Ehrlich and colleague Stephen H. Schneider made five years later (when the spotlight of media attention, the put-up-or-shut-up moment, had long since passed): they would bet not on commodity prices but on twelve very specific and measurable indicators of environmental health—such things as "The three years from 2002 to 2004 will on average be warmer than 1992–1994," "There will be more carbon dioxide in the atmosphere in 2004 than in 1994," more nitrous oxide, more tropospheric ozone globally, less fertile cropland per person, less agricultural soil per person, less rice and wheat grown per person, less fuelwood per person in developing countries, less tropical moist forest acreage, smaller per capita fisheries harvests, fewer plant and animal species still extant in 2004 than in 1994.

Simon declined. This move was seen not as a lack of confidence in his optimistic projections but as an affirmation of his fundamental principle: what matters, he said, is not any particular objective condition that presents a challenge to humans, but the nature and quality of the human response. The proposal from Ehrlich and Schneider turned on measurements of environmental conditions; and as Simon saw it, environmental conditions don't control human well-being, for human ingenuity will solve those problems in ways that can't be foreseen. So what if fuelwood becomes scarcer in developing countries? Given enough time, people in those places will be heating and cooking with electricity from nuclear power or other sources. So what if per capita harvests from ocean fisheries decline? Fish farming will increase, and per capita consumption of fish will remain steady or increase; or people will turn to other sources of protein. Climate change? Here the grounds for rejection were rather thin: the Ehrlich-Schneider approach, one of Simon's defenders explains, made no attempt to specify how, if it happens, climate change would have a measurable and negative effect on humans. Despite his offer to bet that "every measure of material *and environmental* welfare will improve rather than get worse," Simon refused this wager on environmental indicators, saying, "I do not offer to bet on the progress [sic] of particular physical conditions such as the ozone layer"—as if, Schneider replied, decline in the ozone layer "were not a negative measure of environmental welfare!"

This failure to reach agreement on the terms of a rematch was taken by both sides as evidence of the failure of nerve of the opponent: both could claim that the other had no confidence in their principles. But the stalemate left the original bet as the test between the two visions, lending greater support to the conclusion that Simon's infinite-planet premises had carried the day. Ehrlich's loss was a loss for the entire environmental movement, a loss for those seeking more rational environmental legislation, a loss for efforts to control population growth. It was also widely interpreted as a victory for the Hayek-inspired faith in the power of free and unregulated markets. As one triumphant recounting of the bet in *American Capitalist* put it, "Simon easily won because he knew that the supply for resources was not becoming more scarce but more abundant, since the economic history of predominantly free capitalist nations had demonstrated how the prices of most major commodities have declined over time."

If Ehrlich and other ecologically minded "doomsayers" were completely and utterly wrong, the alternative was Simon's optimistic thesis that economic growth would not hit scarcity limits. And if economic growth would never be constrained by environmental factors or resource scarcity, why, it followed — as Simon actually asserted — that the whole notion of a finite planet was bogus: "The idea of finiteness is a prejudice and . . . is not supported by available facts." As he put it in his reply to critics in *Science*: "The relevant system [i.e., human civilization on the planet] has a long enough horizon that it makes sense to treat the system as changeable, and not finite in any operational sense."

Perhaps in retrospect historians of our era will credit Simon with making the infinite-planet assumptions of our perpetual-growth, free-market economy explicit and obvious and therefore more clearly subject to disputation and correction. But the exhumation of those premises came at considerable cost: whatever impetus there had been in 1990 for forward-looking policies on population, renewable energy, and limiting resource throughput by increasing the efficiency of our use of them was stymied. Thanks to Simon's efforts, discussion of what to do about the consequences of the economy's increasing ecological footprint was replaced by argument about whether or not anything needed doing at all. The result of the bet confirmed a policy consensus among conservatives, who had gained power in the Reagan era, that resource constraints were shibboleths — that human ingenuity expressed in unregulated markets would solve any and all environmental problems.

Reagan, symbolically and notoriously, had the solar panels on the White House taken down: sunk cost or not, they simply sent the wrong message. Conservative America wasn't interested in turning down thermostats and being frugal; it aimed squarely at increased economic growth, and a recovery of the sense of infinitely expansive well-being that the country had known earlier. Under Simon's influence, and with strong support from its anti-abortion and anti-family-planning constituencies, in 1984 the Reagan administration instructed its representative to an important population conference in Mexico City to insist that "population growth is, by itself, a neutral phenomenon." (This was, one demographer remarked, "a choice piece of nonsense." If per capita well-being—wealth divided by population—is the problem, pretty obviously both the numerator and the denominator play a role in shaping it.) The Mexico meeting came ten years after a population summit in Bucharest, at which the Chinese had blocked progress on population control by remaining true to Marx: population was not and could not be a problem because every person is born with their own labor power, which enables every person to get their own living and more besides. In the ten years between the two meetings, developing nations had increasingly come to appreciate that the Marxist doctrine was wrong; controlling population growth would be a useful, perhaps necessary strategy in achieving higher per capita well-being. (This failure of Marxist population policy is an underappreciated contributor to the worldwide decline in influence of Marxist ideology and, ultimately, the dissolution of the Soviet Union.) Now the United States was saying the same thing. The labor theory of value lay behind both.

Considered solely as a public relations device, Simon's proposal of the bet was a stroke of genius; if his ideas had been "fringe" before the bet, his win made them mainstream. Environmentalist concern about population growth and resource scarcity were displaced to the periphery of public conversation. Simon's victory was taken to affirm his broader thesis: that with economic growth, every day and in every way (except, of course, for some temporary bumps and glitches—the expectable result of a free and open system) things were getting better and better. Simon summarized that optimism in a brief piece published in the *San Francisco Chronicle*'s editorial pages in 1995:

> The real prices of food and other raw materials are lower than in earlier periods, a trend of increased natural-resource availability rather than scarcity. The major air and water pollutions in advanced coun-

tries have been lessening rather than worsening. Every measure of material and environmental welfare in the United States and in the world has improved rather than deteriorated. All long-run trends point in exactly the opposite direction from the projections of the doomsayers.

So Infinite-Planet Theory prevailed and became the foundation of globalized economic practice, and the ecological footprint of the globalizing economy continued to increase, even though by many measures it had transgressed sustainable limits in the late 1970s or early 1980s. In the halls of power, scarcely a thought was given to forestalling the category of problems that Ehrlich and others had foretold. The solution to the problems of growth was going to be more growth. The consequences of this counterintuitive commitment have included a worldwide increase in human population and a reduction in the planet's carrying capacity — changes that will have large and unpleasant consequences and will increase the sum total of human pain and suffering in our civilization's course through history.

Thus, "the most important bet in history" was also "the bet that ruined the world," in the words of Paul Kedrosky.

What had happened? Why did Ehrlich lose?

The bet has been analyzed and replayed quite a bit — with notably varying results, depending on who is doing the analysis and replay. At the Property and Environment Research Center (which offers a fellowship named in honor of Simon), David McClintick and Ross B. Emmett reran the bet for each of the ten decades in the twentieth century, finding that Simon "would have won five of the ten decades by large margins, and would have won the bet over the entire century." They allowed that "to some extent Simon was lucky," but they didn't take that as any sort of claim against Simon's underlying theory: Simon hadn't claimed that prices would trend inevitably down without variation, just that they would trend inevitably down; "he had said simply that he was more likely to win than to lose in any given decade."

Other researchers, going at the issue a bit differently, came to a different conclusion. In 2008 Katherine Kiel and colleagues in the Department of Economics at Holy Cross used the same data tables but asked a different question: how did the prices of those metals fare in all possible ten-year periods for which we have data? From 1900 to 2007, there are ninety-eight such ten-year intervals, and in their analysis, Ehrlich and company would have won in 61.2 percent of those intervals, with an average return of 10.5 percent — a good deal greater than the return Simon got for the years 1980–1990. "The story that the Ehrlich-Simon bet really tells is not that natural resource scarcity does not exist, but rather that in any gamble it is always better to be lucky than good. Simon happened to place the bet during one of the 38.2 percent of years since 1900 during which he would have won." The most recent trend, visible since the late 1990s, is up: Simon would have won a ten-year bet in only four of the ten start years in that decade. And in the new millennium, so far Ehrlich is nine-for-nine.

As interesting as they are, attempts to rerun the Simon-Ehrlich bet are a bit beside the point, for they accept all of the fundamental conceptual flaws that lie behind the original bet itself. As any economist ought to be able to recognize, drawing conclusions about resource scarcity from a straight-up look at prices is foolish. A host of factors affect the price of natural resources in the marketplace, and unless those factors are effectively held constant over time, any conclusion about scarcity drawn from the behavior of prices is invalid. One such factor which was not foreseen by Ehrlich (and which accounts for quite a bit of the luck that even his sympathizers acknowledge Simon had): a recession at the start of the 1980s led to a decreased demand for the five metals in the wagered basket, which had the predictable effect of suppressing their price.

One recent and surprising confutation of Simonism comes from within the investment banking industry: in April 2011 the manager of a major hedge fund registered a carefully reasoned argument that resource prices, trending up, would never come back to the low levels we've known in the past. Jeremy Grantham, the head of GMO LLC, a hedge fund with $100 billion under management, published a letter to investors for the first quarter of 2011 headlined "Time to Wake Up: Days of Abundant Resources and Falling Prices Are Over Forever." He set out not to prove or disprove Simon, or to rerun the infamous bet, but to predict markets in order to make money. His newsletter reports his analysis of the volatility in the prices of key natural resources: how big, exactly, are the swings, as measured against average variability over time? He found that sharp increases in the prices of significant commodities since

2002 fall well outside the standard deviation. For iron ore, the rise has been 4.9 times the standard deviation, a result (Grantham tells us) that has a 1 in 2.2 million chance of being "normal" variation. More likely, he warns, it signals a new and different reality. For coal, copper, corn, silver, sorghum, palladium, rubber, and so on, the odds are not as long, but still pretty sizable: 1 to 48,000; 1 to 17,000; 1 to 14,000, and 9,000, and 4,000. Grantham concludes that a basic, deep-seated trend of increasing prices has reasserted itself. A fundamental and increasing scarcity lies beneath the statistical noise — the price spikes and troughs that characterize price history, including ups and downs created by speculation and subsequent "market corrections," including the downward pressure on prices created by increase in the rate of flow we extract from fixed and finite stocks.

Our ability to increase that rate of flow depends, ultimately, on the amount of energy we dedicate to extraction and the technological efficiency with which that energy is used. Based on a review of human energy use that reaches back to when wood was our primary fuel, Grantham concludes that we have entered a new era: we are on the cusp of what he calls the Great Paradigm Shift, "one of the giant inflection points in economic history" — the moment, he warns, that lies at "the beginning of the end for the heroic growth spurt in population and wealth caused by . . . the Hydrocarbon Revolution." To put it clearly: the enormously favorable energy return on energy invested (EROI) of coal and oil drove down prices of minerals and other extracted commodities over the past two centuries, as thermodynamically cheap energy was used to extract ever larger flows from finite stocks; with the passing of Hubbert's Peak, the prices of extracted minerals have begun to increase.

The basic failure to distinguish between stock and flow, along with lack of agreement about the role and relevance of other considerations (including, at some basic level, physical reality) accounts both for the torturous, drive-you-crazy quality of the debate, and the fact that it shifts from reasonably discussed facts and analysis to ad hominem exchanges and — on Simon's part — blatant disregard for the truth.

The subject is, frankly, a morass, one whose depth gradually becomes apparent as you read Simon, his critics, Simon on his critics, and his critics' replies to his rejoinders. The considerable surface commotion of the debate has origins deeper than a clash of personality; all the insult and invective is but the superficial chop created by the meeting of ocean-sized currents of thought rooted in incommensurate views of reality. Resources are infinite? Impossible! No, it's true! No, it isn't; I've done the math! Your math is wrong! Oh yeah? Yeah! There's a great deal of this kind of is-not, is-too back-and-forthing about factual matters — sometimes over issues as small as typos, other times over such plainly and simply discoverable facts as what the history of UN population projections has been. (Simon played fast and loose with these numbers in order to "prove" that the UN's population projections were declining. The first number Simon offered was the UN's high-range projection; the next, from a later report, was the UN's mid-range projection; and the final projection wasn't from the UN at all, but from Lester Brown at the Earth Policy Institute — and represented not a projection but the target he advocated. Simon defended the inclusion of Brown's number with the completely irrelevant observation that his Earth Policy Institute sometimes received support from the UN.)

Simon was unapologetic about his persistent and willful misrepresentation of factual matters. He seems to have felt justified in lying. He saw himself as engaged in an epic struggle over the quality and fate of civilization on the planet and thought his opponents had no qualms about lying to advance their cause; it seems probable that he saw himself as responding in kind.

And here you see how easily a debate that's crucial to the fate of civilization becomes centered on personalities and ad hominem arguments.

Before his death in 1998, Simon was an academic economist. Blatant misrepresentation of the sort Simon engaged in, and the logical and factual errors in his arguments, are not generally tolerated in the academy. Economists especially pride themselves on their mathematical rigor. Presumably they police their discipline, holding it to standards implied by that pride. But revelation of Simon's errors and misrepresentations and mendacities had no noticeable effect on his career or influence. Simon was, in this and in so many other matters, given a pass. Why? Why did the discipline of economics not read Simon out of the discipline, despite his rejection of a disciplinary foundation, the concept of diminishing marginal returns, and despite his explicit acceptance of a thoroughly discredited labor theory of value, a theory shared with neoclassical economics' arch-nemesis, Marx?

We can't know without surveying the members of the profession who remained silent about his work—and even then, the explanations they offer might not indicate the deeper underlying cause. One workable hypothesis: economics did not rise up against Simon and his work because that work supported a thesis that had become fundamental to the discipline, more fundamental than the law of diminishing returns—the faith that economic growth is always and everywhere a good thing and is achievable, infinitely, forever. It's possible (and here we are admittedly thrown back on conjecture) that disciplinary economists approved of Simon's purpose and therefore were willing to overlook his bumptious neglect of some of the discipline's canonical standards and ideas. (Did they even "tsk tsk" mildly to themselves?)

As with the conservative management of public perception of climate change, the commotion of is-not, is-too argument and the clear structuring of the Simon-Ehrlich disagreement as a "half-full versus half-empty" impasse works to the advantage of the side that holds the field through inertia. In principle, if not in practice, factual disputes ought to be relatively easy to resolve. But the arguments here frequently illustrate the Kuhnian insight that facts say different things to people with different mind-sets and as a consequence often don't change minds. What does have "illocutionary force" is the integument that holds facts together—the idea systems and mind-sets that string those facts into meaning and give them context. As Simon himself said (undercutting his oft-repeated claim that his views were completely data-driven and fact-based), one's point of view depends on one's "thema" (roughly, a Kuhnian paradigm), and "which thema is better for thinking about resources and population is not subject to scientific test." (He's right, of course: a fully scientific test would mean running a controlled experiment by taking two planets, operating one on one thema and the other on another, and submitting the results for peer review after several millennia.)

Thema versus thema, supposed optimists versus supposed pessimists, Infinite-Planet Theorists versus those who propose we face environmental limits: is there a way out of the impasse? Ehrlich offered one, a form of Pascal's wager: given two paths with uncertain outcomes, choose the path on which a mistaken choice of path is less costly. "If I'm right, we will save the world [by curbing population growth]. If I'm wrong, people will still be better fed, better housed, and happier, thanks to our efforts. Will anything be lost if it turns out later that we can support a much larger population than seems possible today?"

Simon countered by trying to disallow any such bootstrapping. He argued that Pascal's wager — basically, "If you gamble on God's existence and are wrong, you lose nothing, but if you gamble against it and are wrong, you lose eternal life" — is a device for making an individual choice, not social policy. He offered no convincing argument to support the idea that the form of Pascal's wager is valid and useful only for individual choice, and he himself used appeals to individual choice when it suited his purposes.

His aggressive assaults on Ehrlichian population analysis are often couched in calls for sentimental appreciation of the lives that won't get to be lived if we listen to environmentalists and take steps to control population growth. But even on those grounds, the debate is a wash: Ehrlich's view, if correct, tells us that controlling population growth and establishing a sustainable level of population now will protect and extend human life in the future. If Ehrlich had been so inclined, he too could have dressed his appeal in sentimental schmaltz. Simon gives no indication — none — that he recognizes that Ehrlich has a strong claim to be aiming at reduced human suffering and misery; he paints Ehrlich as a callous grandstander more interested in personal influence and publicity than in the quality and fate of civilization.

It's easy to pick nits with Simon, and his style of argument strongly encourages it: over and over he makes personal attacks (while protesting that his opponents have wronged him by doing the same); misrepresents the views of his interlocutors; and crows in triumph over victories that are invented or irrelevant. Over and over he appeals to data that tell a partial story, to facts that either aren't facts or are drawn far out of context in order to spin their meaning — from the large consideration that unless other relevant factors are held constant, the price history of raw materials tells us nothing about their ultimate scarcity, to what seem minor cases of prevarication, misrepresentation, incomplete data, and faulty logic that appear in his work and in his rejoinders to his critics. Contesting with Simon can degenerate into picking a near-infinite amount of nits.

Any parent whose kid brings home lice from school is grateful for Quell, the patent medicine that, applied topically, saves you from having to remove each and every one of those unpleasant little egg cases. Is there, for this debate, a methodological version of Quell?

Yes: the second law of thermodynamics.

Simon acknowledges the second law—not by name, but in principle—when he allows in *The Ultimate Resource* that "energy differs from other resources because [in use] it is 'used up,' and cannot be recycled." And he acknowledges that energy is crucial—though it isn't on a par with humans, who are the ultimate resource, it is still "the master resource," because "if the cost of usable energy is low enough, all other important resources can be made plentiful." He might have used these recognitions to run his thinking this way: "Falling prices mean resources are becoming more plentiful in the market. Increased use of energy can make resources more plentiful in the market. Therefore, to infer anything useful about scarcity of resources from their prices, we have to hold energy use constant. But this is an experiment that history didn't make, as energy use has increased in the fossil fuel era." Simon sees the trend in energy use—ever upward—as an additional cause for optimism, rather than as an explanatory factor lying behind all the other upward-trending lines he offers in support of his infinite-growth argument. In this he perpetuates the mistake encoded deep within neoclassical economic theory: energy is seen as a commodity like any other, rather than one of three factors of production (matter and intelligence being the other two) that are brought to bear in our efforts to create wealth and economic value.

With the advent of the fossil fuel era, and then especially with the advent of the petroleum-based economy, human appropriation of resources became possible on a scale never before known in planetary history. It's true, as Simon argues, that in the course of the fossil fuel era, the available supply of quite a few natural resources has become larger and larger. And it's true that the pace of our extraction has frequently been sufficient to outpace growth in demand, which has, at those times, suppressed prices. It's also true that as you blow up a balloon, every point on the surface gets farther and farther from every other point on the surface: balloons do grow. That doesn't mean they can grow forever. Like breath pumped into a balloon, our systematic exploitation of vast quantities of antique solar income has expanded our economy and brought more and more of nature within our grasp; stocks of accessible resources have increased. But as it stands, that statement is incomplete because there's a key term missing. The *thermodynamically* accessible stock of numerous raw materials has increased. Because it depends on a finite stock of past solar income, our ability to pump the economy ever larger is as finite as the lungful of air we use to expand a balloon. (And like an inflating balloon, an economy also has an outermost limit that can't be sustainably breached.) Our ability to inflate the economy is limited by the laws of thermodynamics: we can't create energy, nor can we use it over and over. And if there are limits to the energy we can find and use, then there are limits to everything else.

If Simon had done more than make an oblique reference to the second law of thermodynamics, he might also have been led to realize something like this: *my argument about decreasing resource prices, and the conclusion I draw from it that resources are unlimited, stands or falls on whether or not energy is for practical purposes unlimited. The laws of thermodynamics tell us that it isn't—and that it can't be.*

Simon addresses the subject of energy in many places in his work, including a chapter in *The Ultimate Resource* titled "Will We Run Out of Oil? Never!" Here he insists that "the most reliable method of forecasting the future cost and scarcity of energy is to extrapolate the historical trends of energy costs," an approach that effectively presumes the Hydrocarbon Era to be the permanent condition of humanity. (He might have been led to sturdier, more realistic conclusions if he had projected forward from the energy cost of energy—the EROI—instead of its monetary cost.)

Simon recognizes that his vision of infinite bounty and infinite growth requires infinite energy, and actually says "energy is infinite." He offers three distinct arguments in support of this remarkable assertion: (1) We'll never run out of oil; (2) even if we do, there are other kinds of energies available to us (biomass and nuclear get favorable mention); and besides (3), we won't be limited to the energy available to us on this planet. At least one of these arguments must succeed if, taken together, they are to reassure us that the supply of energy available to us is infinite.

To take the last one first: no technology that we can invent will change the fact that it takes one horsepower to raise 550 pounds one foot in one second; nor will we ever change the fact that the escape velocity of the Earth's gravitational field is eleven kilometers per second.

Gravity is a constant, a given, an immutable limit. It takes large amounts of energy to lift mass off the Earth and to accelerate it into orbit (and much of the mass that has to be lifted — up to 90 percent of the weight of the rocket — is fuel for continued acceleration in the lifting). It is extremely unlikely that the energy return on energy invested of any extraterrestrial source of energy would ever be positive, let alone exceed the EROI of exploiting sunlight, the sustainable and renewable form of off-planet energy that is delivered to us every day, cost-free, here on the surface of the Earth. (Even it if were thermodynamically feasible, importation of additional off-planet energy would have consequences for terrestrial systems, all of them unknown and some of them not good. The tried-and-true economics adage "There is no such thing as a free lunch" is supported by Barry Commoner's First Law of Ecology, which warns us of unintended consequences: "You can't do one thing.")

Neither is biomass an infinite source of energy. Simon asserts that "there is no meaningful limit" to the amount of biofuel we can exploit, "except the sun's energy," and the sun will last for billions of years, so this potential source is also infinite. But his argument here has a definitional slide, as infinity-in-time (which is granted) becomes infinity-in-current-expansion (which is what's at issue). There are two easily identifiable limits to expansion of the rate at which we exploit the temporally infinite flow of sunlight by turning it into biofuel: one, increasing our take of Net Primary Product leaves less for nature, and at some point the resulting loss in ecosystem services imposes greater costs on humans than the benefits humans can gain from increased use of biomass fuel. Two, the amount of solar energy falling on the planet is limited by the Earth's diameter. Simon doesn't talk about the first, because his theoretical frame doesn't acknowledge it: all value comes from human labor, and so the category of ecosystem service is one he does not and cannot acknowledge. Nor is the diameter of the Earth a limit: "There are energy sources on other planets," and "there may well be other suns elsewhere." Thus, this second argument reverts to the first: for biofuel to be the source of infinite energy, the EROI of space-based exploitation of energy has to be economic, which means it has to be greater than the EROI of alternative and renewable energy exploited here on Earth. Thermodynamics says we have a very low — infinitesimally low — chance of accomplishing that.

Will nuclear power be an infinite source of energy? In its current form, certainly not. It is, by many estimates, an energy sink, costing the human economy more in energy than it usefully returns (though much of the energy cost is imposed on posterity, who will have the burden of storing wastes and guarding nuclear infrastructure sites against trespass in perpetuity). It takes quite a bit of energy to find and refine uranium, to fabricate and assemble the reactor, to transport wastes and ores and construction material. As you can imagine, net energy analyses of nuclear power are the subject of intense debate, much of it rooted in ideological and faith-based conviction. Should the energy cost of building highways and trucks to transport the necessary materials be included or not? If so, what percentage? (Will these things be used up in the production of nuclear power, or will they benefit society more broadly?) What about the energy costs of storage of nuclear wastes; what number should the analysis use for that? Since we don't have a suitable system for permanent storage of nuclear waste, the number that's used has to be based on a guess.

But nuclear power doesn't have to be an energy sink to be technically uneconomic. It only has to have an EROI lower than an alternative — and the EROIs of solar photovoltaic and wind power stand between fourteen and nineteen, and are rising with invention, innovation, and returns to scale.

Deciding nuclear energy on the sheer technical grounds of EROI leaves out the political, social, and moral concerns that for many of us are the dominant considerations. Even supposing that technological progress would allow nuclear power eventually to deliver on its long-ago promise of offering "energy too cheap to meter," if that energy came at the cost of contaminating parts of our planet for hundreds of thousands of years, should we accept it? In the wake of the tsunami and core meltdown of the nuclear plants in Fukushima, Japan, the always-present risk of catastrophic, civilization-threatening nuclear accident has a reality it formerly lacked for many of us. Are we wise to impose those risks on ourselves? Do we have the moral warrant to impose those risks on future humans — the "unborn" that Simon professes to care so much about? And, given that a nuclear-power infrastructure is incompatible with a high degree of civil liberty and social freedom, should we continue to trade away political and social values for economic ones? Larger and larger numbers of us are answering no to such questions—questions that can't be decided on technical grounds.

Simon's argument presumes that the only consequences of nuclear accidents worth considering are the consequences for humans, and also that whatever negative consequences humans might experience from nuclear power (or, indeed, any aspect of human economic activity) can be forestalled, corrected, or remediated by humans—using more energy. His argument for infinite energy thus is circular: it needs a source of energy that is infinite. Nuclear power, under any technology that we have today, is not that source; and it depends on a fuel—fissionable uranium—that's available in finite quantities on a finite planet. "But the whole point is there are other planets," comes the rejoinder. "They probably have uranium on them. We'll go there, get it, bring it back." And, "What about fusion?"

We do, in fact, benefit from fusion reaction today, in a system that has withstood the test of time by having the generating facility located a good 93 million miles away from the closest human settlement. (The delivery system is efficient and equitable, and though it's intermittent, its night-and-day cycles are easily predicted.) A fusion reactor in a more proximate location would have serious safety issues, and in any case the technology for such a thing lies well beyond our current capacities.

For nuclear power to be an infinite source of energy, it needs to be an infinite source of energy. The attempt to break through that conundrum by appeal to discoveries yet undiscovered, inventions yet uninvented, and developments yet to be developed is an appeal to faith and hope, not fact; and the faith can be maintained only in ignorance of the laws of thermodynamics.

As to oil: Simon's assertion that "we'll never run out of oil" is, as I said earlier, technically true but irrelevant. Some oil will remain unused because it is thermodynamically inaccessible to us (it would cost us more energy to find and exploit it than we will derive from exploiting it). In yet another definitional slide, "We'll never run out of oil" is taken to mean "Oil will never become scarce and expensive." Simon supports that conclusion with a bit of flawed argument that should embarrass a college sophomore: "The oil potential of a particular well may be measured, and hence it is limited. . . . But the number of wells that will eventually produce oil, and in what quantities, is not known or measurable at present and probably never will be, and hence is not meaningfully finite." The argument has this form: "Infinity is a number we can't know. We can't know a number x. Therefore, x is infinity." You would be equally justified in concluding that because Julian Simon is a man, the next man you meet will be Julian Simon. "Julian Simon" belongs to the category "man," as does the next man I meet, so they must be the same thing.

You can see why some of Simon's critics are led to characterize him in intensely unflattering terms. With arguments like this, Simon concludes that "except for temporary fluctuations caused by bad luck or poor management, the world need not worry about energy shortages or costs in the future."

The rest of Simon's discussion of energy in *The Ultimate Resource* is, for the most part, elaborately beside the point. In discussing the history of human fuel use, Simon attacks some easily attacked prognosticators, from Stanley Jevons (whose nineteenth-century concerns about scarcity of coal were widely treated as having been made moot by the advent of petroleum, a carbon pool he hadn't foreseen), on through the parade of oil industry observers who have predicted an impending oil shortage — predictions which, in truth, have been a feature of oil-driven society all along. But the fact that such predictions have been wrong in the past does not mean that they are of necessity wrong for all time — not the next ten years, let alone "seven billion years into the future," the time frame that Simon expresses optimism about.

In sum, on Simon's world, the laws of thermodynamics do not operate: in contradiction to the first law, we have the capacity to "invent" new sources of energy as the old sources run out. This is, again, a straightforward consequence of holding a labor theory of value: human ingenuity and effort can do anything, including making energy in violation of the laws of thermodynamics. Bottom line: "Careful thinking leads to the conclusion that the potential amount of oil . . . is not finite." Oil is infinite, biofuels are infinite, solar energy is infinite, nuclear power is infinite — in Simon's universe, there's infinity everywhere you look. And so, "it's reasonable to expect the supply of energy to continue becoming more available and less scarce, forever."

How would Simon reply to criticism grounded in thermodynamics? We don't have to guess: one critic, a professor of sociology, raised the specter of the second law, summarizing his critical evaluation of the first edition of *The Ultimate Resource* with these words: "Simon has ignored the basic physical realities of entropy." Simon's argumentative style, and the weakness of his argument as a whole, are evident in his rejoinder, a brief passage in his lengthy "Reply to Critics" in the second edition. "In other words," Simon wrote, "a sociologist instructs us that the physics of cosmology . . . as embodied in that old chestnut entropy, makes nonsense of what I write about population economics." First, the condescending ad hominem swipe (a sociologist presumes to know something about physics); then, inaccuracy (the implication that application of the laws of thermodynamics is limited to cosmology); then a pooh-poohing of "that old chestnut, entropy"—as if the second law had been definitively discredited. For good measure, Simon went on to prevaricate: the physics of cosmology, he said, is "a subject now enlivened by fundamental speculative differences"—implying that where once there had been certainty about the first and second laws of thermodynamics, there is now uncertainty and legitimate academic debate. That is not true. (Even if it were, the point wouldn't be relevant: we live in the physical reality of Earth, not in the weird and counterintuitive realms of black holes and singularities and curved space.) To dismiss the application of the laws of thermodynamics to terrestrial life because they also find application in cosmology, whose energy balances and mechanisms we don't fully understand, is rather like asserting that you can't drive a car on the clearly gridded streets of New York if cars just like it are being driven on the confusing streets of Rome.

Simon also took aim at the law of entropy in "Entropy and Energy Accounting: Are They Relevant Concepts?," an unpublished essay available on an homage-purposed website titled *Julian Simon: 1932–1998. An Appreciation.* (The site was evidently created with Simon's participation before his death; the first-person voice in the writing on the site is Simon's.) The answer Simon gives to the rhetorical question of his title is, of course, no. In the essay he trots out arguments familiar to readers of *The Ultimate Resource*, the most substantial of which is grounded on the assertion that the sun won't burn out for at least 7 billion years. (Again, extension in time is confused with extension in physical space.) This plenitude of energy, Simon says, means that "the notion of entropy . . . is entirely irrelevant to us." He throws in the additional consideration that evolution can be taken to prove that entropy is no constraining factor:

the entropy law tells us that systems move from greater order to greater disorder and from greater differentiation to greater homogeneity, yet all around us is evidence of evolution, which, perking along in planetary history, has proliferated species and given us an increasingly complex, increasingly differentiated world. Simon's confusion here is an elementary one, a point long since taken up, and answered, by the relevant sciences. (This may explain why the piece remained unpublished.) Biology and physics tell us that evolution is no violation of the second law. Solar throughput is the engine that drives ecosystem organization — the increasing complexity and differentiation visible in evolution — and the entropy account is balanced by the increasing entropy of the solar furnace. That the furnace will last 7 billion years is neither here nor there; as noted above, the issue is the finitude of the Earth's energy budget in the present, not its extent in time. Because the solar energy arriving on the planet is finite (though generous), our ability to capture solar flow for our purposes without depriving ecosystems of the energy they need in order to maintain themselves and support us is also finite.

At one point Simon quotes Stephen Hawking's koan-like assertion that though the universe is bounded, "the boundary condition of the universe is that it has no boundary," which Simon takes to be authoritative support for his infinite-planet assumptions. The ultimate character of the universe is indeed mysterious, and there is room for mystical and poetic expression in our attempts to describe it within a language that is otherwise ill-suited to the purpose. But when all is said and done, we live on a finite planet, not in the far reaches of space-time whose character is unknown, perhaps unknowable to us. Here on Earth this passage from A. S. Eddington remains as apt today as when it was written:

> The second law that entropy always increases holds, I think, the supreme position among the laws of Nature. If someone points out to you that your pet theory of the universe is in disagreement with Maxwell's equations — then so much the worse for Maxwell's equations. If it is found to be contradicted by observation — well, these experimentalists do bungle things sometimes. But if your theory is found to be against the second law of thermodynamics I can give you no hope; there is nothing for it but to collapse in deepest humiliation.

Would that Simon, in response to criticism, had collapsed in deepest humiliation; the world would have been a demonstrably better place for it. Instead, he enjoyed a long and influential career (although he never achieved the influence he thought he deserved). His faith in technological success without limit, like the labor theory of value that is its foundation, is an artifact of our previous life on Garden Planet, where the difference between what nature could offer to and absorb from us, on the one side, and what we actually took from and emitted into it, on the other, was sufficiently large to mask the planet's finitude — and to mask the necessary role that nature plays in economic life as the source of the flows of matter and energy we transform to create economic value. On Earth, Simonism is a luxury good that we can no longer afford to buy. For decades the true price of Infinite-Planet Theory was obscured by cheap energy, the once-in-planetary-history exploitation of past solar income to accomplish work and generate wealth in the present. That subsidy is no longer possible. Both literally and figuratively, on a finite planet we can't afford to think the way Simon wants us to think.

freakonomist cheap shots jane fonda

You don't often see academic economists blaming liberal movie stars for climate change, but that's what University of Chicago economist Steven D. Levitt did in one of his syndicated columns, coauthored with journalist Stephen J. Dubner. (Their first book, the best-selling *Freakonomics*, was subtitled "a rogue economist explores the hidden side of everything," so it seems that economist Levitt had the major hand in picking the subjects that the pair has taken up, including going after Fonda.) Their joint book offers Levitt's analyses of an impressive array of subjects: how data can be used to identify teachers who cheat; how data can be used to show that the drop in the US crime rate in the 1980s had less to do with conservative get-tough-on-crime policies than with the reproductive freedom women got under *Roe v. Wade* in 1973 (which meant fewer teen moms, fewer unwanted babies, and eventually fewer badly parented adolescent males); how data can be used to answer the question, "Do parents really matter?"; how data can be used to show that your realtor doesn't really have your best interests at heart.

You see the pattern. If the authors themselves say, "There is no unifying theme to *Freakonomics*," they do allow that there's "a common thread": "It has to do with thinking sensibly about how people behave in the real world" — using data to test hypotheses about people's behavior within the incentive systems they face, even if those responses are sometimes counterintuitive and unexpected.

For instance: people are supposed to respond to price incentives, right? But an Israeli daycare center that instituted a $3 penalty for late pickup of children was dismayed to find that the problem simply got worse. No wonder, *Freakonomics* says; by substituting a cash incentive for a moral one, the policy allowed people to buy off their guilt on the cheap. Interestingly, the effect wasn't reversed when the penalty was rescinded; once the must-avoid-guilt motivation was snuffed out, it stayed out. (Levitt and Dubner don't make the connection, but there's a cautionary lesson here for those of us interested in achieving sustainability by putting monetary prices on unpriced ecosystem services. Currently, guilt is a factor in leading some people to reduce their ecological footprint. If the effects of conscience disappear when a system of price motivation is implemented, we'd better get the prices right.)

If you think like a Freakonomist, "you might become more skeptical of the conventional wisdom; you may begin to look for hints that things aren't quite what they seem; perhaps you will seek out some trove of data and sift through it . . . to arrive at a glimmering new idea." And it turns out that if you think like a Freakonomist, you might package your result with an attention-getting headline that makes an unsupported inferential leap, like the one Levitt and Dubner took when they suggested Jane Fonda is responsible for climate change.

Levitt is a recipient of the John Bates Clark medal, awarded to the most influential economist under the age of forty; he's also director of the Becker Center on Chicago Price Theory at the University of Chicago's Booth School of Business. *Freakonomics* has plenty of new glimmering new ideas—many of which are rooted in conservative, Chicago school economic theory. The book presents Levitt as cultivating the conceptual ground staked out by Nobel laureate Gary Becker, "the original Freakonomist," who started his career tackling subjects that weren't seen as part of the discipline as it was then practiced: "crime and punishment, drug addiction, the allocation of time, and the costs and benefits of marriage, child rearing, and divorce." It's all a matter of asking the right questions of the right data; and—heretical thought in an arithmomorphic discipline dominated by econometricians—"an approximate answer to the right question is worth a great deal more than a precise answer to the wrong question." Economics as practiced needs this kind of heresy. Freakonomics wants the discipline to tackle even such nontraditional questions as "how people . . . choose someone to love and marry, someone perhaps to hate and even kill." The book's conversational, accessible style and its engaging "did you ever think of this?" subject matters helped to make it a best seller, and that helped get the pair of coauthors a regular (if short-running) column at the *New York Times Magazine*, where Dubner was formerly an editor. And that's where they took on Jane Fonda.

In a piece titled "The Jane Fonda Effect," Levitt and Dubner insinuated that Fonda is "one of the biggest global warming villains of the past 30 years." I enjoy seeing conventional wisdom shaken up as much as the next guy, but there's not a whole lot of convention-shaking here; among conservatives Fonda-bashing has long been ritual and standard practice, ever since as an antiwar activist in the 1970s she visited North Vietnam and was photographed sitting in an anti-aircraft-gunner's chair. ("Traitor" was one of the kindest epithets leveled at her.) The charge that she is responsible for climate change may have sent some conservatives into cognitive dissonance — "climate change is a total hoax, but it's also real and Fonda is to blame." Being able to blame a liberal for climate change may encourage conservatives to be more open to reason and evidence on the issue, but to get there they'd have to accept a notably flawed argument from Messrs. Levitt and Dubner.

As the scientist Steven Schneider noticed (in a bit of analysis that was the cause for a dustup with Julian Simon), in a sound-bite culture it's difficult for complex ideas to break through the cultural noise and gain enough attention to be appreciated in all their complexity and nuance. It does help if the idea is tagged with a strong, provocative hook, and Levitt and Dubner are good — very good — at coming up with those. (The subtitle to their follow-up book, *Superfreakonomics*, offers three such hooks right up front: "Global Cooling, Patriotic Prostitutes, and Why Suicide Bombers Should Buy Life Insurance.") But their search for "The Jane Fonda Effect," with its pandering to deep-seated conservative convictions and its scapegoating, is not the punchy-but-accurate presentation of complex truth that Schneider described (a description that Simon seized on and misrepresented in order to charge that Schneider advocated lying for political purposes). It's more like the one-sided, inaccurate, and logically flawed spinning that got Julian Simon where he wanted to go — which is to say, it falls outside the realm of reasoned, fact-driven discussion. Pandering and scapegoating aside, the argument beneath Levitt and Dubner's hook just doesn't hold up.

The two are careful never actually to *assert* that Fonda, through the movie *The China Syndrome* and her vocal opposition to nuclear power, is directly responsible for increasing emissions of greenhouse gases; instead, they insinuate this conclusion by asking a question. Their first two sentences: "If you were asked to name the biggest global-warming villains of the past 30 years, here's one name that probably wouldn't spring to mind: Jane Fonda. But should it?" Later in the piece they write that "anyone hunting for a global-warming villain . . . can't help wondering" if she played a major role. They're not saying, they're just sayin', is all.

They get there with this reasoning: Fonda made an influential movie that persuaded people to oppose nuclear power. Nuclear power is not carbon-based energy, so if we had more of it, we'd have less CO_2 in the atmosphere. Less CO_2, less climate change. Conclusion: you just might want to think of Fonda as a villain.

The China Syndrome opened on March 16, 1979, back when people actually had to go to theaters to see movies, which no doubt contributed to the power that Levitt and Dubner attribute to it: the movie shaped cultural perception about nuclear power. As pure movie, *The China Syndrome* was really pretty good. Starring Fonda and Jack Lemmon and Michael Douglas, it told an engaging story with interesting characters who happen to run smack into evidence of corporate corruption and the dangers of nuclear power. Fonda plays a TV reporter doing a routine stand-up at a nuclear plant for an upbeat piece on energy, when she and her cameraman (Douglas) film what the plant spokesperson later describes as "swift containment of a potentially costly event"—an accident, with a near meltdown. Lemmon plays a whistle-blowing engineer who's upset to discover that X-rays of important welds have been faked. The nuclear industry itself contributed by accident to the movie's popularity—the accident being the one that happened at Three Mile Island twelve days after the movie's release, when one of two reactors lost coolant and had a partial core meltdown. Reality created buzz for the movie, and the movie buzzed a particular take on that reality: the dangers of nuclear power are grossly underrepresented by the industry, which is huge and powerful and cares about its own bottom line, not our health and safety. (It's a lesson that was reinforced by experience in Japan, where two reactors in Fukushima lost coolant in the tsunami.) Result? "Widespread panic," Levitt and Dubner assert, and an industry "already foundering as a result of economic, regulatory, and public pressures" stopped expanding. "And so, instead of becoming a nation with clean and cheap nuclear energy, as once seemed inevitable, the United States kept building power plants that burned coal and other fossil fuels." Jane Fonda, climate villain.

It may be that economist Levitt was offended by the anti–Adam Smith narrative offered up by the movie: in the neoclassical understanding of free-market capitalism, a business's pursuit of its own selfish gain is supposed to work out for the common good, and here you had a Hollywood story showing us very graphically and compellingly that sometimes corporate pursuit of profit runs dead counter to the public interest. Whatever the motive, the reasoning by which Levitt and Dubner accuse Fonda of being responsible for climate change depends on two key points: nuclear power is clean, cheap, and sensible, and we'd have more of it—and hence less greenhouse gas emissions—if Fonda hadn't made that movie.

Consideration of the second point is where Levitt and Dubner can stretch the discipline with what they're calling Freakonomics. With Becker's work, rational choice theory began to acknowledge and study something that advertisers had known for years: people don't always make strictly rational choices; rather, they can be influenced by images, narratives, "themas" (as Julian Simon called them), strong metaphors, emotional triggers, "frames" (as George Lakoff calls them). Because economics sees humans as rational, value-maximizing actors, choices that are monetarily irrational must, by definition, be value-maximizing within some other, perhaps larger context. (If you make an absolutely stupid, totally irrational decision, an economist has to say that you've obviously chosen to minimize the opportunity cost of thinking, or have a taste for risk and surprise, or don't want to pay the information costs of informing yourself enough to make a better choice.)

It's possible to grant Levitt and Dubner their Beckerish point—that what economists call the "preference structures" of Americans for nuclear power were significantly affected by Fonda's movie—without following them all the way to holding her responsible (or, to be precise, suggesting that maybe you wouldn't be wrong if you thought she was responsible) for climate change. Holding her responsible is irresponsible, because to do so you have to commit an elementary fallacy. Levitt and Dubner's "blame Jane" implication is valid only if there was and is a straight-up choice between carbon-and-climate-change, on the one side, and climate-stability-and-nuclear-power, on the other. And that's not true; there were then and continue to be other choices: solar and renewable, conservation, and so on. By not mentioning these, Levitt and

Dubner structure the argument as a false dichotomy. Even if you grant that Fonda's movie had a role in halting development of nuclear power in this country, you can't hold her responsible for climate change unless nuclear power was the *only* alternative to carbon-based energy systems.

That's such a deep and telling flaw that there's no real need to go further—and it may explain why you won't find this piece listed on Levitt's academic curriculum vitae, even though other newspaper pieces, including ones published in the *New York Times*, are listed under "Popular Writing." Hypothesis: Levitt doesn't want to remind anyone that he coauthored a newspaper column built on such an obviously flawed argument.

But let's go further, because doing so will give us a chance to think like a Freakonomist—and to see how even prominent economists sometimes botch things in support of their faith in infinite economic growth on a finite planet.

If we're going to accept Levitt and Dubner's suggestion that Fonda can be held responsible for climate change, they have to convince us that nuclear power is clean, cheap, and sensible—which means they have to gloss over the reasons for those "economic, regulatory, and public pressures" that were evident before the movie came out. In their view, the accident at Three Mile Island was inconsequential and was blown out of proportion only because of the movie. "There was no meltdown through to the other side of the earth—no 'China syndrome,'" they report, and there was "no . . . significant damage, except to the plant itself."

The "significant damage" to the plant was the melting of fuel rods—half of the core. It didn't breach the containment and head for China, but no one knows by what margin of luck that outcome was avoided. (And we won't ever know, not unless an accident breaches the containment in a similar reactor, so we can compare. Here ignorance isn't so much bliss as it is continued health and security.) And despite what Levitt and Dubner assert, there was significant damage off-site: an official report by the us Nuclear Regulatory Commission (hardly a hotbed of antinuke sentiment) notes that "TMI-2 suffered a severe core meltdown, the most dangerous kind of nuclear power accident," which led to "a significant release of radiation from the plant's auxiliary building." Evidently, in Levitt and Dubner's view, a significant release of radiation is not significant damage.

It took a year for radiation inside the damaged plant to decay enough that workers could enter for brief, one-shot shifts and stabilize the melted core. At considerable expense, the plant was defueled and moth-balled and now sits idle on the site. In cold, calculating economic terms, this financial loss is a kind of overhead—the cost of doing business with an unforgiving technology in which a few small mistakes, in train, have large consequences. It would be helpful to see some calculations about the risk of incurring more such costs in the future; just as a company has to set aside some of its income to replace its capital equipment because everything eventually wears out, if we're to make rational calculations about the nuclear industry we need to know the odds—the risk—of seeing another expensive accident, because accidents do happen, and dealing with them is part of the cost of doing this kind of business. Experts in the private sector—the insurance industry—won't make that calculation for us. More precisely, they made the calculation and refused to get involved; nuclear power couldn't come online until passage of the Price-Anderson Nuclear Industries Indemnity Act of 1957, which has the American taxpayer on the hook for liability claims beyond a $10 billion cap. (That number sounds impressive but comes nowhere near covering the foreseeable cost of an accident at a nuclear plant, especially one in a densely populated and propertied area. In the wake of the Fukushima accident, the US Nuclear Regulatory Commission recommended to American citizens that they evacuate at least fifty miles from the site. If the same evacuation zone were to be applied to the Indian Point reactors in Buchanan, New York, every resident of New York City would have to be relocated. Ten billion dollars is enough to compensate the city's 7 million residents with just $1,430 each.) Without Price-Anderson's short-circuiting of the Smithian free market, we would not have had nuclear power, ever.

If entropy is the ghost in our machines, haunting them with a relentless degradation that wears out their usefulness, we can also see the specter of the second law here, in the risk of accident, as well. The law of entropy is a law of probability. It tells us that valuable arrangements of matter and useful stocks of energy are rare and improbable, and over time the less probable state gives way to the more probable state. Think of it this way: there are billions of ways for a given quantity of lumber to be arranged as a jumbled pile, but only a few hundred thousand ways for it to be assembled into a useful structure. Over time and left to it-self—with no inputs of matter, energy, and intelligence in the form of maintenance—a useful barn will become a random jumble of boards. It's irrational to bet against those odds. Entropy warns us that when we employ an unforgiving technology, chances are very good that eventu-ally we'll do something that wants forgiving. Given that, we'd be wiser to build and make use of systems that are more resilient.

But neoclassical economists don't have any truck with entropy, so Levitt and Dubner's gaze falls elsewhere. Reporting a visit to the site, they focus on the other reactor, which "continues to quietly churn out electricity for 800,000 customers," close to a vegetable garden—a ra-diation test bed—"badly in need of watering . . . [but] otherwise fine." No one died on-site or nearby (they mean: not immediately, and so far as we know), and the levels of radiation released can be presented as minimal: "Estimates are," according to the passively voiced US NRC re-port, "that the average dose to about 2 million people in the area was only about 1 millirem," one-sixth the dose of the average chest X-ray. No (human) harm, no foul, right? But the same report notes that "the maxi-mum dose to a person at the site boundary would have been less than 100 millirem." We can presume that the number wasn't much less than 100, or the report would have specified it—like advertisers, the NRC knows the irrational appeal of staying just under a round number. One hundred millirem is the low end of the range the report gives for the normal background dose in the area. That doesn't sound so comforting when you know that radiation doses are cumulative. The information can be cast this way: to someone near the plant, the radiation release just about doubled the normal background dose they receive. Whether or not that exposure led to measurable human harm could, with some effort, be teased out of statistical data on mortality and cancer rates in the area—a Freakonomics project that Levitt and Dubner don't pursue, here or anywhere.

Whatever does show up in that data, analysis of it will have to take another variable into account, another fact not mentioned by Lev-itt and Dubner: in a joint decision by Pennsylvania governor Rich-ard Thornburgh and Nuclear Commission chairman Joseph Hendrie, pregnant women and preschool-age children were advised to evacuate a five-mile-radius area around the plant. Our Freakonomists, who are interested in using data to answer questions that economists haven't traditionally asked, don't seem to be interested in asking about the significant damage — the economic and psychic costs, including fear and maybe even terror — brought on by emergency evacuation under threat of harm from an invisible and invidious poison.

The Freakonomics point that Levitt and Dubner pursue in the piece has to do with an insight from economist Frank Knight, who drew a distinction between risk and uncertainty: the former can be calculated, but the latter cannot. People tend to accept known risk — clear odds, like fifty-fifty — and avoid the ambiguities of uncertain odds. One excellent illustration of this is the insurance industry's unwillingness to write liability coverage for a risky enterprise with no track record; professional risk-assessors steered clear of the nuclear industry's uncertainties. But Levitt and Dubner cite Knight's work to point us in the opposite direction, to bolster their speculation about reasons for (what they assert to be) renewed interest in nuclear energy. This is another point offered by insinuation, through a question: "Could it be that nuclear energy, risks and all, is now seen as preferable to the uncertainties of global warming?"

Maybe. Maybe, as one of their other social-science anecdotes concludes, people are being reasonable when they prefer the devil they know to the one they don't, and maybe fifty years of operation under Price-Anderson is enough of a track record to let us think of nuclear power as the devil we know. One certain sign of that would be repeal of Price-Anderson and a willingness of private insurers to underwrite nuclear power's risks. That hasn't happened. If there's renewed interest in the industry, that may be because the Energy Policy Act of 2005, passed by a supposedly pro-free-market Congress and signed by a supposedly pro-free-market president, renewed Price-Anderson and offered other large, market-trumping incentives to create new nuclear plants in the United States — a factor that Levitt and Dubner don't mention, though it happened two years before they wrote about Fonda.

The weighing of benefit against risk and uncertainty is a form of cost-benefit analysis, which in its classic, monetized form is the bread-and-butter of economic thinking. Freakonomics stretches the discipline to extend cost-benefit analysis into areas that aren't measurable in money — analyses that include status, guilt, and the other nonmonetary motivators of human behavior. But if Levitt and Dubner had wanted to be extend their iconoclastic practice even further and bust a few more of the boundaries and outdated conventions of the discipline, they might have brought a different kind of cost-benefit analysis to their discussion of energy infrastructure: net energy accounting. The relevant factors in a choice between energy systems aren't limited to monetary cost-benefit analysis, aren't confined to the question "Do we get the most energy for our dollar from this system, or that system?" The fact that nuclear power is cheaper than coal, as Levitt and Dubner report, isn't the only cost consideration and shouldn't be the controlling one. (As I've argued elsewhere in this volume, for a whole host of reasons the price of a thing, especially energy, is not a good indicator of its cost.) The more fundamental economic question for an energy system is "Do we get the most calories out per calorie invested from this system or that system?" This approach — looking at energy return on energy invested, or EROI — moves beneath price to look at physical reality.

As noted previously, the EROI of nuclear power is a hotly contested issue. One expert assessment by Charles Hall of the State University of New York found that "much, perhaps most, of the information that is available seems to have been prepared by someone who has made up his or her mind one-way or another . . . before the analysis is given." Hall surveyed EROI studies of nuclear power, reporting results that range from 93:1 (an outlier; that study neglected to include the energy costs of refining the fuel) on down to 3:1 and lower — down to zero and negative numbers, which if accurate would mean that nuclear technology is an energy sink, not a net energy producer. Two key factors explain this range of answers: disagreement over the appropriate boundary for the analysis (should it include, for instance, a prorated portion of the energy cost of the vehicles and roads that construction and mining and enrichment consume?) and disagreement over the estimated energy cost of waste storage and protection for dozens of centuries — a figure that is sheer postulation, since there is no historical experience to base it on. Proponents of nuclear power draw the boundaries of the analysis tightly and discount future energy costs severely, in part because they imagine a world filled with nuclear power plants. (Yes, there's logical circle here: nuclear energy has a net energy payoff in the present when we discount future energy costs because the future will have nuclear power; and we know the future will have nuclear power because it has a net energy payoff in the present.) Opponents of nuclear power tend to draw more inclusive boundaries and to arrive at much larger estimates for "back-end" energy costs.

Cost-benefit and net energy analysis hardly ever line up, because of the perverse incentive structures that have accumulated over the years in which we've enjoyed cheap (and high-EROI) petroleum. In much of their work in *Freakonomics*, Levitt and Dubner examine perverse incentive structures. Here, when it comes to energy, they drop their curiosity and fall into line with disciplinary convention.

As any economist, icon-buster or not, can tell you, cost-benefit analysis based solely on monetary prices leads to an inefficient — "sub-optimal" — result if the negative and positive externalities of the alternatives haven't been captured by price. The foundation of Levitt and Dubner's sally against Fonda is that climate change is a negative externality of burning coal and that climate stability would be a positive externality of going nuclear. The first of these is certainly true, and the second may or may not be. But those are just two externalities, one apiece, for two very large systems that have many other externalities; and those two systems aren't the only choices we face. Stopping there leaves the largest and most relevant considerations completely unconsidered. The question that needs to be asked is not "Should we hold Fonda responsible for climate change?" but "How do all the positive and negative externalities of nuclear power stack up against all the positive and negative externalities of both carbon-based and non-carbon-based energy systems?"

As we come down the backslope of the global Hubbert's Peak, the choice of energy systems to replace oil is the most consequential economic and political choice we will make. Levitt and Dubner don't address it anywhere in their work. They can't even begin to get at it in this short piece on Jane Fonda, because on their way to bashing her they don't talk about externalities at all, even though their analysis is centered on one. Their exposition hints at others, including two of the major negative externalities of nuclear power: there's that annoying tendency of humans to be fallible, even when their technology demands perfection; and there's that razor-wire-topped chain-link fence and the bulletproof sniper's stands that surround the bunker office in which they interview the chief operating officer of the remaining Three Mile Island reactor. Nuclear plants are complex, inherently fragile systems in which a few mundane disruptions (a stuck valve, a failed gauge) can, in combination, produce enormous and disastrous effects. That makes them terrorist magnets. Part of the cost of adding nukes to our energy infrastructure is the risk of terrorist attack—and the additional cost of whatever we do in our efforts to prevent such attacks. That cost comes partly in money (hardening the site, patrolling those fences) and partly in real but intangible losses, like the loss of civil liberties we experience if we choose to adapt our society to our technology, instead of choosing a technology that's compatible with the social and political values we hold.

Not just the plant itself but the entire fuel chain is vulnerable. Because radioactive material in any concentrated amount could be used to make a "dirty" conventional bomb, it's increasingly likely that we'll perceive a need for armed motorcades to move nuclear fuels and waste from its point of generation to wherever we eventually decide it will be safe—or "safe"—to store. As we dangle the low-hanging fruit of a vulnerable nuclear infrastructure in front of malefactors and malcontents of every stripe and variety (both domestic and foreign), the foreseeable effect will be that we're forced to accept ever more intrusive and more effective surveillance of the American population to catch and deter those who move among us who might intend to cause nuclear harm.

Just as no one ever commandeered a train and ran it into a building, there's little likelihood that a solar voltaic cell will provide a terrorist with the materials to make a weapon of mass destruction. (Solar and other renewables have their externalities, to be sure, but not anything nearly so risky.) If instead of developing solar and other renewable energy systems we build a nuclear energy infrastructure that is incompatible with the exercise of the civil liberties we hold as Americans, the cost of that infrastructure includes, as an externality, the degradation of our heritage of constitutional freedoms. Most Americans would say that our constitutional freedoms are priceless. But in economic calculations about nuclear power, because "priceless" is vague (and infinity is a difficult number to work with), we mark it down to zero.

So in practice neoclassical economists treat negative civil-liberties externalities as if they didn't exist. The discipline can see those civil-liberties externalities only when they're positive, as when Hayek and other conservative political economists (like Milton Friedman) celebrate free markets as the only allocative mechanism consistent with our political freedoms. Focus on the positive social externalities of markets and disregard for the negative social externalities of energy systems seems hypocritical—a bias, a prejudice that's manifest in the discipline. Many of us who value civil liberty would count its loss or diminution as a big externality, and it's just the kind of thing you'd want a renegade, think-outside-the-box economist to be talking about (especially one like Levitt, who is coeditor of the *Journal of Political Economy*; he can't say that political subjects are forbidden territory for the discipline). But you'd be disappointed if you bring that expectation to Levitt and Dubner. Had they discussed the bias and hypocrisy of the neoclassical approach, they could have remained true to their Freakonomics manifesto and scored a few easy points against the failing icons of standard economic theory. Instead they fell in line with conventional thinking and its ideologically motivated limits on the reach of rational economic analysis—and they cheap-shotted Jane Fonda.

got terrorism? blame economists

et's do a little Freakonomics analysis of our own.

Obviously economists aren't mailing packages filled with explosives, aren't offering training and assistance to hate-filled zealots meeting in camps deep in Afghanistan, aren't sending support checks to al-Qaeda (or if they are, that's got nothing to do with their practice as economists). So how could economists be in any way to blame for causing terrorism?

The acknowledged expert on causation is Aristotle, whose treatment of the kinds and categories of causes has scarcely been improved upon in two millennia. He allowed that everything that has a cause has in fact four kinds of cause: material, efficient, final, and formal.

Material and efficient causes are easy to see. The suicide bomber or hijacker is the efficient cause of terrorist violence — the agent who causes it to happen — while the weapon is the material cause. Behind the particular efficient cause may be a larger system of efficient causation. To operate effectively terrorist groups need financial support — and US law will hold you liable for complicity in terrorism if you make financial contributions to any of the groups that the State Department designates as foreign terrorist organizations (FTOS). Besides money, these FTOS presumably need ground on which to organize and operate — havens where sympathetic authorities are disinclined to track them down and submit their activities to judgment before the law, or states that are "failed states" — places where the machinery of justice simply doesn't operate. Similarly, material causation can have multiple strands. If the Twin Towers had been built on a different design, they might have withstood the effects of the fire that ultimately caused their collapse.

If you want to stop terrorists, you can straightforwardly tackle both the material and the efficient causes: you can track and control dangerous explosives (and the materials that can be used to make dangerous explosives), and track and control people who have shown themselves willing (or who we think might be willing) to commit terrorist violence, and work to keep the two from coming together anywhere near a likely target. If we're to be rational about it, we weigh expected cost against expected benefit and do the work that has the biggest payoff in risk reduction. And because there's a chain of efficient causation that includes financial support and safe havens, and a chain of material causation that includes design vulnerabilities, it's reasonable to consider the costs and benefits of going after those, too.

The material and efficient causes of anything — terrorism included — explain *how* it happens. The final and formal causes begin to explain *why* it happens. These two categories of cause are being ignored in our current antiterror strategy, and pursuit of them may well be more economic: it may have a higher payoff per unit of effort than continued pursuit of efficient and material causes. To tackle them, we need to think beyond the usual borders of economic analysis; we need to think like Freakonomists — and like ecologists.

Part of the final cause of the terrorism directed against us is the imposition of expense and cost on the United States, in which we have to understand "cost" as *Freakonomics* authors Levitt and Dubner do, in terms that include considerations besides money. We would pay money to reduce risk, uncertainty, fear, and death (as we do every time we pay an insurance premium or pay for health care); therefore, the imposition on us of risk, uncertainty, fear, and death is a cost. We value our constitutional system: clearly we will sacrifice blood and treasure in order to defend and preserve it. The imposition on us of unwelcome changes to our system is thus also a cost, and terrorism succeeds when it imposes this cost on us, which it tends to do even if it fails to accomplish specific acts of terror. As Levitt and Dubner explain in *Superfreakonomics*, Richard Reid, the failed shoe bomber, may not have succeeded in igniting the explosives he smuggled onto a plane in his sneakers, but he imposed costs on us anyway. "Let's say it takes an average of one minute to remove and replace your shoes in the airport security line." Multiply by 560 million annual airplane trips in the United States alone, and that works out to 1,065 years; divide by average US life expectancy, and you get 14 lifetimes. Though he failed to kill anyone, Reid "levied a tax that is the time equivalent of 14 lives a year." Or, casting the net a bit broader, we can compare the amount of time that travelers spent in airport security four decades ago (basically, zero) to the time spent there today. If the typical traveler budgets an hour for airport security — surely an underestimate — that's sixty times what Reid alone cost us: 840 lifetimes a year. (And if you consider that most people sleep eight out of twenty-four hours, you've got to increase that number by a third, to 1,120 lifetimes.) Less easily calibrated are the psychic, social, and political costs of increased security screening — the loss in personal freedom and privacy, the clear distinction between fast-tracked business class and the complacent herd of economy class, the citizen's resolute acceptance of a process in which he or she can be nothing but a passive subject. Taken individually these burdens are small to the point of insignificance, but it's possible that they, like the minutes lost to shoe removal and replacement, cumulate into something consequential.

Increasing American security costs is clearly what al-Qaeda is aiming at. After the thwarted Federal Express attack in November 2010 (in which authorities intercepted two explosive-packed printers being shipped to addresses in the United States), al-Qaeda in the Arabian Peninsula devoted an issue of its online magazine to the attempt, proclaiming, "This supposedly 'foiled plot' will without a doubt cost America and other Western countries billions of dollars in new security measures. That is what we call leverage." They also called their attempt to use Federal Express to deliver explosives "Operation Hemorrhage," likening their strategy to "the death of a thousand cuts." In the wake of the collapse of the Twin Towers, bin Laden proclaimed that the entire operation had cost al-Qaeda $500,000 and had imposed costs on the United States of "more than $500 billion, meaning that every dollar of al Qaeda defeated a million dollars." (Bin Laden's estimate didn't include a category of "collateral costs" of 9/11 that Levitt and Dubner track down with data. In the three months after September 11, 2001, there were one thousand extra traffic deaths in the United States. Some came from increased highway usage as travelers stayed out of airports; but most of the extra deaths were on local roads, concentrated in the Northeast, and were more likely than usual to involve alcohol. "These facts, along with myriad psychological studies of terrorism's aftereffects, suggest that the September 11 attacks led to a spike in alcohol abuse and post-traumatic stress that translated into, among other things, extra driving deaths.")

When it comes to formal cause, we need to think like ecologists. In nature, life proliferates into opportunities. Wherever there is a niche — an energy opportunity, a food source — existing species colonize the niche or, through evolution, gradually adapt to make use of it. Live things produce seeds by the dozens, thousands, tens of thousands, playing the odds, trying to ensure that at least some few among them will grow and flourish and reproduce. Each seed contains assembly instructions for new life, and most also carry a bit of stored energy to give that new life a head start in the world. (The less energy the seed carries, the more of them the organism can make. Energy is a limiting factor, because it's in scarce supply: the second law, again.) Within that spray of seed is genetic variation. Because the environment that receives the seed is continually changing, in any particular springtime some of this variation will represent a desirable adaptation and some of it (including sometimes the same-old, same-old genetic coding of the previous generation) will prove maladaptive. Genetic variance, mostly the result of the mingling of genes in sexual reproduction, means that life continually presses outward, experimenting, rattling the doorknobs of possible niches, looking for opportunities to exploit.

In a common analogy, ideas are like seeds. ("Seminary" originally meant seed storehouse, and gradually came to mean a school, then a particular kind of school.) The analogy can be extended. Every culture, in every generation, produces within its population a great variety of ideas. Most are comfortably mainstream, but the bell curve has its tails: there are beyond-the-pale ideas present within every culture all the time, beliefs and policy ideas that deny conventional wisdom and assert the applicability of a differently defined truth. Most of these ideas are not successful at replicating. Their purveyors are dismissed as crackpots and cranks, and they dry up and blow away, sterile, like a maladaptive genetic variation. As with seeds, whether and how some ideas survive and replicate — whether and how they take root in the world — depends not just on the energy with which they've been sown but also on the hospitality of the larger system into which they're cast. Some times and places have a niche for them; others don't. In this view, it's likely that every generation in every culture produces someone with ideas like Hitler's or Osama bin Laden's (or, for that matter, like Dick Cheney's or John Yoo's) — you just never hear about most of them. Whether those ideas are taken seriously or not depends on whether they can be represented as successful solutions to conditions as people experience them. The politics of resentment advocated by Hitler and his Nazi Party wouldn't have made as much headway in interwar Germany if that country hadn't been suffering severe economic hardship (hyperinflation, mass unemployment, risk of starvation, and in general a high degree of material insecurity) as one result of the extremely punitive peace terms imposed on the nation at Versailles. The ensuing genocide directed against Jews and others wouldn't have become official policy if good Germans hadn't accepted the gradual demonizing of Jews, acquiescing in the scapegoating that targeted them as the cause of all of Germany's troubles. Dick Cheney's ideas about the Unitary Executive, and Yoo's justification of tactics forbidden by the Geneva Convention, wouldn't have gained nearly as much ground in the United States if the World Trade Center towers hadn't collapsed due to a diabolical assault.

The formal cause of terrorism: Osama bin Laden wouldn't have been able to recruit and inspire suicide attackers to carry out operations against the United States if the populations from which his followers are drawn did not have reasons for the large and passionate resentments they feel. Bin Laden didn't create those resentments and grievances out of nothing; he gave voice to and articulated reasons for resentments and grievances that people had already been feeling, just as Hitler did in his culture.

Besides being relevant to our hypothesis, this analysis has implications for how we pursue our campaign against terrorists. As others have noticed, as long as terrorists can succeed in imposing costs on us by failing, we fight them on lose-lose territory; there is no path to victory. (Levitt and Dubner don't take their analysis this far. They allow that shoe bomber Reid imposed costs on us, but don't follow the logic to a macroscale to question the utility of addressing only material and efficient causes of terrorism. If protecting ourselves from terrorism is a kind of overhead — part of the cost of going about our business, a cost that has to be paid out of a finite amount of income generation — how much increase in that overhead can we absorb before we start experiencing a declining standard of material and cultural well-being?)

We won't succeed in our War on Terror until and unless we can get off the lose-lose ground on which we now wage that war. One way to do that is to discover why and how this fertile niche for terrorism was created and decrease its scope. Louise Richardson, executive dean of the Radcliffe Institute for Advanced Study and a longtime student of terrorism, advocates this when she suggests a two-track strategy for dealing with terrorists. We should, she says, use good information, allies, and judiciously employed force to destroy terrorist groups, while simultaneously addressing the grievances that lead people to embrace terrorism. "Our objective should not be the completely unobtainable goal of obliterating terrorism; rather, we should pursue the more modest and attainable goal of containing terrorism recruitment and constraining resort to the tactic of terrorism." If hatred of the United States is the formal cause of terrorism, the ground on which the seed-idea of violence against the United States grows, then the most effective strategy may be to deplete the nourishment at its roots.

With this Aristotelian (and Freakonomic, and ecological) framework in mind, we can see that there are two ways to get to the conclusion that economists are at least partially responsible for terrorism. The first looks to efficient cause. Terrorism breeds in failed states; states fail for many reasons, including ecological degradation and the pressure of population on resources; and ecological degradation and pressure on resources are encouraged by neoclassical economic theory. The second looks to a combination of formal and final causes. Terrorism feeds on real and perceived grievance; globalization of market economic relations of the sort we have today gave rise to grievances in many parts of the world; neoclassical theory brought about that globalization.

Let's examine each argument and see if the hypothesis holds up.

Does terrorism breed in failed states? Quite a few authoritative observers think so. Condoleezza Rice, speaking as secretary of state in 2005, declared, "The greatest threats to our security are defined more by dynamics within weak and failing states than by . . . strong and aggressive ones." The *National Intelligence Strategy of the United States* of that same year says failed states are "breeding grounds for international instability, violence, and misery." The us National Intelligence Council made clear just what kind of violence and instability that included: failed states "can become sanctuaries for transnational terrorists like al-Qaeda." That's a conclusion shared by John Yoo, who served in the Department of Justice's Office of Legal Counsel under George W. Bush (and who authored the notorious memos justifying "enhanced interrogation techniques" — torture — of prisoners of war captured in Afghanistan): "Failed states become anarchic areas where terrorists can build resources, train operatives, and create bases from which to launch attacks." The World Bank, too, agrees.

The idea that failed states breed terrorism is part of the conventional wisdom — at least, among members of the administration of George W. Bush, and within the National Security bureaucracy that his administration politicized, and at the World Bank, headed by his appointee. The idea does have intuitive appeal: outlaws need a hideout somewhere outside the law. But intuition has led many a thinker astray, and like good Freakonomists we shouldn't accept conventional wisdom just because it's widely shared or intuitively appealing. The Freakonomist has got to check the data.

The first problem you face if you want to check for a correlation between failed states and terrorism is, of course, definitional: what counts as state failure, and what counts as terrorism? Experts have been having at those questions for more than a decade. One clear assessment of failed states comes from a nonpartisan think tank called the Fund for Peace, which, in cooperation with *Foreign Policy* magazine, has compiled an annual Failed State Index since 2004. It uses indicators in twelve different categories to rank nations on a scale of failure from one to ten, with ten the worst. Its rankings are taken seriously by the world; Kenyan officials recently expressed pride that their country's ranking in the index had improved and dismay that it hadn't improved further. The twelve categories remind us that if we're going to create indicators of sustainable, delivered well-being that encompass the benefits of social and natural as well as economic capital, and we want those indicators to be broadly applicable throughout the world, then we need to look beyond the experience of secure and developed countries and make sure we also measure some basics that developed nations may tend to take for granted. The twelve categories:

1 Demographic pressures, including high population density relative to food supply and other life-sustaining resources
2 Movement of refugees and internally displaced people, creating complex humanitarian emergencies

3 A legacy of vengeance-seeking group grievance or group paranoia
4 "Human flight," meaning brain-drain and emigration by
   entrepreneurs, artists, and the professional classes
5 Uneven economic development, with the benefits of development
   being distributed along group lines
6 Sharp or severe economic decline
7 Corruption and other factors (like boycotted elections) that erode
   the legitimacy of the state
8 Deterioration in public services
9 Suspension or arbitrary and politicized application of the rule of
   law, including widespread violation of human rights
10 A security apparatus — secret police, or militias or factions in the
   armed forces — that operates as a "state within a state"
11 Elites that are factionalized along group lines, often with nationalist
   sloganeering directed against a scapegoated "other"
12 Intervention in the internal affairs of the state by outside powers

It's a comprehensive list. Using it, the Fund for Peace ranks the
world's 177 recognized nations according to their index score, from
"most failed" to "least failed." In 2010 the winner was Norway, 177th in
the failed state rankings, with a combined score of just 18.3 (12 would be
perfect). At the top of the list stood the definitively failed state of Somalia, with a total score of 114.7 out of a possible 120. (The United States
came in 159th — eighteenth from the bottom — with a score of 34.0, edg-
ing out the United Kingdom, Germany, and France at 35.3, but behind
Japan at 31.2. None of these five highly developed nations made it into
the exclusive company of the 20-somethings — nations that scored in
the 20s or lower — that were listed as "sustainable." That group takes in
all of Scandinavia; Canada; Iceland; Austria; Switzerland and Luxem-
bourg; the Netherlands and Ireland; and Australia and New Zealand.)
    The Failed State Index captures the idea that there is no single cause
of state failure, even as the data show variation but consistency across
the twelve categories. States that scored a 9 or higher in one or more
categories rarely scored lower than 7 in any of the other categories. This
makes sense, because clearly conditions that affect the score in one category also affect the scores in others. Marauding militias (one of the
elements in category 10) that systematically violate human rights (cat-

egory 9) would lead some citizens to emigrate (category 4). Group grievance (category 3) might lead to boycotts of elections (category 7), as
happened in Iraq in the first election held after the US invasion. While
we can analytically distinguish different facets of state failure, in practice there are connections and correlations between them, though the
index doesn't sort these out. (And this means there's a niche open to
an enterprising political scientist, who might use the index to come to
interesting conclusions about what influences what, or at least what
covaries with what.) We can use the data to look for an answer to our
question: do failed states breed terrorism?

To do that, we still need a definition of terrorism — and some data
about it. The definitive data set on terrorism worldwide has been compiled by the National Consortium for the Study of Terrorism and Responses to Terrorism (whose lengthy title was no doubt directed at
producing the acronym NC-START). Their Global Terrorism Database,
funded in part by the US Department of Homeland Security, was built
at the University of Maryland by a team of specialists in and out of the
academy. In order to be counted as an act of terror in the database, an
"incident" has to meet these criteria: it has got to be intentional, something willfully done by perpetrators; it has got to entail violence or the
threat of violence, against civilians or property; and the perpetrators
must not be agents of a national government (which would make their
violence an act of war, not terror). Since 1997, an act of violence has been
coded into the database as terrorism only if it meets two out of an additional three criteria: it was aimed at attaining a political, religious, or
social (but not economic) end; it offers evidence of an intent to coerce,
intimidate, or send a message to an audience beyond the immediate
victims; and it falls outside "the precepts of International Humanitarian Law," that is, if it were an act of war it would violate the Geneva
Convention.

So: we've got data on state failure, and data on terrorism. It should be
a simple matter to compare the two, testing whether the conventional
wisdom — that failed states breed terrorism — is correct. Unfortunately,
it's not that simple. The 87,000-plus incidents logged into the database
have been tagged with a variety of searchable labels and variables (including country, region, perpetrator) but not with the one that our hypothesis would find most useful: country of origin of the perpetrator.

And even that tag wouldn't capture all of what we want: it's possible that a terrorist whose life experience (and desire to commit terrorism) was shaped by residence in a failed state became an immigrant and resided somewhere else before the attack was launched. It's also possible for terrorist acts to be committed by citizens-in-good-standing of a relatively less failed state acting in sympathy with or directly on behalf of a cause that has its genesis, or strong support, in a failed state. (To put it in Aristotelian terms: it's possible that state failure is not just a potential efficient cause of terrorism, but a potential formal cause as well.)

One researcher who tested the assertion "Failed states breed terrorism" by using this database found no strong correlation because terrorism happens not just in failed states but in other places, too. Well, that's no surprise: if one of the goals of terrorist violence is to delegitimize or force behavioral changes on the government of the citizens it attacks, an attack on citizens of failed states for those reasons is redundant or futile; the legitimate authority is already dissolving and incapacitated. But the hypothesis (and conventional wisdom) we're testing here says that failed states breed terrorism, not that failed states breed terrorism directed against people in failed states. Terrorism could be fostered by state failure even when its targets are Western industrial democracies, or those who are seen as collaborating with them. Indeed, since Western democracies are frequently terrorism's targets, the assumption that terrorism is caused by something in the nation where it happens leads to a conclusion that's a reductio ad absurdum of the argument that produced it: "The more democracy, the more terrorism."

But even this study, which tried to discount the conventional wisdom that failed states breed terrorism, had to admit that "it would be an exaggeration to say that failed states never facilitate terrorism." There are clear instances in which terrorist organizations have benefited by making themselves at home in failed states — and that correlation was reason enough for the Bush administration to identify failed states as the key causative factor in world terrorism.

To summarize: we can't be certain that there's a firm causal connection between the existence of failed states and terrorism, because the studies that have looked for it have gone about it the wrong way. The thesis is not disproved; hypotheses that might test it have not been pursued, and the best data we have don't admit this kind of exploration.

Nevertheless, researchers investigating the link report that the thesis has some empirical support.

The next step in this thread—one of two by which we could find economists to be a contributing factor in the existence of terrorism in the world—is the step that connects ecological degradation to state failure. Here the results are considerably clearer. The first category of factors measured by the Failed State Index is "demographic pressures"—including "high population densities relative to food supply and other life-sustaining resources," like water and other necessities that come to us as ecosystem services. Ecological degradation registers in this category, and we would expect it to play a contributing role in other categories as well—ecosystem degradation creates refugees, leads to human flight, and can play out as a group grievance (as Jared Diamond, in *Collapse*, asserts that it did in Rwanda). It also leads to economic decline, with a consequent effect on the ability of a government to collect revenues to support public services. Scarcity of resources leads to scarcity of goods, including staples, and that scarcity can lead to black markets, corrupt systems of distribution, the rise of alternative (and armed) authority systems, and so on. How to check for a correlation in this confusion of possible connection?

One way is to look for relationships between ecological degradation by region and the incidence of failed states in the region. If ecosystem degradation leads to state failure, then we'd expect the Failed State Index number to be high for states that are in ecologically degraded regions. And there is indeed a correlation. The UN Millennium Assessment Report identified sub-Saharan Africa as a region particularly vulnerable to climate change because its ecosystems are degraded and lack resilience. Most of the states in that region scored 90-plus on the Failed State Index, putting them in the red zone—failed state.

Another way to test our premise is to check whether states with a high score in the first category, "demographic pressures," have failed or are among those states most at risk of failure. Here too there is a strong correlation. The 2010 index counts thirty-eight states as failed, which means their average score across all twelve categories was 7.5 or higher. If there were no correlation between ecological degradation and state failure, we would expect half of the thirty-eight to score above that average in this category and half to score below it. But of the thirty-eight failed states, only three scored below 7.5 in the first category; thirty-three scored 8 or higher, and fourteen scored 9 or higher. At the other end, among nations ranked as having a "moderate" risk of failing or as "sustainable," only one nation scores a six or higher in this category (Panama, moderately at risk, with a 6.6). Among the rest, the average score in this category was below 3.5. Within the data, then, the first category's measure of ecological degradation and the pressure of population on resources is a very good predictor of overall score on the index.

Thus, if the scoring that lies behind the Failed State Index is accurate, it's safe to conclude that ecosystem degradation and pressure on resources is a major determinant of whether and to what extent states fail. Given, then, that policies rooted in a faith in infinite economic growth lead to ecological degradation (a point I've argued elsewhere in this volume), then it's fair to say that neoclassical economists share in the responsibility for the incidence of failed states in the world. Whether this then leads to the conclusion that neoclassical economics is a contributory cause of terrorism depends on whether failed states breed terrorism, which isn't so clear. At the least we can say that if you want to believe that the Bush administration's campaign to turn failed states into democracies is an appropriate strategy in the war on terror, you've also got to hold economists responsible for terrorism.

The second argument linking neoclassical economics to the production of terrorism in the world looks beyond failed states as part of the chain of efficient causation to examine formal and final causes — to terrorist motivation and the factors that produce the discontents that are the fertile ground on which terrorism breeds. If terrorism is rooted in grievances that spring from the globalization of market relations, and if the grieved harms were not accidental creations of globalization but were generated through a by-the-book application of neoclassical economic theory, then neoclassical economists share responsibility for terrorism.

That the Arab and Muslim world is much aggrieved with the United States and its policies is beyond doubt. In an annual survey of public opinion in five Arab countries, Shibley Telhami found in 2008 that a remarkable 88 percent of all respondents named the United States as one of the "two countries that you think pose the biggest threat to you." This is the ground on which bin Laden cast the seed of his call for terrorist vengeance. Fourteen percent of respondents in Telhami's survey said that Osama bin Laden was the world leader outside their own country that they admired the most, and another 8 percent picked him second. This 22 percent of the Arab population is nowhere near a majority, but acts of terror aren't produced by majority vote. What terrorist organizations need is a small supply of avid recruits, and 22 percent of the population is a very large pool from which to draw.

The attitudes, beliefs, and orientations of many of the remaining 78 percent of the Arab population also play a role in supporting terrorism. John Horgan, who directs Pennsylvania State University's International Center for the Study of Terrorism, has interviewed around sixty former terrorists in an effort to understand why and how individuals are recruited, are radicalized, and become open to using violence against civilians. Among the factors: having friends or family who are sympathetic to the cause, even if those friends and family members specifically reject the methods chosen. Many of the 78 percent of Arabs who don't rank bin Laden highly as a world leader no doubt do so because they expressly reject his methods, even as they approve of his efforts to reduce US presence and influence in the Middle East. With 88 percent of Arabs marking the United States as one of the two countries by which they feel most threatened, there's plenty of sympathy in the Arab world for the ends al-Qaeda pursues.

But are the grievances that Arabs feel attributable to neoclassical economic theory? Some are and some aren't. Among the grievances that aren't a result of neoclassical economic theory are US support for Israel, which in Arab and Muslim nations is widely perceived as systematically violating the basic human rights of Palestinians. Others: US intervention into the affairs of Middle Eastern nations, and the quartering of "infidel" US troops in Saudi Arabia, which many fundamentalist Muslims see as profanation, since that country is home to the holiest sites in Islam. Rhetoric about a world-historic "clash of civilizations" and a "crusade" to make Arab nations over in the image of Western democracy hasn't helped, either. (But if Hayek is right about the connection between free markets and democracy, then the effort to make Arab nations over into democracies does have a root in neoclassical economic theory.) Also telling: the pain and suffering inflicted by the US-led economic boycott of Saddam Hussein's Iraq, in which half a million children died from lack of medicine and other causes that could have been alleviated by trade. When Leslie Stahl asked Secretary of State Madeline Albright about this in a 1996 interview, Albright gave a chilling answer that was widely reported in Arab countries: "We think the price is worth it." (For many Americans, policies pursued in the 1990s are ancient history, too remote to influence thought and feeling today. But the American presumption that what's past is past and unimportant is not widely shared in the Arab world. They remember the embargo on trade with Iraq, and to many it stands as a clear example of America's callous disregard for the lives of innocents.) To many in the Arab and Muslim world, US policy looks to be a coherent campaign of abuse, victimization, and disrespect.

Other sources of Arab grievance are rooted in neoclassical economic theory, though of course neoclassical economists would deny this. Globalization — the integration of national economies into a single world economy operating on the principles of free trade offered by neoclassical economics — is supposed to make everyone better off; there's no room in the theory for harms and resentments. The basic justification for globalized free trade is that if nations concentrate on producing the things they are most efficient at producing, and trade for everything else, everyone in the system can enjoy more of everything — and more of everything is the *summum bonum* of economic life as the neoclassical model defines it. Everyone should be happy with the additional consumption that globalized trade makes possible. And if the consumption isn't distributed equitably enough to make everyone happy, well, that's just a matter of time. Through its Kuznets Curve the neoclassical model reassures the world that income inequality in developing nations increases at first but then moderates and declines. And if the increased consumption has costs in environmental degradation, the Environmental Kuznets Curve reassures everyone that time, and more growth and development, will take care of that, too. Neoclassical theory suggests that if residents of developing countries feel aggrieved by income inequality or environmental degradation, they're being impatient or just don't understand the theory well enough. But as we've seen, the Environmental Kuznets Curve is not a valid representation of the relationship between development and environmental degradation, and some of the same criticisms that apply to the EKC apply to the Kuznets Curve as well.

Income inequality and environmental damage are not the only results of globalization that give rise to grievances. When two countries trade because trade will leave both countries with more material goods, there's nothing in neoclassical theory that says both partners have to benefit equally. The exact terms of that trade—how much of one thing is given up for an increase of something else—are determined by extraeconomic considerations like the relative strength of the two economies, the degree of dependency one partner has on the other, even the implicit or explicit threat of punishment—up to and including war—if the trade isn't consummated favorably to nation that is economically or militarily more powerful. Trade can create international inequalities in income distribution—inequalities that do not automatically disappear with additional trade (although, true to the spirit of the Kuznets Curve, neoclassical theory suggests that they eventually will). While free-trade theorists in the United States see the United States as having brought the benefits of trade to underdeveloped countries worldwide, some residents of those countries see the United States as having used its overweening economic and political power to secure terms of trade that unjustly favor its interests and corporations, consigning the developing country to serve as a source of extraction and a sink for the absorption of waste. When a developing nation does on occasion break out of the source-and-sink ghetto to develop a consumer-oriented economy, not all of its citizens welcome that as a benefit. Some elements of Western consumer culture are inconsistent with the habits, mores, traditions, and folkways of the countries being invited (or coerced) to join it, and wholesale revision of those elements of culture is a cost that some members of those societies think is too high a cost to pay. To them, globalization offers some forms of material wealth that they don't particularly want. There's not much of a market for alcohol, pornography, or miniskirts in Saudi Arabia; the cost in cultural change is a cost they've decided they don't want to pay.

To the neoclassical economist, rejection of globalization can be explained only as the selfish response of narrow segments of the population who are seeking to protect their own interests. As one introductory text puts it: if "everyone can enjoy more goods and services [when] nations specialize in those products in which they have a comparative advantage," then "why do politicians so often resist free trade and 'globalization'?" The reason — the only reason offered — is that "although free trade benefits the economy as a whole, specific groups may not benefit," and those groups exert influence on the politicians who represent them. This view is ideologically biased, myopic, and Eurocentric.

The ideological bias is evident in the way workers worried about losing jobs are defined as a "special interest," while the factory owner who seeks liberalization of trade laws so production can be moved to wherever costs are lower is not. (This is consistent with the reassignation of the term "special interest" that Ronald Reagan offered in the 1980s: in his accounting, special interests include abortion rights activists [but not anti-choice activists], feminists, minorities, the ACLU, the NAACP, public interest research groups, and others of a generally progressive bent.) This corporate-centric view of productive life is not widely shared outside Westernized nations that accept neoclassical free-market theory.

Nor does neoclassical trade theory look beyond increased efficiency in the production of goods and services to examine the ecological, cultural, and political externalities that come with trade. One political externality is increased dependence. Smaller national economies that specialize in goods for export become dependent on their trade relations, and that dependence undercuts the ability of those nations to chart their own course — in world and even domestic affairs. It's reasonable for a small nation to restrict the integration of its economy into a global free-trade regime in order to preserve some degree of economic and hence political independence. A key feature of representative democracy is that citizens feel that they have some say in making the decisions that affect their collective lives, and their national government is one instrument by which they gain, or fail to gain, that sense of effective participation. If integration of their economy into a global system restricts the range of policy options available to their elected representatives, then major decisions that affect the society are made elsewhere, reducing the scope of national sovereignty and, with it, the efficacy of the country's democracy. Under these conditions, preserving democracy requires resisting globalization. Because the neoclassical model slices politics and economics apart so completely (except when it doesn't, à la Hayek and Friedman), it can't make this connection — and can't understand the perspective of those who do.

One analysis that makes these connections is offered by Fathali Moghaddam, of Georgetown University's Department of Psychology, in the provocatively titled *How Globalization Spurs Terrorism: The Lopsided Benefits of One World and Why That Fuels Violence*. Moghaddam argues that rapid globalization has forced disparate cultures into contact with one another and is threatening the domination or disappearance of some groups whose way of life is undercut by consumerist values. Fundamentalist Muslims place higher value on religious observance than on material consumption, a choice they ought to be free to make; some of them fear losing that choice as their nations are drawn into Western orbit. "You can interpret Islamic terrorism as one form of reaction to the perception that the fundamentalist way of life is under attack and is about to become extinct." The neoclassical model has no theoretical grounds on which to appreciate an individual's attachment — sometimes passionate attachment — to his or her religion and culture, and no theoretical grounds on which to see how economic life affects that attachment.

Clearly, al-Qaeda does not accept the logic of the standard neoclassical model. Equally clearly, their rejection of it is part of the organization's appeal for many citizens in Arab countries and for other Muslims around the world. Bin Laden called for Muslim societies to reject trade and become more self-sufficient economically. He also advocated a halt to shipment of oil to the West, urging oil-bearing Muslim nations instead to preserve oil as "a great and important economic power for the coming Islamic state" — a policy goal that finds no theoretical support in neoclassical theory, where all of humanity is presumed to want to enjoy citizenship in the Republic of Consumption.

Bin Laden's program (and more generally many of the resentments that his program articulated) makes no sense within the neoclassical model. To the neoclassical economist, the cultural losses, social dislocation, and ecological degradation brought by the development of a market-based consumer society are not just a small price to pay, but are not counted as costs at all — and in any event they will, the theory says, soon disappear. They'd disappear all the sooner if people whose values and way of life have been adversely affected by globalization would simply accept neoclassical economic theory and switch allegiance from their existing culture to the one offered by market-based consumer society.

There's a word for people who think that fundamental disagreement over values can be solved by getting everyone to accept the values that they themselves hold. We call these people *zealots*. It should not be surprising that zealotry is met by zealotry.

Partisans of free-market globalization can indeed point to impressive data to show that in the industrial era, as trade has increased, many of the markers of global well-being have improved: longevity, per capita production, and literacy rates (in most places) have increased; deaths by disease and infant and maternal mortality have decreased; and so on. Trends like these were what led Julian Simon to assert—incorrectly, as we saw—that with economic growth and increasing integration of national economies into a global system of (relatively) free trade, "every measure of material and environmental welfare in the United States and in the world has improved rather than deteriorated." The standard litany of development successes is impressive, but it doesn't take into account the full cost of that development in terms of loss of services from the kinds of capital—social, ecological, cultural—that the neoclassical model has never valued. In an exact parallel to how economic theory on Garden Planet could take ecosystem serves for granted because they were so plentiful as to seem infinite, it also took for granted the benefits that people derive from the social and cultural systems in which any economy—developed, developing, traditional, even hunter-and-gatherer—is grounded.

Because the grievances on which terrorism feeds are rooted in part in the loss of social and cultural capital in societies that are drawn into the Western consumerist orbit, and because the neoclassical model took those forms of capital for granted and didn't value them at all, it's fair to say that neoclassical economists contributed, through oversight, to the development of terrorism.

Of course terrorism has no single cause, and nothing I've said here is meant to deny that. Nor do I excuse terrorists from culpability for their acts. Good Freakonomists know that to understand or explain an act is not to excuse or sympathize with it. If we're to "think . . . sensibly about how people behave in the real world," including understanding how people "choose someone to . . . hate and even kill," we've got to look beneath apparently irrational behavior and find the implicit rationality within it. When we do that, we discover that neoclassical economic theory is implicated for having contributed to the grievances and resentments that motivate rejection, sometimes violent rejection, of Western values. And because neoclassical economic theory also produces the ecological degradation that is one main cause of failed states, we're justified in concluding that neoclassical economic theory contributes to both the formal and final causes of terrorism. As good Freakonomists we have to say: Got terrorism? Blame economists.

ending the culture war

emember the culture wars? The term has lost currency, but the thing it labeled, a deep division in the American polity, is definitely still with us. And the phenomenon is global: world economic integration has brought increased contact and conflict between national and supranational cultures and, with it, fundamental conflicts over values and vision. Even without the pressure of globalization there has always been plenty of opportunity for friction and ill-will between cultures. Historic wrongs—some of them dating back centuries, even half-millennia—are kept alive in memory as sorrow-and-vengeance tales that justify animosity and retaliatory and preemptive aggression. Often those tales are built from a common stock: Turks and Armenians, Kurds and Iraqis, Palestinians and Israelis see the shared events of their joint histories through dramatically different lenses. In some cases the difference in historical understanding is mostly symptomatic of other conflict, rather than part of its progenitive cause, but wherever two cultures come into conflict the interpretation of history soon emerges as a central ground on which the conflict finds expression. Irreconcilable difference expressed in historical understanding makes political compromise and accommodation more difficult. To find a ground on which groups with apparently irreconcilable cultural differences could meet and agree would be a useful thing, in the United States and in the world.

The roots of our domestic culture war can be traced as far back as you'd care to trace them. One strong root lies in the decade of the 1960s, which brought polarization over habits of dress, taste in music, patterns of life choices, attitudes toward politics and authority—and over such substantial matters as voting and other civil rights for African Americans, the means and ends of American foreign policy in Vietnam and elsewhere, and, on into the 1970s and 1980s, the role and status of women. The 1960s, in turn, were shaped by the rejection of material consumerist culture articulated by the Beats in the 1950s, who were in turn influenced by an American romantic tradition, reaching back to Emerson and Thoreau, that rejected the increasing commercialization of culture and the industrialization of the landscape. The battles over civil rights for African Americans trace back to Jim Crow segregation laws, and behind them to Reconstruction and the Civil War before it, and from there back to the American Constitutional Convention of 1787 and the infamous Three-Fifths Compromise — the moment that determined just how much representation the "slavocracy" (as John Adams called it) would have in the new federal government. Behind that compromise lay the inherent divergence of interests between two different kinds of economies: in the South the soils and climate and heritage were favorable to plantation-scale agriculture, in which slavery was economically "efficient"; in the North, rocky soils gave rise to smaller freehold farms on which slavery was impractical, and widespread hydropower brought greater diversity in manufacturing and trade.

The phrase "culture war" seems to have been invented by Pat Buchanan, the conservative columnist and commentator who has been a sometime presidential candidate and former adviser to Presidents Nixon, Ford, and Reagan. Speaking at the Republican National Convention in 1992, he offered a call to arms that would have registered to the country's discredit on the Failed State Index (under "factionalized elites offering nationalist sloganeering") had the index been compiled back then. "There is a religious war going on in our country," he warned. "It is a cultural war, as critical to the kind of nation we will one day be as was the Cold War itself." Buchanan was describing the competition between interests that is politics-as-usual in a democracy; but to that ferment he brought a narrow, uncompromising, absolutist, essentially moral vision, which led him to see political and ideological difference as a religious war in which no true patriot could refuse to serve — or accept compromise with the enemy. "And in that struggle for the soul of America, Clinton & Clinton are on the other side, and George Bush is on our side." Certainly Buchanan knew that as a matter of duly ordained electoral procedure, George Bush was in fact running against Bill Clinton and Al Gore. His casting of the enemy as "Clinton & Clinton" traded on the deep and passionate antipathy many conservatives felt toward Hillary Clinton, who personified the changed role and larger ambitions of women that had been made possible by the feminist movement. The elder Bush had been a navy pilot in World War II; William Jefferson Clinton was a baby boomer, born after the war, who came of age in the 1960s. (During the campaign it came out that he'd been seen with a joint to his lips at a party when he was a Rhodes Scholar in England. "I didn't inhale" was his much-derided response.) The election that Buchanan styled as a jihad was a contest between candidates from generations with markedly different cultural values.

Having been called to action, conservatives responded. In 1994 a strong salvo was fired by Lynne Cheney, former chair of the National Endowment for the Humanities, who launched a preemptive strike against a set of as-yet-unpublished standards for the teaching of history in America's schools. In an op-ed piece in the *Wall Street Journal* titled "The End of History," she attacked the work of a group of professional historians who had produced new guidelines for the teaching of American history. That work had been organized by the National Center for History in the Schools at the University of California, under the guidance of the National Council for History Standards (NCHS), a nongovernmental advisory group drawn from various organizations of professional historians practicing at the university and secondary school levels. Their efforts were, by the account of many participants, a model of an open, consensus-building process. The project was initiated by the Department of Education, responding to a diagnosis offered in its widely distributed report *A Nation at Risk*, which was produced under Reagan and published in 1983. The standards were developed with funding from Cheney's own National Endowment for the Humanities and the US Department of Education. They were completely voluntary: no law dictated their adoption.

Cheney's attack began with inflammatory misrepresentation. "Imagine an outline for the teaching of American history," she wrote, "in which George Washington makes only a fleeting appearance and is never described as our first president." She continued in that vein, listing supposed omissions and ignoring an essential distinction: standards for producing and delivering curricula are not the curricula themselves. (One might as well rail against the screw-pitch standards and testing criteria set by the American Society of Engineers for not being shiny and made out of metal.) The Constitution is dealt with extensively in the NCHS document; she claimed that it wasn't, but allowed that "it does come up in the 250 pages of supporting materials"—which were, in fact, the standards themselves; she seems to have mistaken the executive summary for the whole. Rush Limbaugh dramatized these invented omissions on his radio show, giving his listeners the sound of tearing and crumpling pages, as from a history book, saying, "Here's Paul Revere. He's gone. Here's George Washington as president . . ."

That the battle was joined over the teaching of history is no accident. The story of who we have been is necessarily the story of who we are and what we value. Cheney's account of the standards was inflammatory and inaccurate, but beneath the demagoguery, misrepresentation, and fallacious reasoning was the kernel of a fundamental truth: history matters, and in America (if, perhaps, not so much among the hundreds of teachers of American history who participated in developing the standards) there are clear cultural differences over how history should be taught. The stories we tell ourselves about how we got where we are today tell us who we are; like national politics itself, "[national] history . . . is about national identity," as one group of historians put it— and Americans have often had dramatically different ideas about who and what we are as a nation.

To the conservatives who rallied against the new standards, the question "Whose vision of history will we teach our children?" became a different one: would we let a select group of academics who had "bullied their way into power positions," and who "worked in secret," teach our kids that "our country is inherently evil"? Would we offer what Cheney characterized as a "grim and gloomy" portrait of the country by including in American history stories about McCarthyism, the Ku Klux Klan, lynchings, smallpox blankets and other genocidal practices against Native Americans? Or would we hold up before the next generation of Americans a sanitized narrative of progress, a call to sustain (and perhaps extend) the noble ideals on which the country was founded?

The hundreds of historians who worked on the project were surprised to learn that they had bullied their way into power and worked in secret and that the curriculum guidelines and pedagogic practices they hammered out amounted to a claim that America is Evil. The question they had taken up was a bit more complex: how can we communicate to students that history is not a settled matter—not simply factual, not simply "what happened," as Limbaugh, in a fit of know-nothingism, told his audience—but the product of an ongoing intellectual effort, a continual reexamination of the past, in which we need to be aware of how the concerns of the day invariably shape the questions and interest we bring to it?

Conservatives rallied around a denunciation of "multiculturalism," the idea that distinct subcultures and groups within America have distinctive points of view on many of the events, dynamics, personages, and stories of American history. Since the 1960s, decades of scholarship had proliferated these alternative lenses on the subject matter of American history. To ignore them in the production of standards for teaching students would have been professional malfeasance; and, on the contrary, to present those alternative interpretations accurately in classrooms promised to engage students in critical thinking—the evaluation of arguments, of evidence, of modes of interpretation—and would have the considerable political benefit of requiring the future citizens of our country to become not just consumers but producers of their own historical understanding. Under the advisory standards, students were to be challenged with historical questions ("Was the atomic bomb used to shorten the war? Or was it done for political reasons?"), given arguments and primary documents from both sides, and be encouraged to make up their own minds.

But for Cheney and neoconservative commentators like Rush Limbaugh, this approach promised a dangerous, nation-threatening loss. As they saw it, history is the nursemaid to citizenship. If American citizens weren't to be taught a particular and laudatory metanarrative about their history—the story of American exceptionalism with its heroic sweep of ambition, statesmanship, and accomplishment—much mischief would ensue. For conservatives, the traditional narrative is a necessary foundation of American political life.

History is in great part an art, not a science. (Indeed, Thomas Kuhn has shown us that science, too, is in some part an art.) In history as in all the other arts, there are standards of excellence that can be learned, and the national standards sought to codify them. Good practice in history, as in scientific understanding, requires sifting evidence, judging sources, thinking clearly and logically, forming hypotheses and testing them against evidence that can be found and brought to bear—exactly the intellectual skills required for effective participation in civic decision making, even the minimal participation of simply voting once in a while. Seen this way, historical education is indeed the crucible of democracy—not because this or that particular interpretation of a nation's history is necessary to legitimize its institutions, but because a critical and informed citizenry, capable of thinking clearly about political matters, is necessary to its practice and preservation.

Ultimately the controversy was resolved, as political struggles often are, through compromise. Committees were formed, and some parts of the guidelines were revised to make explicit what had been taken to be implicit—the inclusion of much of the standard presidents-and-battles content. Since the conservative position was styled as a moral rather than political position—Cheney et al. wanted complete purity in the return to a monocultural history teaching of yore—the compromise looked like a victory for the multiculturalists. "At all levels of education," said cultural historian Todd Gitlin in 1998, "the traditional story of steady progress in American history has been shattered by stories of the battles fought by women, Native Americans, and members of other disadvantaged groups. Non-Western history has a more-honored place alongside Western civilization."

But what if the conservatives had a point? What if, in the absence of any other strong unifying force (shared fealty to a king, say, or faith in a common God, or widely shared hatred of some scapegoated other), by default a shared narrative of national history becomes the crucible of national identity? If we fragment our history into a set of competing and contradictory histories based on ethnic, class, gender, religious, and racial categories, we risk undercutting the core of shared vision and values that is necessary to the functioning of our system, or any other.

At bottom, American conservatives don't fully accept this reasoning. They reveal themselves to be perfectly willing to revise history in ways that undercut a core of shared vision and values when it suits their ideological agenda. An example: In one of the longest-running controversies in American historiography, some southern conservatives see the American Civil War in terms that many other Americans—northerners and African Americans among them—find inaccurate to the point of being offensive. Among some southern conservatives, the Civil War is "the War of Northern Aggression," a war that valiant Southerners fought defensively against an oppressive central government that wanted to constrain the freedoms they enjoyed. Celebrations of the start of the Civil War in Virginia and South Carolina have drawn strong criticism for leaving out what is taken by many to be a crucial fact: the main freedom that seceding states sought to preserve was nothing more noble than the freedom to hold African Americans as slaves. The first shots fired in the so-called War of Northern Aggression were fired by southerners, as Rebel forces shelled the federal fort in Charleston, committing violent treason against the us government. Those are the facts on which national unity must be built, a unity that includes African Americans and the descendants of those men who left their towns and families all throughout the northern states, offering their lives to preserve the Union and help abolish slavery. A large proportion of southerners have always dissented from that interpretation, and lately conservative politicians have felt freer to model and mirror that dissent in public. To date, no strong conservative voice has taken up the Limbaugh-Cheney case against this practice.

But even if conservatives did offer their argument for traditional history honestly and consistently, it has a fatal flaw: it's blind to the true foundation of American exceptionalism. It fails to represent or even to accommodate the beautiful, bold, noble premise that underlies the American founding. What holds the American polity together isn't a language, an ethnic identity, a common religion, or a common narrative, but a Constitution — an unprecedented, purposeful act of self-definition that is at once a document, a plan for government, and an embodiment of fundamental principles that give a particular sort of answer to the questions that underlie any political and social system. America is founded on, and derives its necessary unity from, a shared commitment to the abstraction of process, to the meta-objectivity of political forms explicitly designed on the understanding that a free and diverse people will worship and think and behave — and even interpret their own history — in ways that confound any expectation of permanent consensus. Our Constitution and its Bill of Rights are epistemologically ecumenical: no single worldview or point of view is given pride of place there. The "machine that would go of itself" doesn't try to define civic Truth. Instead, it defines the processes by which that truth is found — and by which it changes.

Unfortunately, appreciation of the value of this bootstrapping out of particular subjectivities and into the objectivity of process is demonstrably weak, not merely among neoconservative politicians and media figures, but among the American populace in general. The self-centered ethos of a consumer society built on market relations — the idea that "greed is good," as the Reagan-era slogan puts it — is in tension with, and has tended to corrode, the civic capital on which our system relies. That civic capital includes an ability to empathize with others unlike ourselves, others with whom we disagree. At a basic level, the machinery of our constitutional freedoms can be derived from nothing more complicated than the systematic application of the Golden Rule to political affairs: What safeguards would I like in place if I were arrested? How would I like others to treat me if I were a member of a minority religion or ethnic group? What rights to speak and live freely would I want if I held an unpopular opinion or had private predilections that differed from those of most people? Empathy, and the quality of imagination from which empathy derives, is necessary for the maintenance of our system of rights. But after three decades of "greed is good" culture, which teaches that empathy is neither politically relevant nor civically necessary, many Americans seem incapable of mustering it in anything like the amount necessary to support civil liberties. The majority of Americans seem all too willing to trade away civil liberties and the integrity of political institutions when doing so promises to bring momentary advantage: success in campaigning or policy making, the silencing of opponents in public discourse, safety from internal and external foes who can be portrayed as a threat. A few decades of historical education under the new standards might begin to rectify this, for then a system whose civil liberties and participatory processes depend on civic empathy would have a citizenry trained up under an approach to historical understanding that encourages its development.

But the conservative argument against the new standards may have another valid point. Complex matters are best learned and retained through assimilation to overarching cognitive structures — theories or metanarratives. It's hard work to sift the welter of detail and evidence and come to nuanced understandings about history without them; the mind craves economy of effort and naturally turns to an overarching story as a way to bring order to experience. Multicultural history that does justice to different points of view runs the risk of being retained as a simple metanarrative about the perpetration of injustice—what Cheney characterized as a "gloom and doom" vision of America.

So we are led to a conclusion that seems to support the conservative position: If our divisive, interest-group-competing constitutional system requires a shared consensual mythos to hold it together against the divisive forces of religion, regional difference, ethnic diversity, competitive self-interest, and difference of moral opinion; if an Enlightenment-era commitment to shared processes—a kind of metanarrative—is too abstract to serve as that consensual mythos; and if students will take the disparate, multivoiced materials of multicultural history and turn them into a single-voiced metanarrative anyway; then perhaps we do need a single, world-ordering metanarrative to serve as the foundation of our polity.

The problem: after what Gitlin calls "the great compromise of 1996," there is no single, authoritative interpretation of American history embedded in the national standards as issued. And, says Gitlin, "we are likely to live without a new, overarching narrative for quite some time to come."

But there is a candidate for a shared, overarching narrative that would fill the bill satisfactorily, and the time for recognizing it has long since arrived.

If today is a typical day in the recent history of the planet, it will see the discharge of more than 15 million tons of carbon into the atmosphere, adding to the burden that causes current and future climate change. One hundred and fifteen square miles of rainforest will be destroyed, with consequent effects on local and global weather patterns. Seventy-two square miles of desert will be created, substantially changing the ability of the planet to feed and support us. Forty to one hundred species will disappear, and 250,000 humans will be born. The rates at which these changes are being wrought have varied, and the particular numbers are estimates; but the damage these numbers measure—the damage we are doing to the planet's ability to support human civilization—is real, factual, and incontrovertible.

Clearly these rates cannot be sustained indefinitely. We are changing planetary systems on a grand scale in a one-off experiment in seeing whether nature can adapt to injury as rapidly as we can give it injury to which it must adapt. If the experiment fails—which seems increasingly likely, if we credit reports from scientists in the field — the changes we are wreaking now will destroy the ability of the planet to support human civilization at anything like a level that we would find commodious, comfortable, even recognizable.

The first step in developing the understanding we need to change this is to see nature historically. We can no longer justify the eighteenth- and nineteenth-century Garden Planet assumption that nature, like God, stands outside history, aloof, infinite, and unchanging. Nature has a history. It has always had a history, and over the past century that history has increasingly become a tale shaped not by its own solar-powered spontaneous processes but by humans. We can accurately assess the implications of human acts only if we take the measure of them across human lifetimes. How are we to know whether greenhouse gases are producing global warming? We study history. How are we to know what the consequences of cutting down the rain forest will be? We look for clues in history — in the change of ecosystems over time in response to changes humans have instigated. As I've argued elsewhere, because nature's rhythms move on a timescale that far surpasses our own, historical understanding is the fundamental precondition for ecological understanding.

An appreciation of environmental history shows us that our current experience of "now" — the brief threescore-and-ten span of our lives as we live them today — is not normal but is instead a remarkable aberration in the history of the planet. Everyone alive today was born into the Age of Oil, an era that may yet prove to have been a brief, century-and-a-half-long efflorescence of frantic human economic activity fueled by an unrepeatable drawdown of stored fossil energy. It is within our power to define the age differently: it could be remembered as an intermediate step toward an ecologically sustainable industrial culture, a culture created through wise use of antique sunlight to build an infrastructure that operates on current solar income.

Ironically, among the ways in which the Age of Oil is unprecedented is that it has seen the intrusion into human life spans of ecological changes that have heretofore been noticeable only in geologic time. Such is the power of oil: it united the human and geologic timescales. Key moments in environmental history used to take centuries, even millennia to play out; they are now reported in the daily paper.

As a meta-metanarrative organizing our thinking about American (and world) history, the story of human culture's relationship to nature has some distinct advantages. First, it is objective: there is no gainsaying its insights, no credible argument holding that the facts of our ecological abuse are simply a matter of opinion that could be changed by adopting a different interpretive lens. Glaciers are measurably retreating, the oceans are measurably warming, weather patterns are measurably changing, soil fertility is being measurably diminished. The truths of environmental history can be discounted only at the cost of discounting most of the edifice of science itself. It takes quite a bit of logical legerdemain to maintain a position that says science is true and right and good when it is coupled to an economic system that brings us wealth, but not credible when it warns us of the dangers of letting that economic system destroy the planet's ecosystems.

Second, environmental history is transcultural and transnational. Every society, every culture, feeds itself from nature; every one of them draws resources from healthy ecosystems in its effort to secure for its participants a certain standard of well-being. Civilizations can clash all they want over whether Abraham or Adam Smith is a better guide to the regulation of our common life, but if we fail to cap carbon emissions and limit fish catches — if, more generally, we fail to learn and apply the lessons that environmental history offers us about wise use of natural capital — succeeding generations will view that sort of controversy as a tragically pathetic distraction of no greater lasting import than the debates among medieval Scholastics over how many angels can dance on the head of a pin.

Third, as an organizing narrative the story of the mutual interaction of culture and nature has a scope and reach unsurpassed by any other metanarrative. Those schemes — God's Righteousness Redeemed, the Progress of Enlightenment, Our Manifest Destiny, Marxist Class War, the (Right) Hegelian End of History tale recently embraced by neoconservatives, right on through the Clash of Civilizations and Onward Forever with Economic Growth, the metanarratives they now embrace — are limited in comparison. It may be true, as Thomas Kuhn said, that the comparison of such alternative visions is more a matter of aesthetic vision and practical utility than logical proof, but one sure guide to utility in practice can be found in two criteria that have themselves proven to be undeniably valid in practice: breadth of application and degree of assimilation of detail. These — scope and reach — are relatively easy to compare. Scope: every civilization has a necessary root in nature, and stands or falls on how well it husbands that root. Reach: the lessons of environmental history apply to matters of large national policy (what's the best way to promote development of a sustainable energy infrastructure?) and petty individual choice (walk or ride?).

And environmental history as meta-metanarrative has this one, paramount, additional virtue: by understanding the history of how humanity has related to the planet, we will have available to us the information and perspectives we need to ensure that the project of human civilization has a good chance of continuing beyond the next few generations or so.

What can be said against environmental history as a candidate for overarching metanarrative? Most obviously, at first (and perhaps even second) glance it doesn't pass Lynne Cheney's "doom and gloom" test: the news from environmental history is bad, and is getting worse. But the test itself is suspect; a commitment to bright-eyed Pollyannadom, come what may, is inconsistent with careful, reasonable assessment of existential conditions, and clear-eyed assessment of the conditions in which we operate is necessary if our collective life is to be founded on wisdom, or even simply reality, rather than delusion. (It hardly needs emphasizing that cultures founded on delusion rarely pass the Darwinian test of survival.) Too much gloom and doom is dysfunctional: if environmental history is going to "save the planet," as Richard Foltz suggests, students of it need to be left with a sense that our end is not foreordained. Whether that sense will prove to be justified is a question that is difficult to resolve before the fact. In the meantime, wisdom counsels that we behave as if our actions matter.

Another objection: the overarching metanarrative of environmental history may be grounded in fact, but this is not a distinctive strength. All such visions have some grounding in fact, and (the objection says) what we should judge is not scope and reach of the vision's factual fit, but the practical result of the system in use. This unabashedly pragmatic approach seems to be at the core of Cheney's argument against multicultural pluralism in history classrooms: teaching multicultural history is wrong not because the facts that are offered aren't true, but because it results in *this* instead of *that*.

Cheney is in good company with this line of argument: it traces to Plato and the Noble Lie he would tell his guardian class, giving them a historical myth by which to understand themselves, their polity, and their role within it. Locke, too, was a proponent of a version of the Noble Lie, suggesting that because the recondite reasoning that supports the metalevel process insights of natural law was beyond the capacity of the mass of humanity, it is better that they should be given a few simple rules, such as the ones offered as a matter of faith by Christianity, to regulate their social and political intercourse: "The vast majority cannot know, therefore they must believe." He didn't envision a culture war, in which the class of people to whom his version of the Noble Lie had been told would flex their political muscle as a majority and rise against the rationalist, Enlightenment principles on which their powers and freedoms are based. (Nor did he foresee the rise of demagogues who would position themselves as leaders of this faith-based rejection of the institutions he aimed to promote.) Besides this practical difficulty, the very notion of a Noble Lie runs counter to the American Enlightenment tradition, embodied in our institutions, of grounding political discourse in reason, evidence, and publicly accessible debate. To have a philosopher-king, or a priest, or a radio host and a former chair of the National Endowment of the Humanities purposely orchestrating mass delusion for political ends, however noble the ends, is inconsistent with the principles and practice of democracy.

Another, more telling rejoinder to this objection can be made if we accept the pragmatic criterion explicit in the argument (as Plato and Locke, if not Cheney, made it). Environmental history should be our meta-metanarrative of choice because environmental history is crucial to establishing human culture within ecological limits. Among all possible metanarratives it is the best and likeliest to lead us to the creation of an ecologically sustainable human civilization that preserves the cultural and political freedoms we currently enjoy.

From the perspective of environmental history, the notion that America's greatness as a nation depends solely on some quality of American character, or on that quality of character in combination with the exceptional quality of its economic and political institutions, is a naive and parochial conceit that can flourish only in ignorance of thermodynamics and ecology. Europeans set forth on this continent a new nation—one that happened to have lucked into history's largest-ever stock of unexploited scarce low entropy: valuable matter and energy in the form of deep soil fertility, standing timber, and easily extractable minerals, including especially fossil fuels. It's a lucky accident that can't be repeated, not on this planet, ever again. From the continent's gift of natural capital we have for several centuries extracted an unsustainable flow of material inputs that were easily turned into wealth, and we've used that wealth to purchase comfort, distance from want, distance from nature, distance from compulsion of nearly every kind. To some extent, we've been able to export this bargain—low entropy in, wealth and freedom out—to other nations, but the global pursuit of it is sustained only by the world's ever-increasing drawdown of natural capital, particularly fossil fuel. When the capital runs out, the bargain is done. And unless we're careful, the freedoms we purchased by cashing out our capital will disappear as well.

The unavoidable conclusion is that a dramatic change is required in the relationship of industrial culture to nature. That change is inevitable; an unsustainable relationship must, by definition, come to an end. The only question is, how intelligently will we face and prepare for that end? That is, how much natural capital will we reserve from current consumption? Our answer will determine how many humans the Earth will support a generation from now. It will also determine both the standard of living and the standard of liberty those humans will enjoy. We can, if we choose, use the lessons of environmental history to ease our global transition to a post-cheap-energy, post-rapacious economy, a world in which democratic freedoms and a decent standard of living are no longer purchased by cheap energy and the destruction of natural capital.

A general appreciation among the American populace of the truths of environmental history isn't anything like the sum total of the intelligence we will need to make that transition. But widespread appreciation of the lens offered by environmental history would make rational anticipation of inevitable change a good deal more likely; and in rationally, purposefully planning our move to a sustainable society lies the best (perhaps our only) hope for continuing to enjoy an advanced civilization of any sort—our own exceptional, noble, constitutional democracy included.

on the oklahoma abortion laws, SUVs, and climate justice

n 2008 and 2009, the Republican-controlled state legislature of Oklahoma passed two of the most restrictive abortion laws in the nation. The laws were quickly challenged in state courts, where they were found unconstitutional for a technical flaw: each had embodied several distinct anti-choice measures and had thereby violated the state's constitutional provision that prohibits laws from addressing more than one subject. The result, predictably enough, was a 2010 legislative session in which the Republicans tackled their separate anti-abortion purposes in separate bills. Seven were sent to Governor Brad Henry for signature in 2010; the House was particularly expeditious, dispatching five on the same day. Governor Henry signed four, vetoed three — and those vetoes were quickly overridden.

HB 2780 might be called the Mandatory Ultrasound Act. It requires that before a woman receives an abortion, the abortion provider has to perform an ultrasound examination on her and has to display the images to her while simultaneously narrating what is on the screen. Leaving nothing to the discretion of the doctor or "certified technician," the law requires that specific anatomic features of the fetus be shown and named, including "internal organs and members." Aside from medical emergencies in which pausing for an ultrasound would endanger life, there are no exceptions — not even for rape or incest. The only grace the law offers is that the woman being subjected to this unwanted, medically unnecessary exam will not violate the law if she declines to look. The law was immediately challenged by the Center for Reproductive Rights (which had brought suit against the two omnibus laws), and in July 2010 an injunction was granted halting enforcement of it while the case is pending.

Another law, one of the three passed over the governor's veto, prohibits any claims for damages from a doctor or medical facility on the basis of "wrongful life" or "wrongful birth." As the Center for Reproductive Rights describes it: "The law essentially gives physicians and other medical professionals permission to lie to or intentionally mislead pregnant patients, including concealing information about fetal anomalies, withholding vital medical information, and failing to perform available tests, without fear of legal consequences."

Another law requires that when abortifactant medicine — RU 486, the "morning after" pill — is administered, the prescribing doctor must be in the room with the patient. This will halt the practice of "telemedicine," in which the prescribing doctor attends by video link and the medication is administered by a registered nurse or physician's assistant. Like the ultrasound law, the law can't be justified as improving medical practice — it addresses only one kind of medication and doesn't prohibit telemedicine in general. Its aim is simply to make abortions more expensive and more difficult to obtain by restoring a burden of expense and travel — a burden that falls disproportionately on poor and rural women. Another law permits employees of health care facilities, and the facilities themselves, to refuse to provide abortion services. Another prohibits abortions done on the basis of fetal gender, which raises troubling issues about thought crime: it's not illegal to know the gender of the fetus before an abortion, but it's illegal to use that knowledge as the basis of a decision to abort, so the crime turns on what's in the woman's mind. Another law requires all facilities that offer abortions to post large signs stating, among other things, that the facility is prohibited from coercing anyone into having an abortion.

And rounding out the seven is one of the most onerous of the laws, also passed over the governor's veto: HB 3284, which might be called the Oklahoma Internet Shaming Act of 2010. It mandates that when a woman receives an abortion, the attending physician must answer a thirty-eight-item questionnaire, collecting information about the abortion that will be placed online immediately. The name and address of the patient won't be posted, but opponents of the law say that in combination several of the responses (age, race, county of residence, number of children, marital status, years of education) will frequently allow particular women to be identified, especially in small communities, and the posting of the information about any woman violates both doctor-patient confidentiality and the woman's right to privacy. Proponents claim that the intent of the law is to collect data about a "social problem," but opponents charge that the real motive is to chill the exercise of a protected right.

The law is scheduled to go into effect in April 2012, by which time state public health officials are to have built a "stable website" where the raw data—the questionnaires themselves—can be posted as a database. The estimated cost of building the website is $286,000. (Oklahoma faces a budget deficit of $1.2 billion in 2011.)

It's common knowledge that demand for abortions is reduced when women of childbearing age have had effective sex education and access to contraceptives. These are avenues of remedying a "social problem" that the Oklahoma legislature hasn't pursued.

The seven bills enacted in 2010 continue an Oklahoma tradition of innovative encroachment on women's reproductive rights. Section 1-738.3 of Title 63 of the Oklahoma Statutes, partially superseded by the Mandatory Ultrasound Act, already required that women seeking an abortion be given "materials designed to inform the woman of the probable anatomical and physiological characteristics of the unborn child at two-week gestational increments"—pictures of fetuses aborted at various stages. These pictures, the law says, "shall be objective, nonjudgmental, and designed to convey only accurate scientific information." They have to be given to women seeking an abortion at least forty-eight hours before the scheduled procedure. Here and in the Mandatory Ultrasound and Internet Shaming Laws passed in 2010, Oklahoma legislators have broken new ground in political and legal theory, with an approach that has yet to draw the attention of legal scholars: they've pioneered lawmaking as passive-aggressive act.

While proponents of the Oklahoma laws want to maintain the pretense that they aim at nothing more controversial than sound medical practice and the collection or communication of "objective" information, their obvious intent was signaled by Republican State Senator Todd Lamb when he acknowledged that the laws were meant to curtail abortions in the state. A small-government conservative, he was nevertheless untroubled by the new laws' unprecedented degree of state intrusion into private life and into professional medical practice. (Evidently, principle doesn't count for much when you really, really want something — which, when you think of it, is the moral stance of a child.) "I introduced the bill [requiring fetal ultrasounds] because I wanted to encourage life in society," he said. "In Oklahoma, society is on the side of life."

Senator Lamb and the rest of the Republican majority in the Oklahoma legislature might consider: Life in society requires that the society be ecologically sustainable. Sustainability requires that we live on current solar income, not on the stored solar income of fossil fuel that must someday run out — and the use of which, in the meantime, produces climate change that threatens human life by destroying the capacity of the planet to support us. A consistently pro-life position demands interest in and action on climate change and renewable energy. What would happen if Oklahoma's precedent-setting passive-aggressive approach to law were applied in pursuit of this other vision of what "pro-life" means?

That line of reasoning was offered to me by my friend Ike, during a visit I had with him when the flurry of Oklahoma legislation was in the news. If he lived in Britain, Ike would be called a "one-off." An avowed anarchist who thinks that things started going downhill when humans invented agriculture (and thus the need for government), he thinks of Marx as a conservative — "just another neoliberal" — who tried to save the industrial revolution's exploitation of nature from its own immediate social consequences. He belongs to the NRA and Ducks Unlimited and hunts with great pleasure — and with ammo that he packs himself in a basement workshop. He can recite long passages from *Hamlet* and Yeats, and has strong opinions on whether Boerling or Caruso was the better tenor. And he teaches political theory at a small rural college.

In response to the Oklahoma legislation, he had an interesting proposal, one that underscores the lack of imagination and empathy that lies behind the Oklahoma legislative barrage. (Yes, lawmakers there have been very imaginative in finding new ways to impede women's exercise of their reproductive rights, and they have a great deal of empathy for pre-born human life, but they're woefully short on the kind of imagination and empathy necessary to have and keep a system of civil liberties rooted in a basic Golden Rule: what if the political shoe were on the other foot?)

Ike's proposal: "Let's have a questionnaire for everyone who wants to buy an SUV. And forty-eight hours before they can drive away in it, they have to look at pictures of the consequences of what they're about to do — starving babies, oil-drenched wildlife, monsoon and flood damage, drought, funerals of US soldiers who have been killed trying to secure our access to oil in Iraq."

Ike's premise about starving babies comes straight from the work of Nicholas Georgescu-Roegen, the economist whose masterwork, *The Entropy Law and the Economic Process*, was the first systematic elaboration of the idea that an economy ought to be modeled as a thermodynamic system (low entropy in, high entropy out). If all goes well with the world, *The Entropy Law and the Economic Process* will take its place alongside Adam Smith's *Wealth of Nations*, Marx's *Kapital*, Keynes's *General Theory*, and Friedman's *Capitalism and Freedom* as a paradigm-shifting text that changed how we think about economics. So far, it's underappreciated.

When you look at modern agriculture as a system of energy flows, you can't help but notice that we're eating antique sunlight. The subsidy from petroleum means that as practiced today, agriculture is a net energy loss for the economy (a point that Ike likes to emphasize when he extols the virtues of hunting and gathering, which had a positive caloric balance sheet). The Earth has a finite energy budget, and energy used for one thing can't be used for something else; if we use a bit of energy to make and operate an SUV, that energy isn't available to feed people. When he discusses this, Georgescu-Roegen reports a folk saying from Rumania, where he was born: "Horses eat people." Before agriculture was mechanized, farmers in Rumania had noticed that they faced a trade-off (what economists would call a production possibilities frontier): land used to grow food for farm animals was land that couldn't be used to grow food for humans. Once you had a horse or two for pulling the plow (which dramatically increases the productivity of your farm), then the more horses you had, the fewer people your farm could feed. (In economists' terms: once the basic need for plow-power was met, the marginal contribution to farm production of additional horses was negative.) The mechanization of agriculture displaced that basic trade-off between horses and people to a trade-off between machinery and people, a trade-off that oil's unprecedented EROI tended to obscure for most of the twentieth century. When oil was offering 100:1 returns and production of it was continually expanding, it seemed we could afford both machinery and people, in increasing amounts, forever. But ultimately our discovery of how to use oil to make wealth and food in the present doesn't free us from the fundamental economic problem of having to make choices about what we do with our finite low-entropy budget. As Georgescu-Roegen updated the Rumanian folk saying in 1971 (when Cadillacs were the iconic gas guzzler): "Every Cadillac produced at any time means fewer lives in the future." Cars eat people, too — and suvs gobble people faster than other, more efficient vehicles.

So, Ike's proposal: he wants an enterprising and progressive state legislature to copy the passive-aggressive approach pioneered in Oklahoma and put it to work for the same end — the preservation and extension of human life — by mandating the collection of information on people who buy suvs. Knowing more about buyers will help us figure out how to minimize this problematic social behavior. And, as Ike says, "if having to answer some questions shames people into not going through with it, so much the better."

Ike was so taken with the idea that he went online to find the questionnaire that Oklahoma legislators have written into law and revised it to apply to vehicle purchases. Where Oklahoma wants to know about number of previous births and how many of these children survive, Ike wants to ask how many internal combustion engines the purchaser has ever owned and how many of them are still in service today. (Besides registerable vehicles like cars, trucks, and motorcycles, his list includes lawn mowers and chainsaws, weed whackers and leafblowers, emergency generators and boats, Jet Skis and snowmobiles.) In sum the questions aim to be just as intrusive as the ones Oklahoma wants to ask, prying into income level, educational level, race, marital status (and asking if the purchaser's spouse approves of what's about to be done).

Notable is his Question 23, which parallels a question on the Oklahoma form: "Was any portion of the purchase process, including the test drive (if any), performed with the use of any public institution, public facility, public equipment, or other physical asset owned, leased, maintained, or controlled by the state, its agencies, or any other political subdivision?" The Oklahoma language hints at further developments in the effort to restrict access to abortion, developments based on the premise, implicit here but made explicit by anti-abortion activists elsewhere, that individual citizens shouldn't have to pay taxes to support in any way a practice they find morally objectionable. (That's a premise that, if consistently implemented, would severely limit the ability of the us government to pay for wars in the Middle East. Do we really want to give every citizen a personal conscience veto for their participation in public revenues?) Here Ike wants to remind the suv purchaser: you're driving on public roads, built at public expense, and that gives the public some interest in what you propose to drive on those roads.

For the last question, Ike wants to ask, "At least forty-eight hours prior to the consummation of the purchase, was the purchaser given information about the consequences of vehicle use, including information on climate change; peak oil and the fact that oil is a finite resource; global food scarcity and the role that oil plays in staving off hunger throughout the world; the costs, in lives and money, of us foreign policy dedicated to protecting and extending our nation's access to oil; and the social, economic, and ecological costs of urban sprawl?" It's his version of the question Oklahoma asks about whether a woman has been shown pictures of fetal development. "Maybe suv drivers just don't realize how selfish they're being," Ike had said to me in our conversation. "If they knew the consequences of their acts, there'd be a whole lot fewer suvs out there." Ike has a bit of faith in the Golden Rule. I suggested to him that his point about hunger might be reinforced if the prospective suv purchaser were confined for forty-eight hours beforehand and fed nothing but the caloric intake of the typical citizen of Bangladesh; if you want to change a person's "thema," it helps to give them visceral knowledge, an experience they can't brush aside. (An even more invasive possibility: require the prospective purchaser to submit to an mri, so they can be shown evidence of how their decision making has been shaped by corporate advertising's influence on their brain's pleasure centers.)

In debate, accepting an opponent's premises and taking them in a different direction to suit your own argument — what can be called the reductio ad "somewhere else" form of argument — can be an effective strategy. ("Hey, they're your premises; I'm just borrowing them.") It can also be personally satisfying to fantasize about shoe-on-the-other-foot strategies like this. One fundamental quality of law is that it is supposed to be equitable and fair, and fairness means, among other things, treating similar cases similarly. If the Oklahoma law represents a legitimate use of state authority to protect and extend human life (a big "if"), then the principles behind it ought to be capable of extension in the new direction that Ike proposes. If you don't like what Ike proposes, you shouldn't like the Oklahoma abortion laws.

No doubt many conservatives would denounce Ike's questionnaire as an unwarranted intrusion into a private act of commerce, an illegitimate do-gooder attempt to influence a personal choice about transportation; but if the two subjects of legislation are similar, such a protest is hypocritical if it isn't joined to an equally vociferous protest over Oklahoma's intrusions into private medical decisions and do-gooder attempts to influence a woman's personal reproductive choices. The discussion thus turns on a key question: is the purchase of an suv like getting an abortion, or not? Are they both so imbued with social effect that they can't be treated as completely private decisions? Ike says yes; and while I haven't asked him, I'd be willing to be that Senator Lamb would say no, they're not similar at all.

That position has merit only if two things are true: abortion ends a human life, and the planet is so expansive that an individual's choice about transportation preferences is nobody's business but his or her own.

On the first question, cultures and religions have disagreed, and objective science offers no help. Only those who listen to a god or gods (or who trust that saints or priests or radio personalities have heard The Voice) can presume to know precisely when life begins. There is no clear marker to tell us when matter becomes spirit, when a fetus becomes ensouled, when human life begins. This makes all but the most ecumenical legislation about abortion necessarily a violation of the separation of church and state — the Western version of sharia law. And Ike might offer a different argument: because the planet's capacity to support humans is finite, and because we've exceeded it, every human life born today ends a human life somewhere else — either now or in the future. Thus, even assuming that abortion ends a human life, on this front abortion is a wash: it ends a possible human life but allows an existing life to continue, or enables a future life to begin. Forcing a woman to carry an unwanted pregnancy to term creates new human life at the expense of imposing death or a much-diminished life on someone else. To prefer that the human life that's created be American and specifically Oklahoman is cultural and state chauvinism, which is not morally defensible high ground.

As to the second issue: before Garden Planet met its limits and was transformed into Factory Planet, we could successfully maintain the fiction that the planet was for practical purposes infinite. On an infinite planet, any one individual's decision about what kind of car to drive (or, more broadly, about the size of the ecological footprint their life choices cumulate into) could be taken to be essentially private; the ecological losses from individual consumption were relatively small and didn't automatically cross the threshold that made them a matter of public concern. But on Factory Planet, where it is clearer that the sustainable flow of low entropy available to us is fixed and finite, we have to face the fact that our apportionment of that flow is necessarily zero-sum. One person's decision to purchase and use an SUV becomes a matter of public interest, because SUV use is not the most efficient way of spending our scarce low entropy. The position I've ascribed to conservatives—that having an abortion and buying an SUV are two completely different kinds of acts—makes sense only on an infinite planet.

There's a stronger case to be made for Ike's Law than for the Internet Shaming Act it's based on. The Oklahoma law violates a woman's right to privacy, and it's intended to constrain the exercise of a freedom that's fundamental to civil society: the right to have property in and control over one's own body. The political philosopher John Locke, to whom we owe the concept of popular sovereignty and the civil freedoms that flow from it, began his argument for democratic, representative government with an assertion: every one of us has a God-given property in ourselves, our own bodies. Against this long-standing foundation, Oklahoma law asserts that society, operating through the state, has a legitimate interest in the operation of every individual woman's reproductive system. But clearly, ownership of one's own body is a more fundamental right than ownership of this or that particular internal combustion engine; if both Ike's Law and the Internet Shaming Act it's based on represent state intrusion into personal decision making, the loss to individual autonomy that Ike proposes is a much smaller and more defensible burden.

Another objection to Ike's Law is that it is hypocritical to decry the passive-aggressive intrusion of law into individual matters of conscience when the matter is abortion, but to support it when the subject is vehicle purchase. But it needn't be hypocritical, if there are differences within the essential similarity that justify the one and not the other. Both abortion and SUV ownership can be seen as moral choices. On Factory Planet a choice of transportation modes is a choice that affects others; it imposes negative externalities on others, and therefore ought not to be treated solely and primarily as a matter of individual conscience. On Factory Planet, where human population currently exceeds the sustainable carrying capacity of the ecosystems that support civilization, the decision not to carry a pregnancy to term also has social consequences, but the externalities are primarily positive: one person's individual choice to limit their reproduction benefits the rest of us. (Of course, if you think the planet is infinite or infinitely capable of supporting human life, you don't see this positive externality at all.)

Ike's Law is rationally defensible on a finite planet and, if implemented, might have its intended effects of discouraging purchase of gas-guzzling vehicles and encouraging purchase of vehicles with higher fuel efficiency. But that doesn't mean it's a good idea. Its passive-aggressive approach is unlikely to be sufficient to stop the behavior it seeks to discourage, and just as partisans of the Oklahoma laws would much prefer to flat-out revoke the privacy rights granted by *Roe v. Wade*, I'd rather see a wholesale movement that would make automobiles less necessary and less desirable altogether. An "Internet Shaming Law, SUV Version" might begin to accomplish that but wouldn't succeed in getting us all the way to a practical, efficient transportation system — and to a pattern of urban development that would make our use of private automobiles less necessary and frequent. Part of the problem is that guilt-tripping doesn't work on those who think they are innocent — and in ecological matters our innocence seems assured by our insignificance. Each of us can genuinely say, "My own contribution to the problem of climate change is so small; certainly my acts don't matter a whole lot." The social benefit that would be produced by an individual act of self-denial is so small that the sacrifice looms large in comparison — and it seems especially large in a society in which many opinion molders and elites (neoclassical economists, conservative politicians, conservative radio talk show hosts) tell us that sacrifice of self-interest in pursuit of public good is a mug's game: it's neither necessary, nor wise, nor wanted.

Ultimately Ike's SUV law wouldn't work because it's based on a category error: it continues to treat as an individual moral issue what is more appropriately understood as an outstanding social and cultural problem. Three decades of moral suasion — of finger-wagging and guilt-tripping in various forms — have done little to curb America's appetite for maximizing low-entropy throughput in the economy, and while it's interesting to imagine that we can devise more effective ways to guilt-trip and finger-wag each other to a smaller ecological footprint, that strategy is unlikely to get us where we need to go. A same-old, same-old strategy is likely to leave the same old problem intact.

And Ike's law doesn't deal with an observable fact: unlike women seeking abortions, who are generally aware that they have made a difficult moral choice, some owner-operators of big resource-wasting vehicles *want* to be perceived as being environmentally oblivious. In particular, owners of Hummers (EPA mileage estimates of just six to twelve miles per gallon) see themselves as true patriots because their use of the vehicle enacts their commitment to the All-American ideals of rugged individualism and faith in the boundless frontier. They want the vehicle because of, not despite, its iconic status as an over-the-top waster of resources. Being required to view a few photographs and to answer some intrusive questions is unlikely to dislodge prospective Hummer owners from their established system of interpretation — their "thema," their paradigm.

One fundamental criterion of good policy advanced by Herman Daly and Joshua Farley in *Ecological Economics* is that "the domain of the policy . . . must be congruent with the domain of the causes and effects of the problem with which the policy deals." Climate change is a global problem. Individual moral choice to limit carbon emissions may be personally satisfying, and would bring individual behavior into congruence with Kant's version of the Golden Rule (his Categorical Imperative: one should act according to precepts that one could reasonably and consistently want to see employed by all others). It would also have the virtue of letting the individual carbon-reducer speak and act against climate change without being susceptible to charges of hypocrisy. But individual moral choice is not going to solve a global problem. For that, global action is required. (Individual change of behavior will have some effect, since the efficient cause of the problem lies in individual choice; but other aspects of cause lie far beyond the range of things that can be affected by individual choice.)

We don't have a global authority capable of creating and administering and enforcing a carbon-limitation policy. (That such a body, remote from influence by individual citizens, seems desirable is yet another manifestation of the way that democracy becomes increasingly threatened on Factory Planet.) In the absence of such a global policy-making body, efforts to address the problem at a global level are dependent on the collaboration of individual nation-states. By default, the operant organization among those nation-states is a Calhounian nullificationist confederacy: in his vigorous defense of slavery in South Carolina, John Calhoun argued that each of the United States remained a sovereign state and thus retained the right to disobey — "nullify" — laws promulgated by the central authority. No sovereign state, he said, can be required by the collective to do something it doesn't want to do; and in his view each of the United States remained a sovereign entity within the Constitution. (This is not merely an abstract point of political theory; it took a long and bloody Civil War to decide the issue in the United States and to establish — more conclusively than some want, less conclusively than others want — that the federal government is the sovereign authority in our country.)

So far, in the effort to establish limits on global greenhouse gas emissions through international treaty, Calhounian political theory has carried the day. No international consensus on climate change has emerged, and there is no international force capable of imposing the terms of such a treaty on nations unwilling to agree to it.

The key sticking point in developing a consensus among nations about climate change policy is the failure of the United States to sign on to significant limits and reductions in greenhouse gas emissions. Reasonably enough, the US position is that there should be equal treatment of nations: it refuses to sign an agreement that doesn't also limit the emissions of developing and underdeveloped nations to the same extent. And reasonably enough, developed and developing nations argue that the developed nations of the world, including the United States, had nearly a century of unimpeded use of the planet's carbon-absorption capacity; as they see it, it is only fair and just that the developed nations reduce their emissions to an even greater degree to compensate for this past use. We can think of the carbon-absorption capacity of the planet as being like a bathtub with an open drain and a flowing spigot. The drain is the capacity of global ecosystems to absorb CO_2 out of the atmosphere and sequester it in material form; the volume of the tub is the inventory of greenhouse gas that can be held in the atmosphere without causing climate change; and the flow from the spigot is the greenhouse gas exhaust our economies emit. (To belabor the metaphor: water splashing out of the brimful tub represents the burden of CO_2 emitted above the volume — 350 parts per million atmospheric concentration — that atmospheric scientists tell us the planet can hold without undue effect.) The US position is that the inflow must be made to match the outflow and that everyone should share equally in constraining the flow from the spigot. The position taken by the developing nations is that the problem isn't just that inflow is greater than outflow, but that some nations filled the tub. Those nations should be assigned a smaller proportion of the flow from the spigot.

Both positions seem reasonable. Is there a way out of this conundrum? One path is offered by the approach taken by John Rawls in *A Theory of Justice.* He proposes that difficult issues be decided by use of the Kantian Categorical Imperative from behind what he calls a "veil of ignorance." The idea: If citizens were to gather to create a social contract, they would most likely try to encode into that contract preferential treatment for themselves. Men would choose patriarchy, women matriarchy; whites might accept the enslavement of blacks, heterosexuals might accept discrimination against gays; the well-to-do would choose a system with low and nonprogressive or "flat" taxes and limited guaranteed welfare, while the impoverished would choose progressive taxes and a stronger safety net. But imagine decisions made about social rules and structure by people who have no idea of what their race and role and status will be once the rules and structure are in place. Behind that veil of ignorance, "no one knows his place in society, his class position or social status; nor does he know his fortune in the distribution of natural assets and abilities, his intelligence and strength, and the like." Whites wouldn't be likely to accept a system of race-based slavery if the decision was "One race will serve the others as slaves, but you can't choose which race you'll be." Men and women wouldn't choose a system of gender discrimination if they didn't know which gender they'd have once the veil was lifted.

By asking us to see that a just system is derivable from a thought experiment, Rawls's veil of ignorance makes obvious the role that empathy and imagination play in maintaining our system of civil liberties. The political system that we would create from behind that veil, Rawls argues, would safeguard minority rights and offer equal opportunity to all; it would achieve justice by being fair to all members.

What if an international carbon-control regime were to be created from behind a veil of ignorance — a gathering of representatives from all nations from whose memories all national affiliation had been erased and who had no idea what nation they'd be joining once the veil was lifted? It's likely that the carbon-justice principles that would emerge would be these: "Every human on the planet has an equal right to use the carbon-absorption capacity of the planet, which is fixed and finite. Every person is thus entitled to an individual, per capita, lifetime share of that fixed capacity, which can be cumulated into an emissions cap for their national economy. The per capita entitlement cannot be diminished by the actions or emissions of others."

This represents a compromise between the two positions outlined above. Against the US position, it says that historical patterns of use — the fact that the tub is full — must be taken into consideration; many Americans (and now many Chinese) have already used their lifetime shares of the planet's carbon-absorption capacity, and their country will have to reduce its average per capita carbon footprint accordingly. Against the position staked out by developing countries, the Rawlsian rule says that consideration of who benefited from filling the tub (and who, therefore, should have a smaller per capita share of the flow from the spigot in the present) reaches only as far back as the lifetimes of those alive today. Americans would not be required to limit their emissions so far as to compensate for the CO_2 emissions of generations past.

An additional principle would emerge from behind the veil of ignorance: nations would be entitled to emit CO_2 only in an amount equal to the sum of the per capita shares they are assigned at the moment the agreement is made. This would prevent nations from increasing their carbon cap by expanding their populations. (Without this caveat, the agreement about per capita emissions offers a perverse incentive: nations would be rewarded with a higher emissions cap for expanding their population more rapidly than other nations.)

After principle comes policy. A specific policy approach to externalities like climate change was proposed by economist Arthur Pigou in

1920. An externality represents a market failure; when the externalities are positive (as with education), private purchase on the market produces less than the socially optimal amount of the good, and when the externalities are negative (as they are with pollution, including emission of greenhouse gases), purchases in markets produce more of the negatives than is socially optimal. Pigouvian taxes and subsidies "internalize the externalities" and make market-based allocations more efficient.

A Pigouvian carbon tax would accomplish what Ike wants to see done. If the price of gas included the costs of the externalities that gasoline use imposes on society, we'd be paying at least eight or ten dollars a gallon at the pump (as Europeans currently do, without any noticeably catastrophic result), and we'd be using a lot less of it. With the Pigouvian tax set high enough to bring total gasoline use under the climate-stability cap for CO_2 emissions, individual consumers would be free to purchase and use gasoline however they choose. (If collectively they use more than can be burned under the nation's CO_2 cap, that's a sign the price is too low; if they use less than can be burned under the CO_2 cap, that's a sign the price is too high.) With a Pigouvian tax on gas, you'd be free to drive a Hummer if you wanted — if that's how you wanted to spend your money and express yourself automotively. Daly and Farley refer to this as "micro freedom under a macro cap."

An eight-dollar tax on a gallon of gas is a mighty whack to take all at once; but it could be phased in gradually, on a known and certain schedule. It would also provide the opportunity to stabilize the retail price per gallon of gasoline, a function that has historically been performed by market demand prorationing, which, for reasons outlined earlier, will cease to be practical in post–Hubbert's Peak oil market. As forces of supply and demand create volatility in the price of gasoline, the tax could be adjusted incrementally to moderate price swings. (If three appointed officials on the Texas Railway Commission could stabilize the US retail price of gasoline through market demand prorationing in the 1940s, 1950s, and 1960s, I'm sure that a similar Carbon Tax Adjustment Board empanelled today could do the same.) That stability would have social and economic benefits. Promotion of commerce and the creation of jobs is a perennial political concern, and any business owner can tell you that business fares better when owners and managers face fewer unknowns. A carbon tax with market-demand adjustment gives them greater certainty about energy costs.

The Pigouvian carbon tax could also be revenue neutral: we could give every household a rebate or "prebate" that represents the tax that would be paid by an average user. Suppose the tax is a dollar a gallon the first year and that the average household uses one thousand gallons of gas. As the tax goes into effect, every household gets a check for one thousand dollars. If it uses less gas than average, it ends up money ahead, while if it uses more, it pays out of pocket. (There could easily be some income-sensitivity feature that ensures that the tax wouldn't fall disproportionately on those least able to pay it.)

The increased costs imposed by the tax would ripple automatically through all the markets in our economy, making command-and-control regulation of carbon emissions unnecessary. Such a tax would make prices tell the ecological truth about carbon use — a necessary condition if we're to preserve free markets while meeting the real-world challenges of limiting our economy to a level of throughput that the ecosystems of the planet can sustainably offer up to us and sustainably absorb from us.

Still, Ike's idea has some appeal. Absent an economy-wide price on carbon emissions through a carbon tax or cap-and-trade, the alternative is to step up the finger-wagging and moral admonition, and Ike's shoe-on-the-other-foot approach is emotionally appealing. It might also be an interesting public relations move: any state's implementation of an suv questionnaire would draw national attention and put the issues it raises firmly into public discourse. And it would be interesting to see the Supreme Court address the Oklahoma case alongside an suv questionnaire case. Recent Court decisions display a want of the same kind of political imagination — the capacity for empathy — that the Oklahoma legislature has been lacking and that Rawls's veil of ignorance asks us to cultivate. In *Kelo v. City of New London*, decided in 2005, the Court held that a city government in Connecticut could exercise its power of eminent domain to condemn and purchase oceanfront property in order to give it to a developer for private use. The case set a precedent by accepting the argument that the increased tax flow from more intensive development (a proposed marina, hotel, and casino complex) is a public good that falls within the purposes of the eminent domain statute, even if the recipient of the property is not a public authority. Citizen interest in the continued quiet enjoyment of long-held property—an interest that is not economically active—was judged inconsequential in the face of the economic benefits that derive from promoting commerce and business activity. The Court might not have reached that decision if the public good being pursued were the condemnation of private property for the purpose of giving the land to a private organization for other purposes—beachfront conservation, species preservation, or the like. Confronting two versions of an Internet Shaming Law, one advanced by conservatives and the other advanced by progressives, might force the Court to put its decisional shoes on both ideological feet and thereby lead it to a decision more respectful of civil liberties and democratic freedoms—the liberties and freedoms that are increasingly threatened on Factory Planet.

what green might bring

ears ago, in an essay titled "Ecology and Guilt," I compared the teachings of ecology to the moral codes offered by an especially rigorous and austere religion. Back then, it seemed to me that one reason the environmental movement wasn't making as much progress as it might was because ecological understanding pointed us toward a life of self-denial, restraint, and extreme discipline: Recycle everything. Turn the thermostat down in winter, up in summer. Don't waste hot water. Walk or bike, don't drive. For every choice you make as a consumer, think: which option has the smallest environmental impact? Not only did ecological precepts teach self-denial; they taught that even if you succeeded in reducing your personal ecological footprint by every reasonable means possible, you would still be part of the problem — a much smaller part, but part of the problem nonetheless. You breathe, exhaling carbon dioxide, a greenhouse gas. We all have to eat, an act by which we make our own small but undeniable contribution to our culture's capture of 40 percent of the planet's Net Primary Product. With 7 billion of us on the planet, it is impossible for anyone fully to meet the standard set by the Kantian Categorical Imperative, sustainability version: "Act so that the principles by which you act, if generalized to all humanity, would establish an ecologically sustainable society." By that principle, each of us is entitled to one seven-billionth of the flow of the matter and energy that can sustainably be drawn from nature. Within our current, petroleum-dependent civilization, only an impoverished life — a bowlful of rice a day, meat once in a great while, dim light, few possessions — comes anywhere close to meeting that ideal.

My essay noted that this kind of moral ground is not a hospitable place on which to build a movement for social change. "Would you," I asked, "join an ambitiously and minutely regulatory church, one that offers no rewards for effort, one that says that even if you succeed in obeying its many rules and regulations, you are still irredeemably guilty, guilty without hope of reform or forgiveness?" Not wanting to let my own rhetorical question go unanswered, I answered. "One wants one's efforts noticed, one's failures forgiven."

My comparison of ecology to a fundamentalist and dysfunctional religion was seized by some conservative readers as evidence that I was a convert, a one-time believer who had seen a better light — the Light of Economic Wisdom, I suppose; or maybe the glow of confidence that comes from a faith in the Environmental Kuznets Curve and its absurd reassurance that someday soon, but not just yet, we'll be wealthy enough to afford the luxury of environmental quality, including a stable climate. To my annoyance, I found my words being enlisted to support some very unecological arguments, despite my having said, as plainly as I could, "I still believe that industrial culture is not sustainable and that therefore it will, in time, change and change drastically," whether we want it to or not. In that essay I criticized guilt-tripping as a vehicle of social change, not the vision of sustainability that tells us social change is needed.

To the problem as I saw it, I gave the best solution I could then see. My diagnosis was that ecology tells us we're guilty, while the moral code that most of us accept within the various Abrahamic traditions holds out to us an ideal of innocence. The two conflict; if innocence is the moral ideal to which we aspire, and ecological understanding says we can't achieve innocence in the world as we've structured it today, then it shouldn't be a surprise that a lot of people simply say "The hell with it" and walk away. The avenue of resolution that I saw then was to acknowledge that circumstances demand we use some other and better form of moral understanding. A moral code that takes innocence as its highest ideal is one suited to infants and minor children and to others who are held in suspension, powerless and weak. "As a species we are not now that impotent, and to pretend to be so is unseemly," I said. What we need, I argued, is a moral code that celebrates something else. Looking back before Christianity to the Greeks I called it nobility: the capacity for selfless action in accordance with principle (a principle as simple as the Golden Rule, in its Kantian sustainability version) in a world that makes complete purity of act, and unity of act and vision, rare and difficult things to achieve.

It was an okay answer, I guess. But I now see that my question was flawed. It wasn't so much wrong as wrong-headed, the product of a misperception of the problem. I neglected to apply something I might have learned from John Rodman, who in his work talked about three levels of analysis that must, for many purposes, be kept analytically distinct: the individual, the social, and the systemic.

The individual level of analysis deals with humans in their individual aspect, treating causes, consequences, and conditions that have their root inside the individual. The social level is comprised of the affairs of the *polis*, of humans in relation, in society, in some aggregate large enough to be more than a collection of individuals. Into the third level goes everything else, everything that lies beyond the boundaries of individual psyche and the collectivity of human society: the systems by which those societies interact, and also nature, the physical world as opposed to the built world. Part of Rodman's project as a scholar and thinker was to analyze the cognitive trafficking across the borders of these three categories. We borrow ideas from one realm (often as metaphor) and apply them in the others in ways that sometimes are and sometimes are not appropriate. Darwin, for instance, got his organizing idea about nature (the one that allowed him to make sense of the variation he had seen among species in the Galápagos) by reading a work in political economy: Malthus on population, which helped him see that competition for food is the driving force of natural selection. After Darwin published *On the Origin of Species*, thinkers such as Herbert Spencer read his work back into political economy, offering us Social Darwinism: the idea that society, like nature, is and ought to be ruled by a struggle for survival and is a place where only the fit should survive.

Rodman's tripartite division is also visible in Kenneth Waltz's classic book, *Man, the State, and War*. Waltz surveyed answers to the question "Why is there war?" and found three distinctly different kinds of answers, categories that correspond to Rodman's. One kind of answer says that we have war because humans are by nature aggressive. As with the other categories, within this group there are optimists and pessimists: those who say we can and those who say we can't reform our natures and solve the problem. At the second level, another kind of answer says that even if humans were angels, when they amalgamate into societies (or into particular kinds of societies: developed, undeveloped, capitalist, communist), they are led into conflict with other societies. (A pessimistic take on this second-order view is captured by the title of Reinhold Niebuhr's *Moral Man, Immoral Society.* Among the optimists at this level you've got Marx and Lenin — and quite a few neoclassical economists — who trace war to particular structural features of some societies and who hold that when those societies are changed to conform to the program the author recommends, war will disappear.) The third says that the fault lies not in ourselves or our societies but in the system within which those societies relate to each other. Internationally there is no legitimate and fully successful institution for promulgating law, none for judging infractions of that law, and none for enforcing those judgments on member nations. (Optimists see a glass half full, noting that since World War II systems of international law have gradually gained moral authority and practical effect; pessimists hold that national sovereignty is "sticky" — nations powerful enough to do so continue to practice Calhounian nullification, denying the encroachment on sovereignty of international law and its practical administration.) Thus, the individual, social, and systemic levels of analysis; or, as Rodman called them, *psyche, polis, cosmos.*

And so, long after I wrote "Ecology and Guilt," I came to see that my rhetorical question about ecology as a rigorous and unforgiving belief system stemmed from what philosophers would call a category error, one I didn't see clearly at the time. I was accepting the presumption that our environmental crisis is, and can be remedied as, a problem in individual behavior when in fact it is something else entirely: a problem at the interface of the other two levels of analysis, a mark of our failure to accommodate our social system to its environment, our *polis* to the *cosmos.* Because that interface is defined primarily by economic activity, it's a problem that is directly addressed by better economic theory, not one that can be solved by promulgation of an environmental ethic. To put it bluntly: if prices told the ecological truth, as Oystein Dahle has suggested, we wouldn't need an environmental ethic at all. Citizens — citizens-as-consumers — could go about their business maximizing their life satisfactions without caring about or concerning themselves with the ecological consequences of their actions.

That's a contentious statement and deserves a bit more explanation. Suppose we aim at achieving a sustainable society through market signals instead of command-and-control regulation. If such a society, populated by ecologically oblivious benefit maximizers, continues to operate beyond the margins of what the planet can sustainably give to us in the form of resources and sustainably absorb from us in the form of waste, that's simply a sign that prices don't accurately reflect ecological reality. The assertion "In a system in which prices tell the ecological truth, human behavior need not be constrained by an environmental ethic" is, at its root, a tautology. Both ethics and prices shape behavior, and on the whole prices are easier to change than ethics. If price signals aren't strong enough to lead to the desired outcome, then prices need to be adjusted.

The role that prices could play in promoting ecologically sustainable behavior wasn't clear to me when I wrote "Ecology and Guilt." Like many others, I fell into defining the problem as a first-order problem — a problem of ethics and morals — partly because that was the one level at which I could respond effectively: I couldn't change an entire social, political, and economic system built on infinite-planet thinking, but I could be responsible for and change my own behavior. And even had I fully seen that the problem is a problem of policy, not morals, I wouldn't have been relieved of the duty to live in accordance with the principles I was expounding for the culture as a whole.

And so it was that many of us, guided by a vision and an ethic, made our efforts to live according to ecological precept. We began to make our economic choices *as if* we lived in a world where prices told the ecological truth. That means we made irrational, uneconomic choices: we paid extra for our energy, installing solar panels even though the price per kilowatt-hour was greater than that of the coal- and oil-fired electricity that was delivered to us by the local utility. We paid extra for organic, post-petroleum produce. We paid extra for energy-saving appliances although the savings, in monetary terms, were nonexistent, negative, or inconsequential. We took the extra time to walk or bike or use mass transit even though time is money and gas was only a dollar a gallon.

I'm not saying we were foolish or wrong to do these things. I'm saying that in a sustainable world, the ecologically rational choices we made — tried to make — would also be the economically rational choice. Until we actually get such a world, for many of us ecological rationality will trump economic rationality, and we'll live by our environmental ethic to the extent that our incomes allow — and we'll feel more or less guilty when we fall short.

Because prices don't tell the ecological truth, being green requires behavior that is "uneconomic." And the willingness of most ecologically minded people to pay a premium for sustainably sourced or resource-saving products is taken by most economists and most conservatives as evidence confirming their mistaken belief that environmental quality is a luxury good — something that only upscale, middle-class people can afford. But living according to one's principles brings a nonmonetary satisfaction. To use an old-fashioned term, it's the essence of integrity — which is not experienced as a "satisfaction" so much as the precondition for a morally defensible life.

Beyond the economically irrational appeal of acting with integrity lie these truths: dramatic change in the structures and practices of society always begins with changes in the beliefs and behaviors of individuals. But the cumulation of one-by-one-by-one individual transformation can't succeed in getting us an ecologically sustainable society, not as long as those transformations are understood as essentially private acts, as personal moral choices. The only effective solution for a social and political problem is social and political change. In this book I've tried to make the case that one efficient step in that direction involves changing the infinite-planet idea systems on which bad — unsustainable — policy is based. The experience of the environmental movement in the past thirty years shows very clearly that moral admonition — finger-wagging in its various forms — will not, by itself, get us where we need to go.

In the United States, the modern environmental movement can be dated to Earth Day One in 1970 or, further back, to the publication of Rachel Carson's *Silent Spring* in 1962 or, even further back, to 1890 and Gifford Pinchot's importation into the United States of the sustained-yield forestry principles he learned in Europe. Wherever you decide it's rooted, throughout its history American environmentalism has expended most of its energy exerting negative pressure on the culture: it has told us what we must not do, what we ought not to do, what we cannot do if we wish to continue to live a commodious life on this planet. We mustn't cut down forests as if they were infinite — when we cut a tree, we ought to plant a tree. We mustn't use DDT — it concentrates in the food chain, fatally weakening the shells of birds' eggs, including those of the bald eagle; eventually it appears in the milk that human mothers offer their babies from the breast. (Appeals to these symbolic values — the purity of mother's milk, the nobility and strength of our nation's iconic symbol — were successful in getting an outright ban on the pesticide — though it continues to be used abroad, on produce destined for US markets.) We mustn't discharge untreated sewage into our lakes and streams; we mustn't let factories disgorge sooty smoke and acidifying sulfur dioxide into the air; we mustn't cause species to go extinct by depriving the last remnant population of this or that animal or plant of its needed habitat. And so on: to many Americans, environmentalism became a set of constraints, a regime of negatives, even (to some) a dictatorship of "no," a tyranny of "you must," administered by faceless bureaucrats who issue commandments according to rules that are increasingly ambitious, increasingly minatory, increasingly inscrutable.

That's what you tend to get when an economy based on infinite-planet thinking collides with the reality of a finite planet.

Rebellion against this control, this loss of prerogative and discretion, easily becomes a rebellion against the authority of the science that tells us this control is necessary: hence the blatant rejection of climate change science by the conservative-dominated 112th Congress's House of Representatives.

When it came to justifying these restrictions, to saying why we mustn't do these things that use scarce resources or damage the environment, environmentalists have offered several distinct lines of argument. None of them find hospitable ground in a society imbued with a belief, based on a shallow interpretation of Adam Smith and on the infinite-planet thinking of Friedrich Hayek and his ilk, that individual pursuit of individual self-interest, unfettered by regulation or constraint, is the only way to define and achieve the common good. One argument is moral: it says we mustn't do these things because *we have no right* — no right to cause a species to go extinct, no right to deprive other life-forms of a commodious and successful existence, no right to foul the planet in ways that affect the ability of other life-forms, and our own progeny, to survive. Reasoning by analogy to relations among humans in civil society (in which my right to do as I please is limited by the necessity of respecting your right to do as you please, which includes the right to quiet enjoyment of your life free of disturbance from my actions), thinkers in the animal rights movement proposed that our problematic relationship to the ecosystems that support us could be remedied by accepting that animals, maybe even all life-forms, have rights. And it's true that the distinction between humans and other life-forms — a distinction that would justify us in excluding animals and other life-forms from our moral universe — dissolves on any sustained inspection. Among other animals, some use tools; some use coded communications that function as language; some are capable of grieving, of feeling pain and pleasure, of establishing troops and pods and hives and colonies that function as culture. If any sort of being has rights, for any but nonarbitrary reasons, then it certainly seems that at least some and maybe all nonhuman animals are the sorts of beings that can have or do have or should be recognized as having rights.

Another argument was not moral but aesthetic, spiritual, and psychological. Something there is, it says, in the makeup of humans — certainly some of us, maybe potentially all of us (if we would only be alive to this aspect of our being) — that requires the experience of "other," of nature free and untrammeled, in order to achieve its fullest expression and development. From Mill with his appeal to a world in which the prospect of human solitude in nature hasn't been completely extirpated, through John Muir's call to commune with transcendent values in the sublime vistas of the Sierras, to Aldo Leopold's insistence that the experience of wilderness — an expanse of territory that could "absorb a month-long mule trip" — was a necessary anodyne to the clotted, stifling, and over-commercialized avenues of self-construction that are offered to us by an increasingly industrialized culture, this argument attempted to put into words (and to give public-policy force) to values that Americans had long since come to believe are deeply private, matters that no public authority had legitimate cause to meddle in: what I think is sublime, what I think is transcendent, or where I choose to hear the voice of God is nobody's business but my own. "Yes, of course" (the environmentalists' answer was and would continue to be), "but please acknowledge that I am different from you, and I deserve my chance to live according to my lights and values, which means that some portion of untrammeled nature ought to be preserved, to allow me this kind of experience."

And when that message was sent, the recipients couldn't help but hear another: "And oh, by the way, you'd be a better person if only you were a bit more like me." No one likes to be condescended to. And moral arguments have their greatest force on youthful and open minds, those who haven't developed the cognitive inertia that tends to accumulate over time, as the values we hold (whether by principle or by unreflective acceptance of what's been taught to us or modeled for us or drummed into our neocortexes by decades of commercial advertising) become solidified in our life choices—our habits, patterns, possessions, and customary ways of being on the planet. Many an unresilient mind resists change with the phrase "What you say may be true in theory, but . . ." —an acknowledgment that theoretical understanding that emerges from a careful review of evidence and argument sometimes fails to outweigh the cumulative mass of habit, routine, custom, the weight of previous choices.

A third line of argument offered more success: enlightened, long-range self-interest suggests that we should care about the world we deed to our progeny, the world that we ourselves will inhabit next year and the year after and the year after. That care and concern is a major factor in most of the successes that the environmental movement has achieved. You see it in the passage of the Clean Air and Clean Water Acts, in the Endangered Species Act, in zoning regulations that bend development pressure away from ecosystem destruction. Confusingly enough, Infinite-Planet Theory made it both harder (in some cases) and easier (in some cases) to bring these changes about. I doubt the Clean Air and Clean Water Acts of the 1970s would pass Congress as it is constituted today (and, indeed, conservatives in Congress have been actively working to undermine and gut key provisions of those laws). In the 1970s, Infinite-Planet Theory could reassure its partisans that the world was large enough to support both an infinite-growth economy and the protection and preservation of environmental quality that was encoded into those Acts. On an infinite planet, there's no trade-off between development and preservation, between cashing out natural capital and preserving it for its social benefit. We can have more of both, forever.

In sum, though, neither the moral argument, nor the pragmatic argument from personal development, nor the pragmatic argument from long-range interest has been successful at preserving enough of the functioning ecosystems of the planet to guarantee the continued existence of our civilization. Clearly, the preservation of enough ecosystem services to sustain civilization requires a different kind of argument, a different kind of appeal.

Throughout this book I've made a rationalist's case for sustainable thinking, taking up individual elements of Infinite-Planet Theory and arguing for their replacement by something more realistic. The EKC is bogus; Julian Simon loses the bet if it's run again, and in any event resource prices signal market, not geophysical, scarcity; Malthus's arguments were never successfully refuted, but the dynamic that demonstrates them in the world was put on hold for a handful of generations by the trick we learned of turning antique sunlight into food, something he never could have imagined; Pareto Optimality is a perverse standard and has got to be discarded; on a finite planet, the road to serfdom is paved with good, free-market intentions; and so on. Of course I hope that these arguments will convince and that they will eventually lead us to adopt a sounder, rationally defensible, finite-planet perspective. I think these arguments have to be made, but I have few illusions that policy change on such a major scale will be the product of a simple falling-of-scales-from-the-eyes, a collective lightbulb moment that will suddenly create an overwhelming consensus for change. We won't get the change we need without broad public support, and the majority of citizen-participants in our system are unlikely to be moved by what must seem recondite arguments about the finer points of economic theory and practice.

What is needed is a vision that will engage, motivate, and inform. And here, ecology as the Unforgiving Dictatorship of No continues to have a branding problem. True as it may be, the negative message — "We must change or die" — is not an easy sell.

We need, instead, a positive vision of what green might bring.

And that vision, effectively articulated, aligns well with the vision implicitly held and sometimes explicitly articulated by a broad swath of conservative voters — including those "values voters" who feel that some important foundation of American life has been degraded in recent decades. Since the Reagan Revolution, conservatives have been selling the idea that the cause of the decline that Americans can't help but feel is liberal thinking and the institution of government itself. Progressives and liberals have offered no clear alternative explanation for that decline, and their silence has allowed conservatives to cast them in the role of villain. Progressive and liberal "messaging" in the (ironically) conservative effort to hang on to our nation's fundamental values — values like toleration, civil liberties, equal access to clean air and clean water, equality of opportunity in education and in life — has not been as effectively organized or as monotonously repeated as the message offered by conservatives.

It's time for that to change. It's time for progressives to package and sell a coherent diagnosis of the condition we find ourselves in and to place blame where blame actually lies: with bad economic theory and the pursuit and use of cheap energy. These together have degraded our neighborhoods, our families, our communities, and our political heritage of a free and open society. The values we hold as Americans have been diminished and continue to be threatened not by growth of government, not by liberals with their all-American commitment to toleration and protection of the civil liberties and dignity of even the weakest among us, not by regulation of the worst excesses of capital and corporate power that, in accordance with established free-market theory, seeks nothing but the augmentation of its own monetary reward (environmental "externalities" be damned). No, the fundamental source of the threat to American values and strength is something else entirely: the centrifugal force of cheap energy and a single-minded dedication to bad economic theory, including the idea that the highest purpose of both economic policy and personal ambition is to increase, continually and forever, the commotion of money in the economy.

In *The Geography of Nowhere*, James Howard Kunstler wrote eloquently and sometimes furiously about the loss of community in America — the loss of that "web of practical interrelationships between neighbors who understand their mutual dependency and honor it by competently caring for their work, their town, their offspring, and each other." In far too much of our broad and accommodating land, that basic texture of life, once so obvious as to hardly need remarking, and once so full and complete that its loss could scarcely be imagined, has raveled into nothing — try though we might to evoke its return through incantatory political rhetoric, or through surly forays against those whom conservatives encourage us to believe are most culpable for its loss. The conservative agenda, with its scapegoating of liberalism, calls for a return to what it sees as the fundamental values and political institutions of an earlier, simpler, better era. When the conservative agenda isn't simply a cynical movement to empower corporations and give them freer reign to manufacture profit by imposing "negative externalities"— costs and harms—on the rest of us, it offers defensive and remedial legislation aimed at restoring the whole cloth of the organic communities—the social capital—we once enjoyed. But it can't do that, not as long as it remains committed to infinite-planet principles, because the infinite-growth, commotion-of-money economy creates wealth by cashing out both social and natural capital. To emphasize: the conservative economic program destroys social capital, then blames liberalism and government for the loss.

The social policies that conservatives advocate do little more than attempt to salvage this or that thread of the thin and palpably unsatisfying tapestry that cheap-energy, infinite-planet commerce has given us in place of the truly satisfying, soul-sustaining, community-building weft of human relations that Americans once knew. Meanwhile, the conservative program's oblivious disregard of obvious market failures, along with its unswerving commitment to increasing the commotion of money in the economy, continues to shred, with great energy, the human connections by which our collective life—our social, political, familial, neighborly life—is held together.

Within the experience of most Americans alive today, genuine community is so thoroughly absent that most know it only indirectly: through empathetic understanding of the lives of elders, through glimmers of the last remnants that have yet to be fully unwoven in this or that town or village that manages, against all odds, to retain a sense of place and of purposed collectivity within that place; and, sadly, through touristy visits to kitschy simulacras of what life on a human, neighborly scale must once have been like. As we stroll about Williamsburg Village or Greenfield Village or await the daily parade at Disney World, on its faux-gaslit, humanly scaled, premodern "Main Street, usa," we think, "Yes: this is the *real* America."

The diagnosis Kunstler offers is that we no longer have the satisfactions of community because we no longer have the sheer physical container, the built landscape, in which such community can abide, let alone thrive. Free-market theory tells us that the public interest is best served by individuals pursuing individual self-interest; the public good is supposedly nothing more than the simple cumulation of private greeds, expressed daily in various markets and biennially in our elections. Because we've lost any sense that the interests of the public might be something different and other than the private interests of the individuals who comprise that public, it's not surprising that, as Kunstler writes, "most of our public spaces are squalid." Nor is it any wonder that our politics—the collective, participatory arena in which we articulate and represent to ourselves the lives we live and want to live in those spaces—are squalid as well. (In federal and state elections, the Money Party—the party that includes one candidate in every contested race, the candidate who spends the most money—wins about 95 percent of the time, a success rate that rivals what dictators achieve in single-party systems.)

We built our public world, and it returns the favor by building us— subtly and not so subtly. It is impossible to do today what nearly any urban-dwelling American could do in the late nineteenth and early twentieth century: fulfill the daily needs of life—shop, work, obtain food, visit family and friends—by walking no more than a quarter mile for any single purpose (and making use of trolleys and various other public conveyances when needed), encountering neighbors, friends, acquaintances, fellow citizens along the way. That see-and-be-seen foundation of civic life has been transsected to death by roads, highways, parking lots built to accommodate the vehicles that speed us on our rounds while encouraging us to see our fellow citizens as little more than impediments—pedestrians who get in the way, fellow drivers who slow us down. The absence of pleasant public space encourages "cocooning"—withdrawal into the private sphere—as does the commercialization and increased capital costs of entertainments and pastimes once less expensively and more publicly shared: music no longer comes from neighborly joint production but is experienced privately, through headphones. Narrative entertainments are enjoyed in private, in home "theaters." Our most attractive public places aren't civically owned but are shopping malls—places where we meet as fellow consumers, not as fellow citizens. More and more of our meals are prepared not in the family kitchen but "out," eaten not with friends and family but alone or in the company of other restaurant patrons—strangers—who don't fully realize that the "break" they "deserve today" is also a break from building and sustaining the social capital that is necessary for democracy, for community, for individual psychological well-being.

Because our economic ideas were suited to an infinite planet with cheap energy and cheap resources and no environmental limit that can't be pushed back through innovation and invention, we've given ourselves a political culture that embodies the presumption that getting and spending for private satisfaction are nearly the sum total of our civic duty. (Remember how, when the towers came down on 9/11, President Bush's great patriotic call was for Americans to keep shopping? That's good, solid infinite-planet thinking at work.) We've given ourselves a built world that presumes that each of us will have an individual, fossil-fueled, discretionary transportation unit whose antipedestrian logic is so compelling that it's completely typical to see a huge suv double-park in the fire lane at the mall, its driver selfishly and carelessly obstructing traffic, to disembark overweight passengers who thereby avoid the necessity of walking an additional ten yards from a parking space.

In service to the freedom of automotive transport, Kunstler tells us, we have built ugly, dysfunctional, soul-numbing places in America. Predictably enough, these cultural containers shape our collective civic life into something that is ugly, dysfunctional, and soul-numbing. It's no wonder that there is a strong strain of disquiet and anger at work in the polity today. Some citizens' entirely understandable discontent with the world as Infinite-Planet Theory has made it has been shaped by conservative messaging into anger at government, at public servants, at those who act or behave or think differently than the majority. If we're to have a sustainable world—and if we're to preserve the democratic freedoms on which our country was founded—progressives have got to come up with their own, alternative, more accurate diagnosis.

A sustainable society, you'll recall, is one that does not draw down any of the capital stocks on which its continued existence depends: natural, built, social, cultural. In the call to care for and tend the latter two, less easily quantifiable forms of capital lies the potential for creating a coalition movement for sustainability that includes those conservative "values" voters who know that something is deeply and horribly amiss in our society.

Granted, the extremists among those voters—the gay-bashers and xenophobes and racists, the anti-abortion activists who feel justified in murdering doctors — are unlikely to be drawn in to such a coalition. But their political programs are properly understood as being grounded in pathology, not principled policy. Homophobia, racism, and hatred of foreigners are symptoms, not solutions; behind them all lies the degradation and loss of the elementary capacity for empathy on which civil society — any civil society other than outright despotism and tyranny — is founded. That capacity for civil empathy is both a product of and a key component of social capital.

Social capital — the stock of trust, mutual understanding, shared values, and socially held knowledge that facilitates our ability to live a satisfying, commodious life with others — flourishes in neighborhoods whose residents have reason to be conscious of their shared enterprise, neighborhoods knit together by time, a sense of shared experience, a sense of shared commitment to place. Its sustenance is civic acquaintance, mutual respect, and basic empathy. Like natural capital (healthy ecosystems seen as providers of economically valuable services), social capital tends to grow of itself when circumstances are right — when the physical container of the built environment allows it, when the human community that occupies that built environment isn't rent by unbridgeable divisions. Because humans are gregarious and necessarily interdependent — the true hermit is a rarity, only slightly less odd than a lone ant — social capital is a naturally occurring phenomenon. It's evident in and strengthened by every act of public courtesy, every act of neighborly care — every casserole delivered to a shut-in, every dog walked while the owner is away, every sincerely offered "Hello, how are you?" It's diminished by selfish disregard of the interests of others; by cynical use of other people as means to an end rather than as ends in themselves; by social isolation (whether by individuals, or by subgroups that maintain a "lifestyle enclave" within the larger community where they reside); by unequal treatment of groups or individuals before the law or the court of public opinion; by disregard for public spaces and shared history; by transience, by civic ignorance, by the commercialization of services (including social entertainments) formerly rendered, without thought of recompense, by neighbors, friends, family. In short, loss of social capital is hastened by the practical application of free-market economic thinking within a rapidly growing population whose political economy is fueled by cheap energy.

American communities enjoyed a high level of social capital in the pre-petroleum era—a stock of it sufficient and sturdy enough to survive the onslaught of oil and economic development for a generation or two. (Hypothesis: the "generation gap" that was much remarked upon in America in the 1960s was the historical cusp of this transition: the older generation wanted to retain the social capital it had known, even as the stock of it had declined to unsatisfactory levels; the younger generation, with little social capital to inherit, adapted to its absence and turned to the development of newer forms, some of them more and some of them less generally satisfactory than the forms their parents had known.) Because a post-carbon, ecologically sustainable world is a world in which social capital fares a great deal better than it does today, it's the world that most Americans want. It's a world with stronger families and neighborhoods, and hence less need of governmental "workarounds" to replace functions once performed by families and neighbors for each other. It's a world with cleaner air and water and enough material and social security to let us enjoy our lives.

It's time for the environmental movement to package that vision and sell it. Failing to do so allows infinite-planet thinking to carry the day. In the infinite-planet vision articulated by conservatives, our communities would be restored to their pre-petroleum level of social capital if we cut government spending, slash social services, make people be more self-reliant, and free up capital from social control and restraint so that it can get on with the business of transforming ecosystems into commodities—the stuff we buy at the big-box store down the highway. That diagnosis-and-proposal is simply wrong.

For decades, many conservative voters have perceived environmentalists as purveyors of "gloom and doom" who issue dire warnings that can safely be ignored. That's changing, as it becomes increasingly evident that environmentalists' warnings about climate change and deforestation and peak oil can't be safely ignored. The weather on Factory Planet—the daily succession of bad news on the environmental beat—increasingly forces us to recognize that something is fundamentally and basically wrong with how we've organized our economic life and our thinking about that economic life. By the time a majority of Americans recognize the need for change and succeed in getting that recognition to be the foundation of electoral politics and subsequent policy, the

steps necessary to retrieve a sound ecological foundation for our culture will be dismayingly difficult. Landscapers and foresters have a saying that applies here: the best time to plant a tree, or to begin addressing
our ecological crisis, is twenty years ago. The second best time is today.

As we stumble toward recognizing climate change to be the outstanding environmental "externality" that we have, through infinite-
planet thinking, imposed on ourselves, many Americans continue to
use an outdated frame to understand environmental politics. That
frame is popular because it offers drama—there's conflict, there's disagreement, there's a clear choice between feel-good free marketers and
finger-wagging moralists, between optimism and pessimism. Given
that choice, many people choose optimism. Recognizing this, some environmental organizations (the National Wildlife Federation, for instance) have joined the Infinite-Planet Theorists in asserting that there
is no trade-off between economic growth and healthy ecosystems—we
can have both, they reassure us. Daly and Farley's distinction between
growth and development is crucial here: in an ecologically sustainable
society, we can have continual improvement in our standard of living,
but what we can't have is a continually increasing ecological footprint.
That distinction is not widely appreciated, and unless it is emphasized,
those who deny a growth-vs.-environment trade-off end up, by default,
in the infinite-planet camp.

Rather than telling the American public that it's possible to have economic growth and ecosystem preservation at the same time, a more accurate and hence better strategy would be for environmental groups
to frame the choice as being between two kinds of optimism: realistic
and unrealistic. "Infinite-Planet Theory" should sound as ridiculous as
"Flat Earth Theory." With effort and persistence, it will. American voters need to be given the opportunity to see that the work of building an
environmentally secure future is not just about building a sustainable
economy; it's about sustaining our communities as well. They need to
hear this message: everything that we value—things like strong families, good neighborhoods, financial security, health, physical safety and
security, clean air and water—is not only possible but is easier to get,
have, and keep within a sustainable economy. They need to hear that
the aspects of modern culture that they don't like—broken families,
families that disperse and live far apart, the fear and anxiety that come

with crime and foreign wars, the incidence of sad people living in isolation who don't know their neighbors and can't rely on them, the dirtier air and water brought by the feverish pursuit of resources, all the environmental threats to safety and health, and not enough time to do the things that bring us happiness and well-being — have their origins in a get-rich-quick economy that tells us, implicitly and explicitly, that using fossil fuel to make and chase wealth is the highest purpose in life.

Both Democrats and Republicans have been partisans of Infinite-Planet Theory, though the most doctrinaire assertion of infinite-planet principles has come from the conservative wing of the Republican Party. Using the conceptual frame offered by Hayek, conservatives have been successful in pandering to people's legitimate desire to preserve their freedoms and enjoy the benefits of healthy communities, even as the conservative political agenda promotes the privatization of public good and the unregulated engines of economic development that impose social and ecological externalities on all of us, damaging the physical and social foundations of our freedoms and communities. Conservatives sell us the disease, then sell us potions and lotions that they say will cure it but in fact can only make it worse.

The choice we face — the most salient division that will shape politics for generations to come — isn't between Republicans and Democrats, between conservatism and liberalism, or even between free-market ideology and social control of capital. The fundamental division that will shape the future of our country and our civilization, our politics and our planet, is the choice between neoclassical business as usual and a new economic vision; between Infinite-Planet Theory and Sustainable Communities.

I'm an optimist: I think that when the choice is offered to them that way, most Americans will choose well.

acknowledgments

The author wishes to express his deep appreciation to the Bogliasco Foundation, whose generous provision of a fellowship month at their Ligurian Study Center contributed enormously to the writing of this book. Thanks are also due to friends, too numerous to mention, whose interest in and enthusiasm for these topics helped sustain my own. My students and colleagues at the Gund Institute for Ecological Economics at the University of Vermont, in the architecture program at the Sam Fox School at Washington University in St. Louis, and in the Prague Program at Empire State College heard many of the ideas and arguments here before they found their way into print, and the writing benefited enormously from that engagement. Portions of the work also benefited from editorial attention by, among others, Joyce Appleby, Eric Ball, James M. Banner, Hal Clifford, Bill Cohn, Brian Czech, Patrick Deneen, Rob Dietz, Mark Lotto, and Adam Siegel. Jon Erickson, Richard Pult, Christi Stanforth, and Bill Vitek offered thoughtful responses to the whole. It almost goes without saying, but I will say it: any and all errors and shortcomings of judgment evident in the text are my own.

Ideas and passages from this book have appeared in various venues, in print and online. Thanks go to the *Daly News*, a publication of the Center for the Advancement of the Steady-State Economy, for permission to borrow as needed from my semi-regular essays there, including especially "The Financial Crisis Is the Environmental Crisis." Thanks are due to the *History News Network* for permission to publish, in revised form, "Is Industrial Civilization a Pyramid Scheme?" and "Reforming Seigniorage: Key to a Sustainable Economy." The editors of the *Front Porch Republic* gave permission to borrow from "Mill, Hayek, and the Other Road to Serfdom," published there in February 2010. "What 'Sustainability' Is" appeared in slightly different form as "Theses on Sustainability: A Primer," in *Orion*, May/June 2010. "Ending the Culture War" is a revision of "Transcending the Culture Wars: Environmental History as Meta-metanarrative," which appeared in *Liberal Education* 94, no. 2 (2008); the author gratefully acknowledges permission to reprint the material here. Thanks are also due to the editors of the *New York Times* for permission to use op-ed material I published there under the titles "G.D.P. R.I.P." and "Mr. Soddy's Ecological Economy," August 10, 2009, and April 12, 2009, respectively.

Finally, I owe the largest debt of gratitude to the patience, forbearance, friendly ear, enthusiastic interest, and sturdy support of my wife, Kathryn Davis.

notes

introduction: the weather on factory planet

x *Fewer than one in a hundred*
Evan Mills, "Insurance in a Climate of Change," *Science* 302, August 12, 2005, pp. 1040–1044, online at www.sciencemag.org/content/309/5737/1040.full. Mills's catalog of the threats climate change poses to the insurance industry is sobering: "Specific technical risks include the following: (i) Shortening times between loss events. (ii) Changing absolute and relative variability of losses. (iii) Changing structure of types of events. (iv) Shifting spatial distribution of events. (v) Damage functions that increase exponentially with weather intensity (e.g., wind damages rise with the cube of the speed). (vi) Abrupt or nonlinear changes in losses. (vii) Widespread geographical simultaneity of losses (e.g., from tidal surges arising from a broad die-off of protective coral reefs or disease outbreaks on multiple continents). (viii) More single events with multiple, correlated consequences. This was well evidenced in the pan-European heat catastrophe of 2003 — where temperatures were six standard deviations from the norm. Immediate or delayed impacts included extensive human morbidity and mortality, wildfire, massive crop losses, and the curtailment of electric power plants owing to the high temperature or lack of cooling water. (ix) More hybrid events with multiple consequences [e.g., El Niño–Southern Oscillation (ENSO)–related rain, ice storms, floods, mudslides, droughts, and wildfires]. And those are just the technical risks; the market-based risks are considerable, as well."

x *State Farm dropped 125,000 customers*
Randy Diamond, "State Farm Pullout Leaves Florida Policyholders Scrambling," *Palm Beach Post*, January 27, 2009; "State Farm Cancels Thousands in Fla.," MSNBC, February 3, 2010, www.msnbc.msn.com/id/35220269/ns/business-personal_finance/t/state-farm-cancels-thousands-fla/. The state Office of Insurance Regulation calculates that more than half of the largest underwriting companies are running net losses in Florida. Their profit-making operations elsewhere are subsidizing homeowners' insurance in Florida, which means Floridians are not paying the full cost of climate change in their state.

xi *The world burns 87.4 million barrels of oil every day*
Statistical Review of World Energy 2011, British Petroleum, at www.bp.com/statisticalreview, p. 9.

xi *9 million barrels of oil*

The US National Academy of Sciences (NAS) estimates that 9 million barrels of oil found their way into world oceans from human activity in 2002; super-tankers—the largest ships ever built, rivaling skyscrapers in volume—can hold 2 million barrels. Not all of the oil released into the world's oceans by human action comes from supertankers and other shipping, of course; I'm just using them as a unit of measurement. Blowouts from underwater drilling contribute. So does runoff from land-based spillage and use of oil. The NAS estimates that naturally occurring seepages account for just under half of all petroleum in the world's waters. This can seem comforting: nature does this to herself, so what's the big deal with human spillage? But aquatic life has adapted to the natural presence of this toxin over millennia, and in a few short decades we have doubled the burden. And seepage from undersea vents doesn't find its way as readily into sensitive coastal wetlands; our spillage represents a short, sharp shock to those ecosystems. See US Department of the Interior Minerals Management Service, "OCS Oil Spill Facts," September 2002, *www.boemre.gov/stats/PDFs/2002_OilSpillFacts.pdf.*

xii *Little resilience in our food delivery system*

The food delivery system has inadvertent resilience in the form of waste. The UN Food and Agriculture Organization (FAO) estimates that as much as one-third of the food raised for humans does not find its way into a consumer. See "Cutting Food Waste to Feed the World," FAO Media Release, May 11, 2011, www.fao.org/news/story/en/item/74192/icode/. Of course that waste should be reduced. Increasing the food system's efficiency, rather than its acreage under cultivation or the quantity of artificial fertilizers it uses, looks to be the least-cost way of feeding additional people, just as harvesting "nega-watts"—savings from conservation and efficiency in electricity production and use—is in many cases cheaper than building additional generating capacity. A realistic target, says one study in the United Kingdom, would be to halve food waste by 2050—leaving something like 17 percent of our food wasted. ("Synthesis Report C7: Reducing Waste," part of the Foresight Project on Global Food and Farming Futures, published by the Government Office for Science, January 2011, www.bis.gov.uk/assets/bispartners/foresight/docs/food-and-farming/synthesis/11-627-c7-reducing-waste.pdf). Like the harvest of "negawatts," comprehensive waste reduction in our food system is a one-shot bonus; while it may ameliorate the problem in the present, the problem recurs if population control policies aren't implemented.

xiv *"Make a whore of his wife"*

The quotation is from Wendell Berry, "The Unforeseen Wilderness: An Essay on Kentucky's Red River Gorge," excerpted in *Words from the Land,* ed. Stephen Trimble (Salt Lake City: Peregrine Smith Books, 1988), 233.

xiv *"What is property but the profits thereof?"*
Justice Scalia, in his majority opinion in *Lucas v. South Carolina Coastal Council*, 505 U.S. 1003 (1992).

xvi *"The multiplier of everything else"*
William Ryerson, "Population: The Multiplier of Everything Else," in *The Post Carbon Reader*, ed. Richard Heinberg and Daniel Lerch (Healdsburg, CA: Watershed Media, 2010), 153–176.

xix *The sun delivers more energy in one hour*
This information comes from the Wikipedia entry titled "Solar Energy," en.wikipedia.org/wiki/Solar_energy, and it checks out. See the data on the webpage of the Stanford University Global Climate and Energy Project: gcep .stanford.edu/research/exergy/resourcechart.html.

xx *Not a completely costless benefit*
This is a nit that might need picking. "Passive solar gain" looks to be costless: the sunlight is falling for free, so why not install a south-facing window and reap it as space heating? In an existing structure, this is (in solar terms) a costless benefit. (In economic terms, you have to remember that installing windows and skylights costs money.) It's costless in solar terms because the cost has already been paid, as the loss of sunlight-as-income to whatever plant and animal life was displaced by the footprint of the building. A structure that doesn't capture the solar energy that falls on it is, in effect, throwing that income away.

xx *Forests being cut at a rate of acres per second*
Two to four acres are deforested per second, according to the World Wildlife Federation. See their press release of December 11, 2007, "Amazon Deforestation Rates Decreasing, Rainforests Still Threatened," www.worldwildlife.org/ who/media/press/2007/WWFPresitem6285.html.

xxi *"We're pond scum," as Gary Flomenhoft puts it*
Personal conversation with Gary Flomenhoft, spring 2011.

xxiv *Land you chase others away from*
This definition of "territory" suggests a common root between *terra*, earth or land, and *terror*, the panic that comes from threat of harm: you protect your territory by creating fear in others. Is there some connection here with terrorism? I think so. Terrorists are people who are not agents of a legitimate government and who use violence for political ends. They do not control the territory in which they perpetrate the violence; often they control no territory whatsoever. (If they did control territory, they would be actors serving some form of government—an insurgency, an aggressor nation or province or city, a splinter regime, a faction in a civil war.) This is no way excuses or justifies the use of political violence to create terror. I merely mean to point out that the term "terrorism" seems to be reserved for violence perpetrated

by individuals or groups who are not agents of legitimate governments, and one criterion of legitimacy — perhaps the ultimate, definitive one — is that a legitimate government controls territory.

the other road to serfdom

2 *Arable land per person*
The arable land figures are from "Global Perspectives," chapter 1 of *Global Environmental Outlook 2000*, a report issued by the United Nations Environmental Programme, available at www.unep.org/geo2000/english/0027.htm #img5b.

2 *One-third of all arable land has become unusable for that purpose*
"Worldwide soil erosion has caused farmers to abandon about 430 million ha of arable land during the last 40 years, an area equivalent to about one-third of all present cropland." Henry W. Kendall and David Pimentel, "Constraints on the Expansion of the Global Food Supply," *Ambio* 23, no. 3 (May 1994): 198–205, quote on 200.

3 *The US Bill of Rights is no longer a particularly ambitious statement of rights*
Other statements of human rights, like the UN's Universal Declaration of Human Rights, have displaced the US Constitution as the model that other nations seek to emulate. See Adam Liptak, "'We the People' Loses Appeal with People around the World," *New York Times*, February 7, 2012, reporting the survey work of David S. Law and Mila Versteeg.

4 *Statement of basic rights from the United Nations*
See the Universal Declaration of Human Rights, particularly Articles 22 through 25, which set a standard that the United States doesn't meet: www .un.org/en/documents/udhr.

4 *The true foundation of our experience of freedom*
Wendell Berry, "Feminism, the Body, and the Machine," *Cross Currents* 52, no. 1 (Spring 2003).

4 *"Every man has a Property in his own Person"*
John Locke, *Second Treatise,* chap. 5. Locke uses this premise to develop his theory of property — the preservation, protection, and extension of which is the great rise of government, in his view. I criticize the infinite-planet premises of Lockean democratic theory in "Fixing Locke: Civil Liberties on a Finite Planet," in *Rhetorics, Literacies, and Narratives of Sustainability*, ed. Peter N. Goggin (New York: Routledge, 2009), 180–201. The notion that civil freedom requires privacy, a privacy that can be styled as property-in-self, comes into play later in this volume in a discussion of Oklahoma abortions laws and SUVs.

5 *Every pound of lobster has been assigned to a use*
It's worth noting that management of the lobster harvest to limit it to sus-

tainable yield doesn't mean that the price of lobster remains stable. In the summer of 2011 the lobster market experienced a "glut"—an increase of supply against a fairly steady demand—which led to falling prices. Regulation of lobstering doesn't set limits to supply by limiting the gross weight of the catch brought ashore; it forbids the taking of egg-carrying females and limits the number of commercial licenses, the physical size of lobsters taken, the length of the season. Stability of market price is not a management goal of the fishery. The recent (2011) surge in lobster harvests in Maine is most probably due to overfishing of species that prey on lobster; the result is a monocultural fishery that is vulnerable to sudden collapse. See Cornelia Dean, "Lobsters Find Utopia Where Biologists See Trouble," *New York Times*, August 23, 2011.

5 *Waiting list for a lobstering permit*
See Sandra Dinsmore, "Lobster Licenses Key to Survival of Maine's Year-Round Islands," *Working Waterfront* (a periodical published by the Island Institute), January 28, 2009, available at www.workingwaterfront.com/articles/Lobster-licenses-key-to-survival-of-Maines-year-round-islands/12937.

7 *Elaboration of a memo Hayek wrote in the early 1930s*
The publishing history of the book is recounted in the introduction to the anniversary edition of the book: Friedrich Hayek, *The Road to Serfdom*, edited and with an introduction by Bruce Caldwell (Chicago: University of Chicago Press, 2007). Unless otherwise noted, this is the edition of *The Road to Serfdom* cited throughout.

7 *Many paradigm-defining works in political economy originate in crisis*
This insight is the organizational theme of Sheldon Wolin's classic treatment of the history of political theory, *Politics and Vision* (1960; repr., Princeton, NJ: Princeton University Press, 2004).

9 *Labour Party pamphlet*
The Labour Party pamphlet titled *The Old World and the New Society* is quoted by Caldwell in his introduction to Hayek, *Road to Serfdom*, 12. I am indebted to Caldwell's introduction for much of the material here on the context in which Hayek wrote.

10 *"A time for revolutions, not for patching"*
Sir William Beveridge, *Social Insurance and Allied Services* (New York: Macmillan, 1942), 6.

10 *"Entrepreneur . . . is replaced by a central planning body"*
Hayek, *Road to Serfdom*, 83.

10 *"Fascism and communism . . . have much more in common with each other"*
Ibid., 23.

11 *The Nazi-industrial system experimented with nutrition*
See Richard L. Rubenstein, *The Cunning of History* (New York: HarperPerennial, 1987).

13 *SLAPP suits*

Through a SLAPP suit, a business or other goal-maximizing organization deprives its target of the free exercise of constitutionally protected speech, and because the legal system is itself the instrument of that denial, a defendant's pursuit of legal remedy simply adds to the burden. Strategic use of the law this way often involves withdrawal of the suit before a decision is reached, which prevents a decision that might set a precedent limiting such suits. They're often brought by developers against environmental critics. See George William Pring and Penelope Canan, *SLAPPS: Getting Sued for Speaking Out* (Philadelphia: Temple University Press, 1996).

14 *"Enough and as good"*

The phrase "enough and as good" is from Locke's derivation of the right to property in *The Second Treatise.* Humans, he says, have an·aboriginal right to appropriate whatever they need from nature as long as they meet two criteria: they don't allow anything to spoil before they use it, and their appropriation leaves "enough and as good" for others. I criticize Locke's infinite-planet assumptions in "Fixing Locke: Civil Liberties for a Finite Planet," cited in note 7 above.

14 *Caldwell summarizes the book's main point*

From Caldwell's introduction to Hayek, *Road to Serfdom*, 26.

15 *A statement Samuelson emphasized twice*

Paul Samuelson, *Economics*, 11th ed. (New York: McGraw-Hill, 1980), 827.

15 *Hayek's letter to Samuelson*

The correspondence is reported by Caldwell in Hayek, *Road to Serfdom*, 28.

16 *The cartoon version of Hayek's book*

The text and pictures from the cartoon pamphlet are being kept in circulation by the Ludwig von Mises Institute, the Austrian school think tank, at mises. org/books/TRTS/, which evidently considers its message timeless: no publication dates are offered there. GM's enthusiasm for free-market capitalism reached no further than its own bottom line; in the 1980s it helped secure quota protection against the competition offered by imports, and little more two decades later it found itself in government receivership.

16 *A "necessary outcome" of socialism*

Hayek, *Road to Serfdom*, abridged version published in *Reader's Digest*, April 1945, 31–32.

16 *Ringing, anthemic statements*

These statements are from Hayek, *Road to Serfdom*, 229 and 212, respectively.

19 *Hayek on guarantees against severe physical privation*
Hayek, *Road to Serfdom*, 147–148. The quotations that follow come from this
passage as well.

21 *"Only within this system is democracy possible"*
Ibid., 110.

22 *Oskar Lange had proposed a central price board*
See Oskar Lange and Fred Taylor, *On the Economic Theory of Socialism*, ed.
Benjamin Lippincott (Minneapolis: University of Minnesota Press, 1938).

24 *Too big to fail*
Those followers of Hayek who railed against bank bailouts in the wake of the
2008 financial collapse were at least being consistent, though to those with
Keynesian principles the Hayekian crowd looked to be mistaking an instrumental end for an ultimate end. Hayekians were all too willing to trash the
world economy, condemning quite a few people to straitened circumstances,
in order to abide by a cherished principle that was supposed to make the
economy sound and productive of benefit.

24 *Prices should "tell the ecological truth"*
The much-quoted epigram by Oystein Dahle is cited by Lester Brown in *Plan
B 3.0* as coming from a discussion he had with Dahle at the State of the World
Conference in Aspen, CO, July 22, 2001. See Brown, *Plan B 3.0* (New York:
W. W. Norton Co., 2008), 267.

25 *Pigouvian taxes and subsidies*
A. C. Pigou, *The Economics of Welfare* (New York: Macmillan, 1920). In the
time since he wrote, "welfare" has come to mean "a system of income redistri-
bution that establishes a base-level standard of living within a society." That's
not what Pigou meant by the term; he meant human welfare in its broadest
sense.

26 *Green tax policy*
One comprehensive proposal for a green tax policy, for the state of Vermont,
was prepared by Gary Flomenhoft of the Gund Institute for Ecological Economics at the University of Vermont. See Flomenhoft et al., "Valuing Common Assets for Public Finance, Green Tax and Common Assets Project,"
University of Vermont, 2008, and Flomenhoft et al., "A Green Tax Shift for
Vermont, Green Tax and Common Assets Project," University of Vermont,
2009.

28 *Green taxes have been under discussion for more than two decades*
See, for instance, Ernst Weizsacker and Jochen Jesinghaus, *Ecological Tax Reform* (London: Zed Books, 1992); Friends of the Earth, *Citizens Guide to Environmental Tax Shifting* (Washington, DC: Friends of the Earth, 1998).

28 *Europe, the United States, and pollution taxes*
Urban Institute and Brookings Institution, *The Tax Policy Briefing Book*, entry 2 and 3 of "Environmental Taxes," at www.taxpolicycenter.org/briefing-book/key-elements/environment/usa.cfm.

28 *The bank will take into account the value of unpriced ecosystem services*
In a speech in Japan on October 27, 2010, World Bank president Robert Zoellick announced a new World Bank initiative to start including the value of ecosystem services in calculations about economic development. See World Bank, "World Needs to Work Harder at Saving Biodiversity," Press Release No. 1022/150/EXC. See web.worldbank.org/WBSITE/EXTERNAL/NEWS/0 ,,contentMDK:22745067~pagePK:64257043~piPK:437376~theSitePK:4607 ,00.html.

28 *Green tax proposals*
Flomenhoft's proposal, "A Green Tax Shift for Vermont," can be found at www .uvm.edu/giee/?Page=research/greentax/greentax.html. The Earth Rights Institute produced a policy paper by Alanna Hartzok, "Financing Local to Global Public Goods: An Integrated Green Tax Shift Perspective," presented at the Global Institute for Taxation Conference, New York, NY, September 30, 1999. Other sources are legion; notable are the proposals from the Canadian and various European Green Parties.

29 *Structural reforms consistent with finite-planet thinking*
See Eric Zencey, "Fixing Locke: Civil Liberties for a Finite Planet," in Peter Goggin, ed., *Rhetorics, Literacies, and Narratives of Sustainability* (New York: Routledge, 2009).

30 *Eliminating subsidies for large families*
We'd want to retain the subsidy to large families given in the form of equal access of all children to public education, since a policy that decrees that third and fourth children are left uneducated is unjust and would have some very foreseeable undesirable consequences. A world in which undereducated younger siblings comprise a sizable demographic is not an attractive world at all; the maintenance of democracy in a complex world requires increasing, not decreasing, the general level of citizen understanding and intelligence.

what "sustainability" is

32 *Economically sustainable, ecologically sustainable, or socially sustainable*
W. M. Adams, "The Future of Sustainability: Re-thinking Environment and Development in the Twenty-First Century," Report of the International Union for the Conservation of Nature, Renowned Thinkers Meeting, Zurich, January 29–31, 2006 (published May 22, 2006; retrieved February 16, 2009, from cmsdata.iucn.org/downloads/iucn_future_of_sustainability.pdf).

34 *Social capital "facilitates the social coordination of economic activity"*

Neva Goodwin, Julie A. Nelson, and Jonathan Harris, *Macroeconomics in Context* (Armonk, NY: M. E. Sharpe, 2009), 48.

34 *Suburban sprawl makes the maintenance and retention of social capital more difficult*

This point is elaborated in the last chapter in this volume.

35 *Five carbon pools*

I first read this idea in an essay by William Vitek, "These Revolutionary Times," North Country Public Radio Essay, published at www.northcountrypublic radio.org/news/newsfacts/fact080722.html, reprinted from *Land Report* no. 91 (Summer 2008). Some energy thinkers, including Vitek, count natural gas as a distinct fifth type of carbon pool.

36 *Many were not*

See Jared Diamond, *Collapse: How Societies Choose to Fail or Succeed* (New York: Viking, 2005).

36 *The Brundtland Report definition of sustainability*

The World Commission on Environment and Development, Gro Harlem Brundtland, convenor; report published as *Our Common Future* (New York: Oxford University Press, 1987).

36 *The highly mathematized discipline of economics*

Nicholas Georgescu-Roegen, whose *The Entropy Law and the Economic Process* stands as the paradigm-defining text of ecological economics, criticized Pareto and the spurious "arithmomorphism" of the discipline. Georgescu-Roegen's early work in economics was econometric, and it was incorporation of thermodynamics that led him to reject what he came to see as a deeply flawed, mannerist preoccupation with mathematical rigor at the expense of geophysical accuracy.

37 *Human preference structures are intersubjective*

As we'll see later in a discussion of Rush Limbaugh's and Lynne Cheney's reaction to new standards for the teaching of American history, neoconservative pundits have railed against liberals for their supposed relativism — their belief that some values and morals differ between cultures and ought to be left to individual choice. Here we see that to the extent that neoconservative ideology is grounded in neoclassical "free-market" economic theory, it accepts in a very fundamental and corrosive way the relativism it claims to reject.

38 *Open thermodynamic system*

This insight belongs to Frederick Soddy; it lies behind a series of works he produced in the 1920s and 1930s, about which more later in this volume. Georgescu-Roegen's *The Entropy Law and the Economic Process* is mentioned in the note above as a paradigm-defining text in the field. Work by Herman Daly, one of Georgescu-Roegen's students, has also developed this view. See

Daly, *Steady State Economics* (Washington: Island Press, 1991); Daly with the theologian John Cobb, *The Common Good* (Boston: Beacon Press, 1994); and, with Joshua Farley, *Ecological Economics: Principles and Applications* (Washington: Island Press, 2004).

39 *"A stationary condition of capital"*
John Stuart Mill, in "Of the Stationary State," chapter 6 of book 4 of *Principles of Political Economy.*

39 *Growth versus progress*
Daly and Farley, in their text *Ecological Economics: Principles and Applications,* offer a useful distinction: economic growth results from increasing the material and energetic throughput of the economy. What they call economic development comes from innovation in our use of a constant flow of throughput (sized to be sustainable) to improve human living standards. This distinction hasn't yet entered the common lexicon and strikes the average ear as technical; the distinction between growth and progress is more readily understood.

40 *Genuine Progress Indicator*
See the entry "Indicators of Sustainable Development" in the online *Encyclopedia of Earth* at www.eoearth.org/article/Indicators_of_sustainable_development.

40 *My criticism of dire apocalyptic warnings*
See "Apocalypse and Ecology," in Eric Zencey, *Virgin Forest: Meditations on History, Ecology, and Culture* (Athens: University of Georgia Press, 1998).

41 *Soil community*
Edward Hyams (in his underappreciated classic, *Soil and Civilization* [New York: Harper & Row, 1952]) encourages us to see humans as members of a soil community and holds up the coevolution of agricultural practice and soil structure in preindustrial Europe as an example of successful human citizenship. Depletion of soil fertility—its drawdown faster than it can be replaced, which he calls "soil mining"—makes the culture that practices it unsustainable.

oil, economic theory, and the moral culpability of a discipline

42 *A Swedish scientist*
Svante Arrhenius, whose *Worlds in the Making* (New York: Harper and Row, 1908) clearly identifies the possibility that burning carbon fuels will increase global temperatures.

42 *"A large-scale geophysical experiment"*
Roger Revelle and Hans E. Suess, "Carbon Dioxide Exchange between Atmosphere and Ocean and the Question of an Increase of Atmospheric CO_2 during the Past Decades," *Tellus* 9 (1957): 18–27.

42 *Over the next half century*

The historical information here comes from Spencer Weart's excellent account of the history of climate change science, *The Discovery of Global Warming* (Cambridge, MA: Harvard University Press, 2008). Weart has put much of the content on a website maintained by the American Institute of Physics at www.aip.org/history/climate/index.htm.

42 *The Pentagon gave President Bush a report*

Peter Schwartz and Doug Randall, "An Abrupt Climate Change Scenario and Its Implications for United States National Security," www.edf.org/documents/3566_AbruptClimateChange.pdf, 5, 1.

43 *Reporters in Britain*

The quotation is from Randall, given by Robert Townsend and Paul Harris, "Now the Pentagon Tells Bush: Climate Change Will Destroy Us," *Observer*, February 22, 2004, www.guardian.co.uk/environment/2004/feb/22/usnews.theobserver.

43 *Republican strategy memo*

Quoted by Chris Mooney in "Earth Last," *American Prospect,* April 13, 2004, www.prospect.org/cs/articles?articleId=7603.

43 *Right-wing billionaires*

On Art Pope, see Sue Sturgis, "Art Pope's Millions Fund Climate Change Denial," *Grist*, October 26, 2010, www.prospect.org/cs/articles?articleId=7603. On the Koch brothers (David H. and Charles G. Koch), see Jane Mayer, "Covert Operations," *New Yorker*, August 30, 2010.

43 *Republican Senator James Inhofe of Oklahoma*

Senator Inhofe's staff reports that he received and read the 2004 strategy memo by Luntz, according to Chris Mooney, "Earth Last," *American Prospect*, April 16, 2004, prospect.org/article/earth-last-o.

44 *Pew Research Center poll*

Pew Research Center, "Wide Partisan Divide over Global Warming," October 27, 2010, pewresearch.org/pubs/1780/poll-global-warming-scientists-energy-policies-offshore-drilling-tea-party.

44 *The Supreme Court decision in Citizens United*

Citizens United v. Federal Election Commission, 130 S.Ct. 876, decided in 2010, broke new legal ground (and threw out much campaign financing law) by holding that corporations have First Amendment, free-speech rights to fund political broadcasts to influence elections.

45 *The 2004 edition of Principles of Economics*

Robert H. Frank and Ben S. Bernanke, *Principles of Economics*, 2nd ed. (New York: McGraw-Hill, 2004), 527–529.

47 *Inventory tends to be limited*

Two hundred eighty-nine million barrels—the estimated inventory of refined products in the United States — sounds like a lot, but given that our country consumes 19 million barrels a day, it works out to be about a two-week supply. On oil use, see US Energy Information Administration, "Oil: Crude and Petroleum Products Explained," data from 2008. On the size of the US inventory, see US Energy Information Administration, "Why Stocks Are Important," in *Oil Market Basics*.

47 *Gas doubled in price*

Jad Mouawad and Simon Romero, "Hurricane Katrina: The Oil Supply; Gas Prices Surge as Supply Drops," *New York Times* September 1, 2005.

48 *Production from other states*

Supply from other states was stable because new discoveries in them were rare and weren't large enough to swing the market, while existing production came under a technical limit: an oil reservoir under a natural, dissolved-gas drive has a maximum efficient rate (MER) of production. To exceed it reduces the amount of oil that can be recovered in the future without expensive pumping and other recovery methods. A self-interested producer sitting atop a wholly owned reservoir with dissolved-gas drive will neither exceed the MER and reduce future income, nor produce under the MER and reduce income in the present.

49 *Worth less than the barrels it was stored in*

In 1901, the gusher at Spindletop signaled the discovery of a huge field whose exploitation drove the price of oil down to three cents a barrel. In 1930, production from the newly discovered East Texas Field crashed the price from $1.10 to ten cents a barrel. See Texas Railway Commission, "Railroad Commission Milestones," www.rrc.state.tx.us/about/history/milestones/milestones.php.

50 *Sitting in their offices in Austin*

Useful information on the Texas Railway Commission is available from their website, particularly the pages on history that open at www.rrc.state.tx.us/about/history/. See also Daniel Yergin, *The Prize: The Epic Quest for Oil, Money and Power* (New York: Simon and Schuster, 2008).

51 *Robert Repetto offered one account*

Robert Repetto, "Accounting for Environmental Assets," *Scientific American*, June 1992, 94–100.

54 *A fairly rapid die-off has happened before*

Jared Diamond, *Collapse: How Civilizations Choose to Fail or Succeed* (New York: Viking, 2004).

55 *A dramatically different introductory economics textbook*

See Herman Daly and Joshua Farley, *Ecological Economics: Principles and Applications*, 2nd ed. (Washington: Island Press, 2011).

55 *Intellectual revolutions*

Thomas S. Kuhn, *The Structure of Scientific Revolutions*, 3rd ed. (Chicago: University of Chicago Press, 1996).

56 *"Biology . . . is our Mecca"*

In this Georgescu-Roegen seconded Alfred Marshall: "The Mecca of the economist lies in economic biology rather than in economic dynamics." (Found in Marshall, *Principles of Economics* [London: Macmillan and Company, 1890; 8th ed., 1920], preface.) The two meant different things by this. Marshall was concerned to get economists talking about dynamic equilibria, rather than the static equilibria that they were modeling, in imitation of (more generously: using methodology approaches influenced by) the examples offered by "hard" sciences like physics and chemistry. Darwin's work had suggested that "nature" — ecosystems — is not static; it moves toward equilibria that are never fully reached. Georgescu-Roegen drew the further lesson that an economy, like a living thing, must take in low entropy.

57 *"The flow of output is circular"*

Lester Thurow and Rober Heilbroner, *The Economic Problem* (New York: Prentice Hall, 1981), 127, 135.

60 *The Einsteinian paradigm, which it emulates*

Einstein began the thinking that developed into his special and general theories of relativity by tackling an outstanding problem in Newtonian physics, the problem of black-body radiation, whose explanation defied classical constructs. It's fair to say that here and elsewhere the Newtonian paradigm didn't account for the laws of thermodynamics (which didn't achieve full statement until the late nineteenth century). Relativity, then, has its origins in correcting Newton through thermodynamics — just as ecological economics seeks to correct the mechanistic, Newtonian assumptions of neoclassical economics by incorporating the laws of energy.

60 *The monetary value of ecosystem services*

R. Costanza et al., "The Value of the World's Ecosystem Services and Natural Capital," *Nature* 387 (May 15, 1997): 256.

64 *Tragedy of the commons*

Garrett Hardin's essay "The Tragedy of the Commons" has been widely reprinted after its original publication in *Science* 162 (December 13, 1968): 1243–1248.

64 *What Daly and Farley propose*
Daly and Farley, *Ecological Economics*, 161.

65 *The stock-flow benefits of the resource*
Daly and Farley, *Ecological Economics*, 158–159.

67 *Individuals simply can't find each other to reproduce*
For some species, that point is reached not when they're too scarce to reproduce, but when other minima are exceeded. Small populations, for instance, can't maintain the genetic diversity that's needed for the species as a whole to adapt to variations in their habitat.

70 *Economic value is produced by intelligence operating on matter and energy*
This insight is directly implied by the work of Nicholas Georgescu-Roegen, but I've been unable to discover who first laid it out. I presented these categories in a talk I gave in 2002 in the Faculty Scholar Lecture Series at Empire State College (Saratoga Springs, April 2002). They are implicit in "Zeno's Mall," an essay first published in 1997 and collected in Zencey, *Virgin Forest*, and in my "Entropy as Root Metaphor" (PhD diss., Claremont Graduate University School of Political Science, 1985).

getting over GDP

72 *Ecological degradation is slowed by recession*
The downturn that began in 2008 led to a decline in several markers of ecological degradation, including carbon emissions and landfill tonnages. James Kanter, "Carbon Trading and the Great Recession," *New York Times Green Blog*, March 30, 2010, green.blogs.nytimes.com/2010/03/30/carbon-trading-and-the-great-recession/. But there is a bit of devilment in the details. Michael Graham Richard at Treehugger.org, in "Counter-Point: 4 Reasons Why Recession is BAD for the Environment" (February 6, 2008), points out that in a recession companies spend less on research and development, including development of greener technologies and alternatives; and with a credit crunch, green start-ups find it harder to finance their efforts. www.treehugger.com/corporate-responsibility/counter-point-4-reasons-why-recession-is-bad-for-the-environment.html. This bears a resemblance to the logic behind the Environmental Kuznets Curve, which holds that environmental quality is a luxury good that we purchase when times are good; that argument is addressed in a later chapter. Richard's argument makes sense if forward-looking, sustainability-promoting enterprises outweigh unsustainable enterprises in the economy; then a slowdown has a net negative effect on the future health of the environment. I don't believe those conditions have been met.

72 *"See off some of this environmental nonsense"*
O'Leary is quoted in "Would Recession Be Good for the Environment?," *Wall*

Street Journal Online, February 7, 2008, blogs.wsj.com/economics/2008/02/07/would-recession-be-good-for-the-environment/.

72 *"Creative destruction"*

Joseph Schumpeter, *Capitalism, Socialism and Democracy* (1942; repr. New York: Harper, 1975), 82–85. By using the term, Schumpeter and his followers in the Austrian school put themselves in some unlikely company: Karl Marx used the term when speaking of how capitalism swept away medieval and mercantilist social relations, and Mikhail Bakunin, anarchist, allowed that "the urge to destroy is also a creative urge." Some conservatives have taken satisfaction in recessions for the economic insecurity they create among workers; with unemployment rates high, market forces drive down wages, increasing the share of production that goes to capital. Recessions also limit labor's ability to negotiate for better (safer, healthier, more secure) working conditions.

73 *"We looked at things like boxcar loadings"*

Economist William Nordhaus, quoted by Jon Gertner in "The Rise and Fall of the GDP," *New York Times Magazine,* May 13, 2010.

74 *Unofficial definition of a recession*

There is no official definition of a recession, in the sense that there is no law defining it or governmental office announcing their arrivals or departures. To keep political influence out of it, US practice is to assign that function to a group of academic economists meeting as a committee of the National Bureau of Economic Research, which is an NGO. Their definition: "a significant decline in economic activity spread across the economy, lasting more than a few months"—which works out to be a declining GDP in successive quarters. See Rex Nutting, "What is a Recession?," *Market Watch,* September 7, 2007.

75 *One economist to whom I spoke*

To name names: Art Woolf, at the University of Vermont, on the phone, fall 2010. Professor Woolf seems to have come around on this point. In September 2011, after flooding from Tropical Storm Irene caused billions in damage throughout the Northeast, Woolf was quoted in the local paper: "There's no way that a disaster can ever be good for the economy and if anybody ever says it is, then the logical conclusion would be that we want big disasters. . . . There's a tremendous amount of wealth that's destroyed, and that's not a good thing." Peter Hirschfeld, "Boost or Bust? Jobs Lost and Gained in Irene's Wake," *Barre Vermont Times Argus,* September 13, 2011, 1.

75 *A marsh is a sponge*

The absorption figure comes from an Army Corps of Engineers study cited by Wendy Wilson Billiot in "Terrebonne's Natural Defenses Nearly Gone," *Louisiana Sportsmen Magazine,* August 2006.

77 *Cantril Self-Anchoring Striving Scale*

For more on the Cantril Self-Anchoring Striving Scale, see www.gallup.com/poll/122453/understanding-gallup-uses-cantril-scale.aspx.

78 *Hayek's warning*

Hayek, as noted earlier, fails to distinguish standards of living from the economic activity that aims to increase it and thus goes astray with his warning: "The one thing modern democracy will not bear without cracking is the necessity of a substantial lowering of the standards of living in peacetime *or even a prolonged stationariness of its economic conditions*" (*The Road to Serfdom*, 215; emphasis added to show wherein he's wrong). Some people will happily perk along with no change or improvement in the material conditions of their lives, especially when there are other arenas of progress and development they can seek and achieve. A populace addicted to consumerist distraction and novelties, and persuaded by the advertising of self-interested producers that increased material well-being is the measure of human satisfaction, will contain fewer such people. If Hayek's full statement is accurate, that may signal a flaw in modern democracy, not an essential quality of the human spirit.

79 *Democratic forms are no certain proof against a slide into repressive forms*

In Germany in the 1930s, a declining standard of living contributed to the rise of the Nazi Party; Hitler was democratically elected to the office of chancellor (and then proceeded to establish himself as *führer*).

80 *"Fish and other products provided by the mangroves"*

Robert Zoellick, quoted in "World Bank Launches New Global Partnership to 'Green' National Accounts," World Bank Press Release No. 2011/155/SDN, October 28, 2010, reporting Zoellick's remarks to the Convention on Biological Diversity Meeting in Nagoya, Japan, that date. See web.worldbank.org/WBSITE/EXTERNAL/NEWS/0,,contentMDK:22746592~pagePK:64257043~piPK:437376~theSitePK:4607,00.html.

81 *Names like "avoided cost," etc.*

The typology comes from Stephen C. Farber, Robert Costanza, and Matthew Wilson, "Economic and Ecological Concepts for Valuing Ecosystem Services," *Ecological Economics* 41 (2002): 375–392. This volume of the journal is a special issue titled "The Dynamics and Value of Ecosystem Services: Integrating Economic and Ecological Perspectives."

83 *2,788 lives a year*

This is the estimate by the National Highway Traffic Safety Commission of lives saved by airbags in 2008. See "Lives Saved Calculations for Seat Belts and Frontal Air Bags," DOT HS 211 806, December 2009.

84 *System of valuation that can encompass ecosystem services*

Farber, Costanza, and Wilson, "Economic and Ecological Concepts for Valuing Ecosystem Services," 383–384.

85 *Germany's environmental economic accounting system*

Karl Schoer, "Policy Use of Environmental-Economic Accounting in Germany," a paper presented at the OECD-Latin America and the Caribbean conference on Environmental Information and Decision Making, November 28–29, 2005, Cancun, Mexico.

85 *The launching pad*

From the press release announcing the opening of the conference; available, with a host of other materials, at the conference's website, www.beyond-gdp.eu.

85 *An international commission*

The Stiglitz Commission, as it's called, is officially known as "The Commission on the Measurement of Economic Performance and Social Progress," and its report is readily available online at www.stiglitz-sen-fitoussi.fr/documents/ rapport_anglais.pdf. Its three sections are titled "Classical GDP Issues," "Quality of Life," and "Sustainable Development and Environment."

85 *Proposed alternatives to GDP*

One good survey of the alternatives is Yanne Goossens et al., "Alternative Progress Indicators to Gross Domestic Product (GDP) as a Means toward Sustainable Development," European Parliament Committee on the Environment, Public Health, and Food Safety, 2007, www.cros-portal.eu/content/ alternative-progress-indicators-gdp.

85 *Fix GDP by deducting costs and adding benefits*

This category includes the Human Development Index, a UN-sponsored measure that factors life expectancy and educational attainment into GDP figures; the system of Integrated Environmental and Economic Accounting that's being implemented in Europe; the separate German Environmental and Economic Accounting system; proposals for Green GDP that would deduct natural capital drawdown from GDP, much as the expense of capital depreciation is deducted from GDP to get Net Domestic Product; and the Happy Planet Index, which corrects GDP by showing it in relation to the ecological footprint of the economy.

85 *Supplement GDP with other indicators*

Into this category fall Environmental Satellite Accounts, which the US Bureau of Economic Accounting was exploring until the work was shelved by the Bush Administration; Sustainable Development Indicators being developed and used in EU countries; the UN's Millennium Development Goals; and measurements of Ecological or Carbon Footprint.

86 *The foundations of life satisfaction*

Nicholas Buetell, "Life Satisfaction (2006)," in the *Sloan Work and Family Research Network Encyclopedia*, offers a good bibliography of recent work, including R. A. Cummins, "The Second Approximation to an International Standard for Life Satisfaction," *Journal of Social Issues* 43 (1998): 307–344.

89 *"Are the following environmental issues of concern?"*
The full text of the survey instrument is available online at the Gross National Happiness website of the Centre for Bhutan Studies at www.grossnational happiness.com/GNHSurvey/gnhquestionnaire.pdf.

90 *Michael Pennock on the future development of the GNH*
Personal communication at the Fifth International Conference on GNH, Foz do Iguassu, Brazil, November 2009.

90 *"Self reporting of . . . experience"*
Karma Ura and Tshoki Zangmo, "An Approach to the Indicators of GNH," paper presented to the World Health Organization's Regional Conference on Revitalizing Primary Health Care, Jakarta, Indonesia, August 6–8, 2008, 7.

91 *Herman Daly and John Cobb*
The precursor of the GPI, the Index of Sustainable Economic Welfare, was presented in Herman Daly and John Cobb, *For the Common Good: Redirecting the Economy Toward Community, the Environment, and a Sustainable Future*, 2nd ed. (Boston: Beacon, 1994).

91 *"An educational tool" and "a complement" to GSP*
The description is from the press release issued by the Maryland governor's office, "Governor Martin O'Malley Launches Genuine Progress Indicator," Annapolis, February 3, 2010.

91 *Quasi-official Canadian Index*
The Canadian Index of Well-Being (CIWB) is supported by the Atlantic Canada Opportunities Agency, a public-private partnership dedicated to promoting sustainable development. A bill to make the CIWB official was introduced in parliament in 2001 but did not become law.

92 *Environmental "Satellite Accounts"*
See Bureau of Economic Analysis, "Integrated Economic and Environmental Satellite Accounts," *Survey of Current Business*, April 1994: "Work on the natural resources satellite accounts was given added impetus and extended in scope in 1993 when President Clinton, as part of his April 21 Earth Day address, gave high priority to the development of 'Green GDP measures [that] would incorporate changes in the natural environment into the calculations of national income and wealth.'" The address can be viewed at www.c-span-video.org/program/39911-1.

92 *Redundancy to isolate and fix errors*
Every language has some degree of redundancy. At the grammatical level, English forms plurals by changes in both the noun and verb, typically adding an *s* or *es* to the noun and changing the form of the verb. This increases the accuracy with which messages are transmitted; a discrepancy between noun and verb suggests that one of the two is wrong, and the receiver of the message is likely to ask for clarification. When blocks of numerical data are

transmitted electronically, inclusion of running totals for columns and rows allows the receiver to perform instantaneous checks on the accuracy of the transmission; a discrepancy in columnar and row totals allows for easy identification of the particular bit of data that got corrupted in transmission.

93 *To turn past solar income into wealth in the present*
One of the foundational insights of the discipline of ecological economics is the idea that all wealth (understood as physical goods and physically provided services, not the accumulation of money that lets us purchase these) has a root in scarce "low entropy" (valuable matter and energy). The idea was articulated by a founder of ecological economics, Nicholas Georgescu-Roegen, in *The Entropy Law and the Economic Process* (Cambridge, MA: Harvard University Press, 1976). It is explained lucidly in Herman Daly and Joshua Farley's textbook, *Ecological Economics: Principles and Applications*, 2nd ed. (Washington: Island Press, 2010), discussed in a later chapter.

93 *Governments pressured to provide services in the least-cost, most efficient manner*
I elaborate this point in "The New Austerity and the EROI Squeeze," *Daly News*, July 18, 2011, at steadystate.org/new-austerity-eroi/.

93 *Results-based accountability*
Mark Friedman, *Trying Hard Is Not Good Enough* (Bloomington, IN: Trafford, 2005). See also Marc Robinson, ed., *Performance Budgeting, Linking Funding and Results* (New York: Palgrave Macmillan, 2007).

94 *The Pew Foundation's Results First initiative*
See the description at www.pewcenteronthestates.org/initiatives_detail.aspx ?initiativeID=61282.

94 *Juvenile offenders "teach each other things"*
Gary Vanlandingham, testimony before the Vermont House Appropriations Committee, Montpelier, VT, October 2011.

94 *GPI Plus*
A précis of what the indicator set would look like, and how it could be integrated with outcomes-based budgeting, is contained in a forthcoming white paper titled "GPI, GNH, and Results-Based-Accountability," available from the author.

the financial crisis is the environmental crisis

104 *Summers' speech*
Lawrence Summers, "Responding to an Historic Economic Crisis: The Obama Program," Brookings Institution, Washington, DC, March 13, 2009.

105 *Testimony to the Financial Crisis Inquiry Commission*
Pierre-Olivier Gourinchas, "U.S. Monetary Policy, 'Imbalances' and the Finan-

cial Crisis," testimony presented to the Financial Crisis Commission's Financial Crisis Forum in Washington, DC, February 26–27, 2010.

106 *"Living wills" for financial institutions*

Randall Kroszner's testimony is published online at the commission's website. "Interconnectedness, Fragility and the Financial Crisis," testimony prepared for Financial Crisis Forum, held by the Financial Crisis Inquiry Commission, Washington, DC, February 26–27, 2010, fcic.law.stanford.edu.

108 *Dewey cautioned*

John Dewey, *Logic: The Theory of Inquiry* (New York: Holt Rinehart and Winston, 1938).

109 *Personal, social, and economic costs of unemployment*

See, for instance, Juanita Muller, Brian Delahaye, Sharon Winocur, and Richard Hicks, "The Psychological Impacts of Long-Term Unemployment, Sex Differences and Activity: A Case Study Analysis," *Journal of Applied Social Behaviour* 3, no. 1 (1996): 3–43, and Iskra Beleva, "Long-Term Unemployment as Social Exclusion," in *Human Development Report*, ed. N. Genov (Sofia: UNDP, 1997), 29–36.

109 *Brink of widespread ecosystem collapse*

To one point of view, this is too well known to require documentation. To another point of view, this can be dismissed as environmentalist fear-mongering hyperbole. The 2005 UN report *Living Beyond Our Means: Natural Assets and Human Well-Being*, a summary statement by the Board of the UN Millennium Ecosystem Assessment Project, indicates clearly that the latter interpretation is wrong: www.wri.org/publication/millennium-ecosystem-assessment -living-beyond-our-means-natural-assets-and-human-we. Among its findings, the report warns of "the dire state of many of the world's fish stocks; the intense vulnerability of the 2 billion people living in dry regions to the loss of ecosystem services, including water supply; and the growing threat to ecosystems from climate change and nutrient pollution," while noting that "human activities have taken the planet to the edge of a massive wave of species extinctions, further threatening our own well-being" (5).

110 *The index to the Financial Crisis Inquiry Commission's report*

The index is available online at www.publicaffairsbooks.com/fcicindex.pdf. Interestingly, "economic growth" gets only one entry in the index. The page listed in that entry notes that by the end of 2000, "the economy had grown 39 straight quarters" (83). Growth is measured, of course, by rising GDP, whose flaws are discussed elsewhere in this volume. Even supposing that GDP growth indicated an increasing level of wealth, from the point of view of an economics enlightened by knowledge of the laws of thermodynamics and an appreciation of the value of natural capital, that sustained growth in wealth is a dubious achievement. Like Ponzi's eponymous scheme, it came about mostly through continual increase in the pace at which the economy expanded its extractive base so that it could cash out natural capital as increased income.

111 *A series of books*
Frederick Soddy, *Wealth, Virtual Wealth, and Debt* (London: George Allen & Unwin, 1926); *Money versus Man* (London: George Allen & Unwin, 1931); *The Role of Money* (London: George Allen & Unwin, 1936).

112 *"The nothing you get for something"*
Soddy, *The Role of Money*, 36.

112 *Ecosystem services*
See Costanza et al., "The Value of the World's Ecosystem Services and Natural Capital," *Nature* 387 (May 15, 1997): 253–260.

113 *"We can and must do better"*
Summers, "Responding to an Historic Economic Crisis."

115 *Irving Fisher at Yale*
Irving Fisher, *100 Percent Money* (1935; repr., London: Pickering & Chatto, 1996).

115 *Frank Knight*
Knight called Soddy's *Wealth, Virtual Wealth and Debt* "brilliantly written and brilliantly suggestive and stimulating" and further judged that his program for monetary reform was "highly significant and theoretically correct." Knight, "Review of Wealth, Virtual Wealth and Debt," *Saturday Review of Literature*, April 16, 1927, 732.

115 *No less an economic eminence than Milton Friedman*
Milton Friedman, *A Program for Monetary Stability* (New York: Fordham University Press, 1960). Friedman's advocacy for a 100 percent reserve system had little to do with Soddy's thermodynamically enlightened approach to monetary policy, but was rooted in a desire to see money creation become less a matter of discretionary choice on the part of bankers and policy makers, and more routinized, automatic, and stable. Still, it would have addressed the dynamic that creates a structural need for debt repudiation.

115 *"Enormous pyramid of debt"*
Herman Daly, "A Steady-State Economy," paper prepared for the UK Sustainable Development Commission, dated April 24, 2008, 9. See also Daly and John Cobb, "Afterword: Money, Debt, and Wealth," in *For the Common Good: Redirecting the Economy toward Community, the Environment, and a Sustainable Future* (Boston: Beacon, 1994). The discussion here owes a great deal to Daly's work, more than is indicated by this brief note.

116 *Capturing seigniorage for the public treasury*
Economists use a variety of measures of money. M1 includes currency and demand deposits — checking account balances. With M1 at $1.333 trillion, the

capture of seigniorage on the entirety of a modest 3 percent annual increase in it would amount to $40 billion a year. And if all the seigniorage on that $1.333 trillion had been captured for the US Treasury, the public purse would have been fatter by about $2.6 trillion. (That's the value of the noncurrency components of M1; the Treasury gets the seigniorage on the currency it issues.) You could put it this way: since the advent of fractional reserve banking, US banks have received a subsidy totaling $2.6 trillion from the American public.

116 *The profit that comes from the issuance of money belongs to us*
I discuss seigniorage in greater, if nontechnical, detail in "Reforming Seigniorage: The Key to a Sustainable Economy," an essay at *History News Network*, May 3, 2010, hnn.us/articles/126156.html.

116 *Uneconomic growth*
The term is an oxymoron within the neoclassical tradition of economic theory, since economic growth is, by definition, always a good thing. But because the neoclassical tradition doesn't count nonmarket and unpriced ecosystem services as economic goods, it can't subtract their loss from the benefits brought by economic growth. If you admit that economic growth has costs in terms of lost ecosystem services, you have to admit that at some point costs could exceed benefits and growth could become uneconomic. See Daly and Farley, *Ecological Economics: Principles and Applications* (Washington: Island Press, 2004), 19–23.

the battle over the environmental kuznets curve

118 *Shut off the water supply to 3.8 million residents*
"Harbin Resumes Water Supply," *Peoples' Daily Online*, November 28, 2005, english.peopledaily.com.cn/200511/28/eng20051128_224182.html. Some details here are reported from other sources by Steven F. Hayward, "The China Syndrome and the Environmental Kuznets Curve," *Environmental Policy Outlook* (American Enterprise Institute, Washington, DC), November–December 2005, 1–6.

118 *Thirty officials were hospitalized, some with serious injuries*
Jim Yardley, "Rural Chinese Riot as Police Try to Halt Pollution Protest," *New York Times*, April 14, 2005.

119 *It was "a pitched battle"*
Howard W. French, "Anger in China Rises over Threat to Environment," *New York Times*, July 19, 2005.

119 *Demonstrations in Xiamen and Chengdou*
Carin Zissis and Jayshree Bajoria, "China's Environmental Crisis," *Backgrounder*, Council on Foreign Relations, August 4, 2008.

119 *"Widespread environmental degradation" in China*
Ibid.

120 *150 million "environmental refugees"*
"*Spiegel* Interview with China's Deputy Minister of the Environment: 'China's Miracle Will End Soon,'" *Spiegel,* March 7, 2005; conducted by Andreas Lorenz, translated by Patrick Kessler.

120 *An increasingly degraded landscape*
See "How China's Taking Over Africa, and Why the West Should be VERY Worried," *London Evening Standard,* July 18, 2008, www.thisislondon.co.uk/news/article-23517837-how-chinas-taking-over-africa-and-why-the-west-should-be-very-worried.do, and Alexei Barrionuevo, "China's Interest in Farmland Makes Brazil Uneasy," *New York Times,* May 26, 2011, www.nytimes.com/2011/05/27/world/americas/27brazil.html.

121 *What Kuznets proposed in 1954*
Kuznets's idea was presented in his presidential address to the sixty-seventh annual meeting of the American Economic Association and was published as "Economic Growth and Income Inequality," *American Economic Review* 45, no. 1 (1954): 1–28.

121 *Income inequality problems take care of themselves*
There's a similarity here to the confidence that Karl Marx had in a different inevitable process: since government exists to enforce and manage class antagonisms, after the Communist Revolution the instruments of state power would, he said, simply "wither away." They didn't, and don't — a fact that calls into question the theory, the diagnosis-and-solution, on which the prediction is based. The recent failure of income inequality to diminish "naturally" ought to call into question the trickle-down, supply-side economics that the Kuznets Curve has so often been used to support.

122 *Jobs are created and wealth "trickles down"*
This sequence has become so firmly embedded in common understanding that now it's difficult to imagine another explanation. But many of the criticisms that can be brought against the EKC can also be brought against the original Kuznets Curve.

122 *The innovation of two economists*
Gene M. Grossman and Alan B. Krueger, "Environmental Impact of a North American Free Trade Agreement" (Working Paper 3914, National Bureau of Economic Research, November 1991). A revised and expanded version of their paper, entitled "Economic Growth and the Environment," was published in the *Quarterly Journal of Economics* 110, no. 2 (May 1995): 353–377.

122 *One review of findings and implications*
Bruce Yandle, Madhusudan Bhattarai, and Maya Vijayaraghavan, "The Environmental Kuznets Curve: A Primer," published online by the Property and

Environment Research Center, Bozeman, MT, 2008. See also, by the same authors, "Environmental Kuznets Curves: A Review of Findings, Methods, and Policy Implications," published in the same place.

123 *Newspaper opinion piece*

M. Robinson, "Growth Is the Key to Protecting the Environment, Not Its Enemy," *Sydney Morning Herald,* September 9, 2008, 10.

123 *"Arithmomorphism" and "methodolotry"*

"The ultimate result is that mathematics has chased away almost completely the truly hard task of coming to grips with the facts." Nicholas Georgescu-Roegen, "What Thermodynamics and Biology Can Teach Economists," *Atlantic Economic Journal* 5, no. 1 (1997): 13–21, quote on 15.

123 *Barriers to entry*

The barrier need not be constructed out of mathematical formulas. Consider this early statement of the basic idea of the EKC from an annual address by a president of the American Agricultural Economics Association, Vernon Ruttan: "In relatively high-income economies the income elasticity of demand for commodities . . . related to sustenance is low and declines as income continues to rise, while the income elasticity of demand for more effective disposal of residuals and for environmental amenities is high and continues to rise. This is in sharp contrast to the situation in poor countries, where the income elasticity of demand is high for sustenance and low for environmental amenities." Vernon W. Ruttan, "Technology and the Environment," *American Journal of Agricultural Economics* 53 (1971): 707–717, quote on 707–708. Of course his audience, economists all, knew what he was saying: environmental quality is a luxury good.

123 *"Very easy to do bad econometrics"*

David I. Stern, "The Environmental Kuznets Curve," *International Society for Ecological Economics Internet Encyclopaedia of Ecological Economics,* April 2003, 1.

124 *One such economist*

Don Boudreau, "The Environmental Kuznets Curve," *Café Hayek* (blog), April 11, 2010, cafehayek.com/2010/04/the-environmental-kuznets-curve.html.

124 *The old* Limits to Growth *myth*

The work that haunts much of the literature on the EKC is the classic survey and argument by Donella H. Meadows et al., *The Limits to Growth: A Report to the Club of Rome's Project on the Predicament of Mankind* (New York: Universe Books, 1972). It said clearly that continued economic growth threatened the life-support systems of the planet.

124 *Boudreau is not a popularizing outlier*

Boudreau is affirming the conventional neoclassical wisdom that is here expressed by John M. Antle and Greg Heidebrink, "Environment and Development: Theory and International Evidence," *Economic Development and Cultural Change* 43, no. 3 (1995): 603–625, quote on 605.

125 *Smaller ecological footprints on top of the base*

This was the finding of Hermamala Hettige, Robert E. B. Lucas, and David Wheeler in "The Toxic Intensity of Industrial Production: Global Patterns, Trends, and Trade Policy," *American Economic Review* 82 (1992): 478–481.

126 *Cumulative burden*

This point is made by Kenneth Arrow et al. in "Economic Growth, Carrying Capacity, and the Environment," *Science* 268 (April 28, 1995): 520–521.

126 *One pair of economists noted with commendable understatement*

S. Barrett and K. Graddy, "Freedom, Growth, and the Environment," *Environmental and Development Economics* 5 (2000): 433–456.

127 *"The quality of institutions related to the enforcement of contracts"*

T. Panayotou, "Demystifying the Environmental Kuznets Curve: Turning a *Black Box* into a Policy Tool," *Environment and Development Economics* 2 (1997): 465–484.

127 *Improvements in political rights and civil liberties*

M. Torras and J. K. Boyce, "Income Inequality and Pollution: A Reassessment of the Environmental Kuznets Curve," *Ecological Economics* 25 (1998): 147–160.

127 *"A robust association"*

R. T. Deacon and S. Saha, "Public Goods Provision under Dictatorship and Democracy: A Survey," in *The Companion in Public Economics: Empirical Public Economics*, ed. A. F. Ott and R. J. Cebula (Northhampton, MA: Edward Elgar, 2006).

127 *Property rights stations*

This is the position taken by Yandle, Bhattarai, and Vijayaraghavan in "The Environmental Kuznets Curve: A Primer."

127 *The result and the methods that produced it have been repeatedly challenged*

The challenge to EKC methodology has probably never been made more obscurely than in this passage: "Levinson and Taylor . . . have recently shown how unobserved heterogeneity, endogeneity, and aggregation issues tend to bias the standard analysis against finding a pollution haven effect." My text translates this technical assessment into normal language. The passage comes from Richard T. Carson, "The Environmental Kuznets Curve: Seeking Empirical Regularity and Theoretical Structure," *Review of Environmental Economics and Policy* 4, no. 1 (2010): 3–23.

130 *An EKC for biodiversity is "a theoretical impossibility"*

S. Dietz and W. N. Adger, "Economic Growth, Biodiversity Loss and Conservation Effort," *Journal of Environmental Management* 68 (2003): 23–35, as quoted by Julianne H. Mills and Thomas A. Waite in "Economic Prosperity,

Biodiversity Conservation, and the Environmental Kuznets Curve," *Ecological Economics* 68 (2009): 2087–2095, quote on 2088. This no doubt explains why Majumder et al. could find "no evidence in support of an EKC relationship" for biodiversity and income; see Pallab Majumder, Robert P. Berrens, Robert P. Bohara, and Alok K. Boharas, "Is There an Environmental Kuznets Curve for the Risk of Biodiversity Loss?," *Journal of Developing Areas* 39, no. 2 (Spring 2006): 175–190.

131 *Generally and everywhere down*
Stern, "The Environmental Kuznets Curve": "Most indicators of environmental degradation are monotonically rising in income," which says the same thing. If the curve were plotted from data, we shouldn't be surprised to find that for some countries or regions it has an inverted N shape; inverted because it plots loss of services rather than presence of pollutants, N-shaped for the reasons given in the text below.

131 *The puzzle solving of normal science*
Thomas Kuhn, *The Structure of Scientific Revolutions*, 3rd ed. (Chicago: University of Chicago Press, 1996), 36.

131 *Annual-income-tipping-points*
Gene M. Grossman and Alan B. Krueger, "Economic Growth and the Environment," *Quarterly Journal of Economics* 110 (1995): 353–377.

131 *"Harms from contaminated water . . . are more clearly visible than those associated with air pollution"*
The conclusion is from Yandle, Bhattarai, and Vijayaraghavan, "The Environmental Kuznets Curve: A Primer," p. 12, drawn from data reported in Grossman and Krueger, "Economic Growth and the Environment."

131 *The cursive N*
Shafik (1994) Nemat Shafik, "Economic Development and Environmental Quality: An Econometric Analysis," *Oxford Economic Papers* 46: 757–777, www.bepress.com/feem/paper35, found this for fecal coliforms in water; S. M. de Bruyn and J. B. Opschoor (1997) found this for sulfur dioxide. Both are cited by J. Barkley Rosser Jr. and Marina B. Rosser in "Institutional Evolution and the Environmental Kuznets Curve," a paper posted online at cob.jmu .edu/rosserjb/Glob.inst.env.Kuznets.doc through the James Madison University Program in Economics, dated April 7, 2005. For other evidence of an N-shaped EKC, see also Massimiliano Mazzanti, Anna Montini, and Roberto Zoboli, "Economic Dynamics, Emission Trends and the EKC Hypothesis New Evidence Using NAMEA and Provincial Panel Data for Italy" (April 6, 2007), Fondazione Eni Enrico Mattei Working Paper No. 35.

132 *The fundamental physical relation reasserts itself*
In planetary terms, the human capture and quarantine of some pollutants—such as we accomplish by lining our landfills—is merely temporary, which

means that over longer periods of time (the time it takes for a landfill lining to decay) the downturn in the cursive N tends to disappear and the relationship modeled by the EKC tends to become a straight-on, linear progression: the more economic activity, the more pollution.

132 *One survey summarizes the empirical research in these skeptical terms*
Arik Levenson, "The Environmental Kuznets Curve," in *New Palgrave Dictionary of Economics*, 2nd ed. (New York: Palgrave Macmillan, forthcoming).

133 *"Little substance lies behind the EKC"*
Richard T. Carson, "The Environmental Kuznets Curve: Seeking Empirical Regularity and Theoretical Structure," *Review of Environmental Economics and Policy* 4, no. 1 (2010): 3–23, quote on 5.

133 *Increasingly cited in mainstream journals*
For instance, see ibid.

133 *This crossing of the boundary portends further change*
Kuhn said, suggestively, that paradigm change might be tracked by paying attention to "formal and informal communication networks including those discovered in correspondence and in the linkages among citations" (*Structure of Scientific Revolutions*, 178).

133 *Conversion . . . to the new way of thinking*
I'll hazard a prediction: while individual economists may understand themselves to have undergone a conversion to the new paradigm, if and when thermodynamic principles and the idea of natural capital are widely accepted in the discipline as a whole it's likely that most economists will aver that the discipline has gone through incremental, not revolutionary change. They'll accept the new foundation of their discipline as the outcome of some dickering between economic theorists with a particularly metaphysical bent. To the extent that it affects their practice as economists, they'll tend to drop those elements of the neoclassical research program that are unsupported in the new paradigm (the hunt for the EKC, for instance) and focus their efforts on the considerable area of inquiry that is common to both the old and new paradigms.

134 *"Yet another mistake in this thinking"*
Spiegel Interview with China's Deputy Minister of the Environment: 'China's Miracle Will End Soon,'" *Spiegel*, March 7, 2005; conducted by Andreas Lorenz, translated by Patrick Kessler. Asked to explain why that assumption was wrong, Pan said: "There won't be enough money, and we are simply running out of time. Developed countries with a per capita gross national product of $8,000 to $10,000 can afford that, but we cannot. Before we reach $4,000 per person, different crises in all shapes and forms will hit us. Economically we won't be strong enough to overcome them." If ecosystem losses lead to an economic crash, China's EKC may well turn out to have a curve shaped like

the upper portion of the number 2: increasing generation of environmental "bads" until per capita income hits a peak and begins diminishing, then further lessening of those bads as economic activity, and income, are reduced.

134 *China's rejection of the EKC*

The premiere was quoted in "China Lowers Growth Targets by 1 Percent," *China Post*, February 28, 2011, www.chinapost.com.tw/china/local-news/beijing/2011/02/28/292700/China-lowers.htm.

revisiting "the bet that ruined the world"

136 *"An Oversupply of False Bad News"*

Julian L. Simon, "Resources, Population, Environment: An Oversupply of False Bad News," *Science*, n.s. 208, no. 4451 (June 27, 1980): 1431–1437.

136 *Landmark environmental protection legislation*

On January 1, 1970, President Nixon signed the National Environmental Protection Act. The Clean Air Act was strengthened in 1970, the Federal Water Pollution Control Act in 1972.

137 *Published in 1690*

Locke's work was taken as justification for the Glorious Revolution of 1688, but was probably written a few years earlier than that, during the Exclusion Crisis. "A truly revolutionary work," Locke's two treatises "may have been intended to explain and defend the revolutionary plot [for an armed and general uprising led by the Country Party] against Charles II and his brother." "Locke, John," *Stanford Encyclopedia of Philosophy* (Stanford: Stanford University Press, 2007).

137 *Locke and Wilderness Planet*

I've explored Locke's use of the labor theory of value, and its result in infinite-planet democratic theory, in "Fixing Locke: Civil Liberties for a Finite Planet," in *Rhetorics, Literacies, and Narratives of Sustainability*, ed. Peter Goggin (New York: Routledge, 2009), 180–201.

137 *Marx credits Adam Smith with the invention of the labor theory of value*

Karl Marx, in *Grundrisse,* trans. by Martin Nicolaus (London: Penguin, 1973), section 3, p. 104. I tinkered with the syntax, moving the word "was" to make it more readable.

138 *"This infamous, vile doctrine"*

Marx's invective against Malthus was usefully collated by William Petersen in *Malthus* (Cambridge, MA: Harvard University Press, 1979), 75.

138 *Simon held a labor theory of value*

You can find unpublished writing of Simon's in which he explicitly rejects the labor theory of value (LTV). If we acknowledge that human ingenuity, embodied in invention and technology, is human labor, it's impossible to reconcile that rejection with the idea that labor is "the ultimate resource" that allows us to transcend any limit imposed by scarcity of other factors of production. Simon's disavowal of the LTV is perhaps best understood as a bit of window-dressing, pure bloviation that worked to allay skepticism and make it easier for fellow economists to accept his infinite-planet paradigm.

139 *As Simon himself saw*

Note 2 to chapter 3 of *The Ultimate Resource* is titled "The 'Law' of Diminishing Returns," complete with "sneer" quotes, and offers a brief (four-paragraph) and wholly unsatisfactory attempt to brush the concept aside. Julian Simon, *The Ultimate Resource*, 2nd ed. (Princeton, NJ: Princeton University Press, 1996).

140 *Only ten countries*

Paul R. Ehrlich, *The Population Bomb* (New York: Ballantine, 1968), 19.

142 *"Blatantly dishonest intellectually"*

Recounted in John Tierney, "Betting on the Planet," *New York Times Magazine*, December 2, 1990.

142 *"Fringe character" and leader of a "cargo cult"*

Both are widely reported; see ibid. Whether or not the cargo cult analogy is apt is probably a matter of taste and ideological orientation; that Simon appealed to expansion of the human domain into space is incontrovertible: in arguing (counterfactually) that copper could be made from other metals, Simon had declared that "even the total weight of the earth is not a theoretical limit to the amount of copper that might be available to earthlings in the future. Only the total weight of the universe . . . would be such a theoretical limit." Julian Simon, *Population Matters: People, Resources, Environment, and Immigration* (Piscataway, NJ: Transaction, 1990), 52.

142 *"Natural resources are not finite"*

Simon, *The Ultimate Resource*, 54. "Yes, you read correctly," is the next sentence. And "on the face of it . . . [this] seems like nonsense." Which it does — both on its face and after reflection.

142 *Simon "felt utterly helpless"*

Recounted in Tierney, "Betting on the Planet." During commercial breaks Carson asked Ehrlich to give him questions to ask next; he did, and was off and running. The "stupefied admiration" that Simon and millions of other viewers saw probably had less to do with the conversation's content than with its form: Ehrlich reports that backstage, after the show, he heard Carson tell Ed McMahon, "Boy, Paul really saved the show." Charles T. Rubin, *The Green Crusade* (Lanham, MD: Rowman and Littlefield, 1998), 76.

143 *"Eagerly" or "with reservations"*

"I and my colleagues . . . jointly accept Simon's astonishing offer before other greedy people jump in," was his widely quoted response (as in, for instance, a profile of Simon titled "The Doomslayer," by Ed Regis, in *Wired*, February 1997, www.wired.com/wired/achive/5.02/ffsimon.html. The account that Paul Ehrlich and coauthor Anne Ehrlich offer in *Betrayal of Science and Reason* ([Washington: Island Press, 1996], 100–104) doesn't deny that but spins it a bit differently: "Paul and the other scientists knew that the five metals [they chose] were not critical indicators and said so at the time. . . . Nonetheless, . . . [they] jointly [bet] a total of $1000 ($200 on each of five metals), rather than listen to him charge that environmentalists were unwilling to put their money where their mouths were. Perhaps it was a mistake, but it can be quite satisfying to skewer an adversary on his own terms, and they thought they had a good chance of winning" (p. 100).

144 *One of Simon's defenders explains*
The defense is sketched out on the web page of John McCarthy, an emeritus professor of computer science at Stanford: www-formal.stanford.edu/jmc/progress/references.html.

144 *"Every measure . . . will improve"*
Quoted in Schneider, "Don't Bet All Environmental Changes Will Be Beneficial," *American Physical Society News*, August/September 1996, no pagination, emphasis added, www.aps.org/publications/apsnews/199608/environmental.cfm.

144 *"Not a negative measure of environmental welfare!"*
Ibid.

145 *"Simon easily won because"*
Joseph Kellard, "Reason vs Faith: Julian Simon vs Paul Ehrlich," *American Capitalist*, April 26, 1998. Note that Kellard portrays environmentalism as a faith and Simon's confidence in the infinite power of technology as reasonable.

145 *"The idea of finiteness is a prejudice"*
Simon, "Natural Resources Aren't Finite," published on the website of the Cato Institute, March 4, 1997. www.cato.org/publications/commentary/natural-resources-arent-finite.

146 *Population growth is a "neutral phenomenon"*
Reported in John R. Weeks, *Population: An Introduction to Concepts and Issues*, 8th ed. (Belmont, CA: Wadsworth, 2002).

146 *"A choice piece of nonsense"*
Paul Demeny, *Population and Development* (Liege: International Union for the Scientific Study of Population, 1994), 10.

146 *Overpopulation declared no problem under socialism or capitalism*
Peter J. Donaldson, *Nature against Us: The United States and the World Population Crisis, 1965–1980* (Chapel Hill: University of North Carolina Press, 1990), 130.

147 *"Exactly the opposite direction"*

Julian L. Simon, "Earth's Doomsayers Are Wrong," *San Francisco Chronicle*, May 12, 1995.

147 *Had transgressed sustainable limits*

Numerous sources, including Mathis Wackernagel et al., "Tracking the Ecological Overshoot of the Human Economy," *PNAS: Proceedings of the National Academy of Sciences of the United States of America* 99, no. 14 (July 9, 2002): 9266–9271, www.pnas.org/content/99/14/9266.long.

147 *"The bet that ruined the world"*

Paul Kedrosky, in an online interview at Techcrunch TV, no date; posted under the title "Paul Kedrosky, 'Markets Uberalis Is Totally Wrong,'" at www .techcrunch.tv/show/keen-on/11OGluMTqOEOlrRZ6pAK4lve1oIkAzL8. See also his "Re-litigating the Simon-Ehrlich Bet," on his website, paul.kedrosky .com/archives/2010/02/re-litigating_t.html. *Infectious Greed: Finance and the Money Culture*, posted February 18, 2010. The piece reports a TED lecture Kedrosky gave the week before.

147 *Simon would have won "over the entire century"*

David McClintick and Ross B. Emmett, "Betting on the Wealth of Nature: The Simon-Ehrlich Wager," *PERC Reports* 23, no. 3 (Fall 2005), www.perc.org/ articles/article588.php.

148 *"Better to be lucky than good"*

Katherine A. Kiel, Victor A. Matheson, and Kevin Golembiewski, "Luck or Skill? An Examination of the Ehrlich-Simon Bet," College of the Holy Cross, Department of Economics, Faculty Research Series, Paper 09-08, 5.

148 *Ehrlich is nine-for-nine*

Kedrosky, "Re-litigating the Simon-Ehrlich Bet." If you chart the prices of the five commodities over the years 1976 to 2010, you get a U-shaped curve — down, then up — the opposite of the inverted U of the EKC. The similarity is not accidental; both record effects of increasing energy use on Garden Planet and a tipping point as limits are approached. Note that defenders of the EKC argue that *this trend will continue* and that here the same shape is dismissed by Simonistas who say *current trends will not continue.*

149 *Grantham on the Great Paradigm Shift*

You can find Grantham's newsletter at www.gmo.com/websitecontent/JG LetterALL_1Q11.pdf. That Grantham is a hedge fund manager, giving investment advice to a sizable number of investors, suggests a new dynamic that may bring about the rejection of infinite-planet thinking: self-interest on the part of investors. If people looking to make money start behaving as though the planet were finite, the economists who theorize about their behavior can't remain too far behind for very long.

150 *Simon played fast and loose*

That's the implication I draw from the criticism offered by Lindsey Grant in "The Cornucopian Fallacies," *Focus* 3, no. 2 (1993), online at dieoff.org/page45 .htm.

150 *Simon saw himself as responding in kind*

In the *American Physical Society News* in 1996, Simon charged that Stephen Schneider—the biologist whose offer of a wager he had declined—had said that "scientists should consider stretching the truth" to get good publicity for their cause. After that issue was in print, Simon had second thoughts about his characterization of what Schneider said and contacted the editors to admit that this damaging attribution was false. He did not offer Schneider an apology. Schneider took exception even to the corrected quote, averring (in "Don't Bet All Environmental Changes Will Be Beneficial," *American Physical Society News*, August/September 1996) that "even what he states to be the 'correct quote' is still an out-of-context misrepresentation of my views"—one that Simon "persists in perpetuating even months after I personally told him of the context of the original quote" (p. 5).

151 *"Not subject to scientific test"*

Simon, in his letter to replying to critics, *Science* 210, no. 4476 (December 1980): 1296–1308.

151 *Peer review after several millennia*

We only get to make the one experiment. This is why we need to look for comparison—the control thema—in the historical experience of other cultures—yet another reason that historical understanding (and a working knowledge of the techniques historians use to validate their interpretations) is crucial to an ecological understanding.

152 *Simon used appeals to individual choice when it suited him*

In his reply to his critics in the second edition of *The Ultimate Resource*, Simon wrote: "Ehrlich bets what he thinks will be the economic gains that we and our descendants might enjoy against the unborn's very lives. Would he make the same sort of wager if his own life rather than others' lives were the stake?" (p. xxxiii). He attacked Ehrlich's statement that "no sensible reason has ever been given for having more than 135 million people" in the United States, writing, "If . . . Ehrlich were to ask those twenty-three million Americans born between 1960 and 1970 whether it was a good thing they were born, many of them would be able to think of a good reason or two" (p. xxxii).

153 *Energy "cannot be recycled"*

Ibid., 180.

155 *Energy is the "master resource"*

Ibid., 162.

155 *Up to 90 percent of the weight of the rocket*
"Even using a minimum-energy trajectory to send a six-person crew from Earth to Mars, with chemical rockets alone the total launch mass would top 1,000 metric tons — of which some 90 percent would be fuel." Bret G. Drake, manager for space launch analysis and integration at Johnson Space Center, quoted in "Houston, Are We There Yet?," *NASA Science/Science News*, September 2002, science.nasa.gov/science-news/science-at-nasa/2002/09sept _spacepropulsion.

158 *"The world need not worry"*
Herman Kahn, quoted favorably in Simon, *The Ultimate Resource*, 177.

158 *"Invent" new sources of energy*
Ibid., 181; "careful thinking," ibid., 178; "more available and less scarce forever," ibid., 181.

159 *"Basic physical realities of entropy"*
The reviewer was Douglas Anderton. See "A Reply to My Critics," in Simon, *The Ultimate Resource*.

159 *An homage-purposed website*
www.juliansimon.com. The essay cited is posted in "Unpublished Writings."

160 *"To collapse in deepest humiliation"*
A. S. Eddington, *The Nature of the Physical World* (Cambridge: Cambridge University Press, 1928), 73–75.

freakonomist cheap shots jane fonda

163 *Once the motivation was snuffed out, it stayed out*
The study that Levitt and Dubner report here (pp. 19–20) was done by Uri Gneezy and Aldo Rustichini, "A Fine Is a Price," *Journal of Legal Studies* 29, no. 1 (January 2000): 1–17. Levitt and Dubner's conclusion: "The $3 fine was simply too small." It would be interesting to know whether and under what circumstances the guilt-and-shame motivation could come back; can it be nurtured into being again, or once it has been replaced by pricing, is it gone forever?

163 *A Freakonomist is "skeptical of the conventional wisdom"*
Steven D. Levitt and Stephen J. Dubner, *Freakonomics* (New York: William Morrow, 2005), 206.

163 *Becker is "the original Freakonomist"*
Levitt and Dubner, *Superfreakonomics* (New York: William Morrow, 2009), 224; see also 12–13.

163 *Becker's early career*
Ibid., 12–13.

163 *"An approximate answer to the right question"*
Levitt and Dubner ascribe this to the statistician John Tukey in ibid., 224.

163 *"How people choose someone to love and marry"*
Ibid., 13.

164 *"The Jane Fonda Effect"*
Levitt and Dubner, "The Jane Fonda Effect," *New York Times Magazine*, September 16, 2007.

166 *As George Lakoff calls them*
See George Lakoff, *Don't Think of an Elephant: Know Your Values and Frame the Debate* (Chelsea, VT: Chelsea Green, 2004).

167 *You won't find this piece listed*
Steven D. Levitt (presumably), "Vitae: Steven D. Levitt," at pricetheory .uchicago.edu/levitt/Levitt-CV.pdf (accessed December 9, 2010).

167 *The China Syndrome*
The phenomenon (not the movie) is actually a misnomer, a bit of drollery that someone thought up to describe the worst-case scenario. A melting reactor core would burn its way into the Earth, right down through rock—until it hit an aquifer, where consensus opinion predicts it would produce a very large, and very radioactively dirty, steam explosion.

167 *"A significant release of radiation"*
US Nuclear Regulatory Commission Office of Public Affairs, *Backgrounder: Three Mile Island Accident*, 2, www.nrc.gov/reading-rm/doc-collections/fact -sheets/3mile-isle.html (accessed December 8, 2010). The report puts the most favorable interpretation possible on the episode; it "led to no deaths or injuries" and "did not produce worst-case consequences," but did bring about "sweeping changes . . . [that] had the effect of enhancing safety."

169 *Random jumble of boards*
This is why maintenance—the intelligent introduction of matter and energy into a built system—is required to stave off system collapse. (Ecosystems accomplish self-maintenance using solar energy and the design intelligence of evolution.) As President Lyndon Johnson put it, talking about efforts to stymie his legislative program, "Any jackass can kick down a barn"; it takes a carpenter to build one.

171 *"Someone who has made up his or her mind"*
Charles Hall, "The Energy Return of Nuclear Power," part 4 of *EROI on the Web*, posted at *The Oil Drum*, April 22, 2008, www.theoildrum.com/node/3877.

got terrorism? blame economists

175 *If the Twin Towers had been built on a different design*
Thomas W. Eagar and Christopher Musso, "Why Did the World Trade Center

Collapse? Science, Engineering, and Speculation," *JOM* (formerly the *Journal of Metals*) 53, no. 12 (2001): 8–11.

176 *"A tax that is the time equivalent of 14 lives a year"*
Levitt and Dubner, *Superfreakonomics*, 65.

177 *"The death of a thousand cuts"*
See David Gartenstein-Ross, "The Death of a Thousand Cuts," *Foreign Policy Online*, November 23, 2010, www.foreignpolicy.com/articles/2010/11/23/death_by_a_thousand_cuts.

177 *Bin Laden proclaimed*
Ibid.

177 *"Extra driving deaths"*
Levitt and Dubner, *Superfreakonomics*, 65–66.

179 *No path to victory*
Among those who make this point are Louise Richardson, in *What Terrorists Want: Understanding the Enemy, Containing the Threat* (New York: Random House, 2006), and General Rupert Smith, in *The Utility of Force: The Art of War in the Modern World* (New York: Knopf, 2007).

180 *"The greatest threats to our security"*
Condoleezza Rice, "The Promise of Democratic Peace: Why Promoting Freedom Is the Only Realistic Path to Security," *Washington Post,* December 11, 2005.

180 *Failed states as "breeding grounds for international instability"*
The report titled *National Intelligence Strategy of the United States* was issued in October 2005 by the Office of the Director of National Intelligence and is available online at www.dni.gov/publications/NISOctober2005.pdf. The quotation is from 1–2.

180 *"Sanctuaries for transnational terrorists"*
US National Intelligence Council, "Mapping the Global Future," December 2004, p. 14, www.dni.gov/nic/NIC_globaltrend2020.html.

181 *"Failed states become anarchic areas"*
John Yoo, "Fighting the New Terrorism," lecture in the Bradley Lecture Series at the American Enterprise Institute, June 6, 2005, www.aei.org/speech/22633.

181 *The World Bank agrees*
Thus the headline "World Bank Lists Failing Nations That Can Breed Global Terrorism," on an article by Karen DeYoung in the *Washington Post*, September 15, 2006.

181 *Kenyan officials expressed pride and dismay*
Kevin J. Kelley, "Kenya Falls in 'Failed State Index' Rankings," *Daily Nation* (Nairobi), June 23, 2010.

182 *Consistency across the twelve categories*
One exception: Syria gets a 9.2 in Refugees and Internally Displaced Persons,

but manages to score 5.7 in Public Services, which makes it a bit of a hero-state—absorbing refugees, but continuing to meet basic needs for public services; though its success at staving off crisis did not last. Another exception: North Korea, ranked seventeenth in failure, with an overall score of 98.3, scores only 5.0 in Human Flight—not because its middle class doesn't want to leave, but because the whole country is under lockdown.

183 *What covaries with what*

It would be interesting to know, for instance, what Chile, Portugal, Namibia, Mali, and Madagascar have in common, besides the fact that on the Failed State Index they are the only nations whose scores on "delegitimation of the state" are two or more points lower—better—than their scores on provision of public services. In these countries failure to provide services is only mildly correlated with delegitimation of the state.

183 *Global Terrorism Database*

Of course the whole thing is available online: www.start.umd.edu/gtd/. Some limitations on the data should be noted. While the Global Terrorism Database includes failed attacks, it doesn't include foiled or thwarted attacks. Some of the data come from a compilation done by the Pinkerton Global Intelligence Services (PGIS), which donated the information to the University of Maryland; PGIS kept the data on index cards, and the cards for 1993 were lost before the donation. The database extends from 1970 up to the present, but inferences about terrorism over time are hampered by major changes in data collection in the years 1997 to 2007. (The data show an increase in terrorist acts after 1997, but that's an artifact of changes in method.)

183 *An act of war, not terror*

This suggests a pair of definitions. National territory: land that an army can scare people away from. Terrorism: political violence perpetrated by people who don't control national territory. I'm not saying, I'm just sayin'.

183 *Two out of an additional three criteria*

The administrators of the Global Terrorism Database recognize that the definition of terrorism is contentious, and they've very generously set up the database to allow searches by the researcher's preferred definition.

184 *Terrorism happens not just in failed states*

Aidan Hehir, "The Myth of the Failed State and the War on Terror: A Challenge to the Conventional Wisdom," *Journal of Intervention and Statebuilding* 1, no. 3 (2007): 307–332.

184 *"The more democracy, the more terrorism"*

Hehir reports this conclusion from a study done by William L. Eubank and Leonard B. Weinberg, "Terrorism and Democracy: Perpetrators and Victims," *Terrorism and Political Violence* 13, no. 1 (2010): 155–164, quote on 160. If we acknowledge that the effort to fight terrorism encroaches on our civil liberties, the fact that there is this observable correlation between democracy and terrorism is additional support for the idea, elaborated elsewhere in this volume, that on Factory Planet we lose the ground on which civil liberties are possible.

185 *The thesis has some empirical support*

An additional wrinkle: political movements happen in time and can change over time. It's possible that a terrorist movement needs a safe haven at a particular stage in its development and that once it has established principles of action and produced a core of dedicated terrorists who are capable of recruiting and training others, it can be effective without a safe haven. An accurate test of the conventional-wisdom hypothesis would have to take this possibility into account.

185 *Sub-Saharan Africa as a region particularly vulnerable to climate change*

Millennium Ecosystem Assessment, *Ecosystems and Human Well-Being: Synthesis* (Washington: Island Press, 2005).

186 *Annual survey of public opinion in five Arab countries*

Shibley Telhami, "2010 Arab Public Opinion Poll," conducted by the University of Maryland in conjunction with Zogby International, available on the website of the Brookings Institution, www.brookings.edu/reports/2010/0805 _arab_opinion_poll_telhami.aspx.

187 *Friends or family who are sympathetic to the cause*

John Horgan's work is reported in Tori DeAngelis, "Understanding Terrorism," *Monitor on Psychology* 40, no. 10 (November 2009): 60.

187 *Arab grievances that aren't a result of neoclassical economic theory*

These are easily inferred from the rhetoric that al-Qaeda leaders use to appeal to Muslims for support and participation. A good overview of these is found in the report prepared by Christopher Blanchard at the nonpartisan Congressional Research Service, "Al Qaeda: Statements and Evolving Ideology," July 9, 2007, document code RL32759. They can also be derived from the annual surveys of public opinion in Arab nations that are referenced above.

188 *The neoclassical model says that income inequality and other problems will self-correct*

It's interesting that the neoclassical model took little notice of negative environmental and income-distribution externalities until it had theory in place to explain how and why these problems would self-correct. This is rather as if medicine had denied the existence of bacteria until antibiotics — ineffective antibiotics — had been invented.

189 *Objectors to globalization are characterized as special interests*

Robert H. Frank and Ben S. Bernanke, *Principles of Economics*, 2nd ed. (New York: McGraw Hill, 2004), 400, 413.

191 *How Globalization Spurs Terrorism*
Fathali Moghaddam, *How Globalization Spurs Terrorism: The Lopsided Benefits of One World and Why That Fuels Violence* (Westport, CT: Praeger, 2008).

192 *Understanding how people "choose someone to . . . hate and even kill"*
Levitt and Dubner, *Superfreakonomics*, 13.

ending the culture war

195 *"There is a religious war . . . a cultural war"*
The whole speech is available on Buchanan's website at www.buchanan.org/pa-92-0817-rnc.html.

196 *An op-ed piece in the Wall Street Journal*
Lynne Cheney, "The End of History," *Wall Street Journal*, October 20, 1994.

196 *Professional historians produced new guidelines for the teaching of American history*
As reported in Gary Nash, Charlotte Crabtree, and Ross E. Dunn, *History on Trial: Culture Wars and the Teaching of the Past* (New York: Vintage, 2000), 3. (The authors were part of the group of historians and academics that produced the National Standards for History.)

197 *Rush Limbaugh used the sounds of tearing and crumpling pages*
Reported in ibid., 5.

197 *"History . . . is about national identity"*
Ibid., 7.

197 *Academics who "bullied their way into power positions" and "worked in secret"*
All phrases from Rush Limbaugh, by way of ibid., 5.

198 *Science, too, is in some part an art*
Thomas Kuhn: "Sometimes it is only personal and inarticulate aesthetic considerations" that lead a scientist to accept one theoretical frame—paradigm—over another (*The Structure of Scientific Revolutions*, 3rd ed. [Chicago: University of Chicago Press, 1996], 158).

199 *"The traditional story . . . has been shattered"*
Todd Gitlin, "A Truce Prevails; for the Left, Many Victories Are Pyrrhic," *Chronicle of Higher Education,* March 6, 1998.

200 *"War of Northern Aggression"*
Southern politicians have recently been freer in using this name for the Civil War even when they're away from their home constituencies, where it passes with less notice. On the morning of February 11, 2009, US Representative Bryan Stevenson, R-Missouri, rose to speak on the floor of the House against the federal Freedom of Choice Act (which aimed to limit the ability of states to restrict access to abortion), calling it the most egregious federal power grab

"since the War of Northern Aggression." Reported by Steve Benen in *Political Animal*, his blog on the *Washington Monthly* website, posted February 11, 2009, www.washingtonmonthly.com/archives/individual/2009_02/016840 .php. Stevenson later apologized at the urging of African American Representative Don Calloway, D-St. Louis, who reminded him that the Civil War helped abolish slavery. Whatever Stevenson was guilty of — egregious historical revisionism, suborning treason — he wasn't guilty of misrepresenting conservative southern belief.

200 *"The machine that would go of itself"*

Michael Kammen took this phrase as the title of his book *A Machine That Would Go of Itself: The Constitution in American Culture* (New York: Alfred A. Knopf, 1986). It comes from a speech by poet and editor James Russell Lowell in 1888, offering a warning that has contemporary application: "After our Constitution got fairly into working order it really seemed as if we had invented a machine that would go of itself, and this begot a faith in our luck which even the Civil War itself but momentarily disturbed." But, he added, "this confidence in our luck with the absorption in material interests, generated by unparalleled opportunity, has in some respects made us neglectful of our political duties" (cited in Kammen, *A Machine That Would Go of Itself*, 125).

202 *The damage these numbers measure*

The numbers are from David W. Orr's *Ecological Literacy: Education and the Transition to a Postmodern World* (Albany: State University of New York Press, 1992).

203 *As I've argued elsewhere*

See Eric Zencey, *Virgin Forest: Meditations on History, Ecology, and Culture* (Athens: University of Georgia Press, 1997).

205 *Breadth of application (scope) and degree of assimilation of detail (reach)*

These are proposed and elaborated by Stephen Pepper in *World Hypotheses: A Study in Evidence* (Berkeley: University of California Press, 1948). Pepper's work predated Kuhn's and clearly influenced it; what Pepper calls "root metaphors" are Kuhnian paradigms at their largest scale.

205 *Save the planet*

Richard Foltz, "Does Nature Have Historical Agency? World History, Environmental History, and How Historians Can Help Save the Planet," *History Teacher* 37, no. 1 (November 2003), www.historycooperative.org/journals/ht/ 37.1/foltz.html. Foltz's essay contains a useful review of recent scholarship in environmental history. Properly speaking, historians can help save civilization. It's likely (but not guaranteed) that life on the planet will continue even if we destroy the ability of the planet to support civilization.

209 *Law "gives physicians and other medical professionals permission to lie"*
Center for Reproductive Rights, *Annual Report 2010*, "Oklahoma," reproductiverights.org/en/document/annual-report-2010-2011 (accessed April 7, 2012).

213 *"Every Cadillac . . . means fewer lives"*
Nicholas Georgescu-Roegen, *The Entropy Law and the Economic Process* (Cambridge, MA: Harvard University Press, 1971), 304.

213 *The Oklahoma abortion questionnaire*
It's embedded in the law, HB 3284, which can be found on the official website of the state legislature: www.sos.state.ok.us/documents/Legislation/52nd/2009/1R/HB/1595.pdf.

214 *Whether a woman has been shown pictures of fetal development*
The original question reads, "Was the information required by paragraph 1 of subsection B of Section 1-738.2 of Title 63 of the Oklahoma Statutes provided to the mother?" Paragraph 1 of subsection B of Section 1-738.2 is the text that requires that a woman seeking an abortion be shown pictures of fetal development.

218 *Rugged individualism and faith in the boundless frontier*
A group of researchers got interested in the moral judgments leveled at Hummer owners (manifest in such things as the gestures recorded on the website www.FUH2.com, which catalogs middle-finger salutes to Hummers and their owners), and found that such criticism merely reinforces driver satisfaction. Their interviews with Hummer owners revealed that they believe that "being under siege by critics is an historically established feature of being an American. The moralistic critique of their consumption choices readily inspired Hummer owners to adopt the role of the moral protagonist who defends American national ideals," especially individualism and a faith in infinite growth in resource use. Marius K. Luedicke, Craig J. Thompson, and Markus Giesler, "Consumer Identity Work as Moral Protagonism: How Myth and Ideology Animate a Brand-Mediated Moral Conflict," *Journal of Consumer Research*, April 2010, pp. 1016–1032.

218 *The domain of the policy must be congruent with the domain of the problem*
Herman Daly and Joshua Farley, Ecological Economics: Principles and Applications (Washington: Island Press, 2004), 363.

218 *The efficient cause of the problem*
Here I'm alluding to the earlier discussion of Aristotle's categories of causation. The efficient cause of climate change is our emission of greenhouse gases, including those released by using carbon-based fuels; the material cause of these is the technology we've developed to burn fossil fuels; the formal causes lie in the structure of an economy and a civilization that has been

designed to employ cheap fossil fuel; and the final cause is, perhaps, a faith that the planet has an infinite capacity to absorb our acts and works.

220 *Once the veil was lifted*
For a discussion of the "veil of ignorance," see John Rawls, *A Theory of Justice* (Cambridge, MA: Belknap Press of Harvard University Press, 1999), 11.

what green might bring

225 *"Ecology and Guilt"*
Published in *Virgin Forest: Meditations on History, Ecology, and Culture* (Athens: University of Georgia Press, 1998).

227 *It was an okay answer*
One problem I now see with that answer is that it merely displaced but didn't change the basic difficulty. I think I correctly identified one of the reasons more people didn't accept the moral frame of ecology, but my solution was to ask them to accept yet another different moral frame.

227 *John Rodman's three levels of analysis*
See John Rodman, "Four Forms of Ecological Consciousness Reconsidered," in *Deep Ecology for the Twenty-First Century*, ed. G. Sessions (Boston: Shambala, 1995), 121–130.

227 *Kenneth Waltz's classic book*
Kenneth Waltz, *Man, the State, and War* (1959; repr., New York: Columbia University Press, 2001).

228 *Prices should tell the ecological truth*
The much-quoted epigram by Oystein Dahle is cited by Lester Brown in *Plan B 3.0* to a discussion he had with Dahle at the State of the World Conference in Aspen, CO, July 22, 2001. See Brown, *Plan B 3.0* (New York: W. W. Norton, 2008), 267.

229 *If prices tell the ecological truth, we don't need an environmental ethic*
Whether an ecologically oblivious citizenry in a democracy would retain an ecologically enlightened system of Pigouvian taxes designed to achieve sustainability is another matter entirely. But what's required to retain popular appreciation of, and political support for, such a tax system is ecological literacy, not an environmental ethic.

230 *Behavior that is "uneconomic"*
Some economists insist that there is no such thing: everyone, by definition, engages in benefit maximization all the time, so all behavior is economically rational. If you're willing to spend more for solar-generated electricity than for coal-generated electricity, this simply indicates that your preference structure and satisfactions are, in this matter, not constructed solely on price. This circular reasoning calls to mind something said by the philosopher of science

Karl Popper, who convincingly argued that if your belief can't be falsified—if there is no possible evidence that would make you discard your belief—then your belief is not a matter of science but something else: faith, myth, fantasy. It beggars the definition of "economic rationality" to assert that everyone is, all the time, perfectly economically rational.

232 *Can have or do have or should be recognized as having*
This parade of verbs is meant to encompass various theories about the origins of rights: do they exist if they aren't recognized, or does the recognition create them? That question, crucial to legal philosophy, is irrelevant here.

235 *"Web of practical interrelationships"*
James Howard Kunstler, *The Geography of Nowhere* (New York: Simon and Schuster/Touchstone, 1994), 241.

237 *The Money Party wins*
"Money Wins Presidency and 9 of 10 Congressional Races in Priciest Election Ever," article published November 5, 2008, on the *Open Secrets* blog maintained by the Center for Responsive Politics at www.opensecrets.org/news/2008/11/money-wins-white-house-and.html. The figures were actually 93 percent of House races and 94 percent of Senate races. All told, the Money Party lost only 30 of 465 races. In California, the Money Party wins 97 percent of all races. See Common Cause, "Taking Elections of the Auction Block," at www.commoncause.org/atf/cf/percent7Bfb3c17e2-cdd1-4df6-92be-bd4429893665percent7D/TAKINGELECTIONSOFFTHEAUCTIONBLOCK.PDF.

index

Ehrlich-Simon bet. *See* Simon, Julian
eminent domain, 223
Emmett, Ross B., 147
empathy, 34, 201, 211, 223, 236, 239.
    See also Golden Rule
Endangered Species Act, 233
energy: crisis, 46–51; dependence on,
    x, 46; as factor of production, 50;
    five carbon pools, 35; inelastic sup-
    ply and demand, 47–51; renewable
    sources, xxvii–xxviii, 73
energy return on energy invested
    (EROI), xxii, 68, 96, 100–101, 149,
    154, 171; fallacy of, 68; Julian Simon
    on, 159; of nuclear power, 155, 158;
    and solar and wind power, 155
enjoyment of life, 57, 85–87
Enlightenment, American tradition,
    206
Enron, 99, 113
entropy, 33, 38, 53, 59, 98, 159, 168–69;
    and evolution, 160; jackass as
    agent of, 278n; law of, 38; theory
    of value, 69. *See also* thermo-
    dynamics, second law of
environmental: crisis, 228;
    externalities, 235; ethics, 228–29;
    degradation, 122; movement, 226;
    quality as luxury good, 122–36, 230;
    sustainable management of, 85
environmental history, xi–xii, 3, 35,
    203–7; and meta-macroeconomics,
    xv, xxvii
environmentalism, as moral vision,
    38, 39, 59, 195, 217, 226
Environmental Kuznets Curve, 46,
    118, 121–22, 125, 188, 226, 234; as
    "beard," 128; and biodiversity, 130;
    and Clean Air and Water Acts, 126;
    compared to electronic type-
    writers, 135; compared to Marx's

doctrine of inevitable revolution,
    121, 267n; as contest ground, 132;
    criticism of, 124–33; crucial to
    faith in infinite growth, 188; data
    problems, 126, 128; ecosystem
    services, 130; and future of civiliza-
    tion, 123; logical problems with,
    125, 130; methodological problems,
    132; as monotonic, 129, 132, 271n;
    N-shaped, 131; peak points of
    pollutants, 131; pollution haven
    effects, 127; and property rights,
    127; role in China's ecological
    degradation, 134; and the World
    Bank, 126; World Bank rejects, 134
ethanol, xiii
European Commission, 85
evil empire, 129
evolution, as design intelligence, xxvi,
    70
excludable good, 62
externalities, 13–14, 60–63, 100, 120,
    172–74, 217–21, 235, 242

fascism, 10–11, 16
Factory Planet, xxv–xxviii, 3–4, 6, 21,
    30–31, 58, 73, 109, 123, 216–19, 224,
    240; and fascism, communism,
    and capitalism, 10
Failed State Index, 181–82, 184–86, 195
fallacy: of circular argument, 157, 171;
    of definitional slide, 62, 68, 155,
    157; of excluded middle, 62; false
    dichotomy, 62, 166; false distinc-
    tion, 20, 50–51; flawed syllogism
    in Julian Simon, 158; of misplaced
    concreteness, 76. *See also* category
    error
Farber, Stephen C., 260n
Farley, Joshua, 55, 57–58, 61–65, 70–71,
    120, 132, 218, 222, 241